The Neuroscience and Neuropsychology of Gambling

Gambling disorder is a behavioural addiction that represents the clinical extreme of a spectrum of gambling-related harm. What insights can neuroscientific and neuropsychological methods provide to help understand this condition and improve existing programs for treatment and prevention?

This volume describes recent research using an array of contemporary tools including structural and functional brain imaging, and neurocognitive assessment. These analyses consider brain activity and psychological functioning in people with gambling disorder under resting conditions, during tasks of reward processing and inhibitory control, and as a function of important sources of individual differences including depression and impulsivity. This volume also synthesizes contemporary research using animal models to examine decision-making under uncertainty from a behavioural neuroscience perspective, as well as synthesizing evidence from pharmacological treatments for gambling disorders. These findings complement research to understand substance use disorders and other emerging forms of behavioural addiction. This volume contains contributions from many of the leading research groups in this exciting field.

The chapters in this book were originally published as a special issue of *International Gambling Studies*.

Luke Clark is Professor of Psychology at the University of British Columbia in Vancouver, Canada. His research on the psychology of gambling combines multiple methods including behavioural analysis, brain imaging, and psychophysiology. He has published over 200 peer-reviewed papers. He is Senior Editor at *Addiction*, and Regional Assistant Editor for *International Gambling Studies*.

Anna E. Goudriaan is full Professor in Addiction: Mechanisms and Treatment at Arkin Mental Health Care and the Department of Psychiatry, Amsterdam University Medical Center, University of Amsterdam. She is a neuropsychologist and mental health psychologist with a combined research and clinical appointment. Her research focuses on the study of neurobiological mechanisms and innovative (neuromodulation) interventions in addictive disorders and dual diagnosis, including gambling disorder, alcohol use disorders and other substance use disorders (cannabis and cocaine). She has published over 180 peer-reviewed articles, book chapters and international papers and co-Editor-in-chief of European Addiction Research.

The Neuroscience and Neuropsychology of Gambling

Edited by
Luke Clark and Anna E. Goudriaan

LONDON AND NEW YORK

First published 2022
by Routledge
2 Park Square, Milton Park, Abingdon, Oxon, OX14 4RN

and by Routledge
605 Third Avenue, New York, NY 10158

Routledge is an imprint of the Taylor & Francis Group, an informa business

Chapters 1-4 and 6-8 © 2022 Taylor & Francis

Chapter 5 © 2018 Tim van Timmeren, Paul Zhutovsky, Ruth J. van Holst and Anna E. Goudriaan. Originally published as Open Access.

With the exception of Chapter 5, no part of this book may be reprinted or reproduced or utilised in any form or by any electronic, mechanical, or other means, now known or hereafter invented, including photocopying and recording, or in any information storage or retrieval system, without permission in writing from the publishers. For details on the rights for Chapter 5, please see the chapter's Open Access footnote.

Trademark notice: Product or corporate names may be trademarks or registered trademarks, and are used only for identification and explanation without intent to infringe.

British Library Cataloguing-in-Publication Data
A catalogue record for this book is available from the British Library

ISBN13: 978-0-367-69113-4 (hbk)
ISBN13: 978-0-367-69114-1 (pbk)
ISBN13: 978-1-003-14045-0 (ebk)

DOI: 10.4324/9781003140450

Typeset in Minion Pro
by codeMantra

Publisher's Note
The publisher accepts responsibility for any inconsistencies that may have arisen during the conversion of this book from journal articles to book chapters, namely the inclusion of journal terminology.

Disclaimer
Every effort has been made to contact copyright holders for their permission to reprint material in this book. The publishers would be grateful to hear from any copyright holder who is not here acknowledged and will undertake to rectify any errors or omissions in future editions of this book.

Contents

Acknowledgements	vii
Citation Information	viii
Notes on Contributors	x

1   Introduction: The neuroscience and neuropsychology of gambling and
gambling addiction   1
Luke Clark and Anna E. Goudriaan

2   Negative interpersonal scenes decrease inhibitory control in healthy
individuals but not in gambling disorder patients   6
Anja Kräplin, Stefan Scherbaum, Gerhard Bühringer,
Thomas Goschke and André Schmidt

3   Regional grey matter volume correlates of gambling disorder, gambling-
related cognitive distortions, and emotion-driven impulsivity   23
Cristian M. Ruiz de Lara, Juan F. Navas, Carles Soriano-Mas, Guillaume
Sescousse and José C. Perales

4   The Rat Gambling Task as a model for the preclinical development of
treatments for gambling disorder   45
Patricia di Ciano and Bernard Le Foll

5   Connectivity networks in gambling disorder: a resting-state fMRI study   70
Tim van Timmeren, Paul Zhutovsky, Ruth J. van Holst and Anna E. Goudriaan

6   Amygdala grey matter volume increase in gambling disorder with
depression symptoms of clinical relevance: a voxel-based
morphometry study   87
Evangelos Zois, Falk Kiefer, Sabine Vollstädt-Klein, Tagrid Lemenager, Karl
Mann and Mira Fauth-Bühler

7   Relating neural processing of reward and loss prospect to risky decision-
making in individuals with and without gambling disorder   97
Iris M. Balodis, Jakob Linnet, Fiza Arshad, Patrick D. Worhunsky,
Michael C. Stevens, Godfrey D. Pearlson and Marc N. Potenza

8 A review of opioid-based treatments for gambling disorder: an examination
   of treatment outcomes, cravings, and individual differences   114
   Darren R. Christensen

   Index   139

Acknowledgements

We would like to express our sincere thanks to Alex Blaszczynski and Sally Gainsbury. In their editorial roles at *International Gambling Studies*, Alex and Sally were instrumental in the initial formulation of this Special Issue of the journal, and have continued to provide much guidance and sound judgment in the preparation of this book edition, including their leadership in the peer review process for this collection of articles. We would also like to express our thanks to all of the contributing authors to the Special Issue, without whom this collection would not have been possible.

Luke Clark and Anna Goudriaan

Citation Information

The chapters in this book were originally published in *International Gambling Studies*, volume 18, issue 2 (2018). When citing this material, please use the original page numbering for each article, as follows:

Chapter 1
The neuroscience and neuropsychology of gambling and gambling addiction: an introduction to the special issue
Luke Clark and Anna E. Goudriaan
International Gambling Studies, volume 18, issue 2 (2018) pp. 173–177

Chapter 2
Negative interpersonal scenes decrease inhibitory control in healthy individuals but not in gambling disorder patients
Anja Kräplin, Stefan Scherbaum, Gerhard Bühringer, Thomas Goschke and André Schmidt
International Gambling Studies, volume 18, issue 2 (2018) pp. 178–194

Chapter 3
Regional grey matter volume correlates of gambling disorder, gambling-related cognitive distortions, and emotion-driven impulsivity
Cristian M. Ruiz de Lara, Juan F. Navas, Carles Soriano-Mas, Guillaume Sescousse and José C. Perales
International Gambling Studies, volume 18, issue 2 (2018) pp. 195–216

Chapter 4
The Rat Gambling Task as a model for the pre-clinical development of treatments for gambling disorder
Patricia di Ciano and Bernard Le Foll
International Gambling Studies, volume 18, issue 2 (2018) pp. 217–241

Chapter 5
Connectivity networks in gambling disorder: a resting state fMRI study
Tim van Timmeren, Paul Zhutovsky, Ruth J. van Holst and Anna E. Goudriaan
International Gambling Studies, volume 18, issue 2 (2018) pp. 242–258

Chapter 6

Amygdala grey matter volume increase in gambling disorder with depression symptoms of clinical relevance: a voxel-based morphometry study
Evangelos Zois, Falk Kiefer, Sabine Vollstädt-Klein, Tagrid Lemenager, Karl Mann and Mira Fauth-Bühler
International Gambling Studies, volume 18, issue 2 (2018) pp. 259–268

Chapter 7

Relating neural processing of reward and loss prospect to risky decision-making in individuals with and without gambling disorder
Iris M. Balodis, Jakob Linnet, Fiza Arshad, Patrick D. Worhunsky, Michael C. Stevens, Godfrey D. Pearlson and Marc N. Potenza
International Gambling Studies, volume 18, issue 2 (2018) pp. 269–285

Chapter 8

A review of opioid-based treatments for gambling disorder: an examination of treatment outcomes, cravings, and individual differences
Darren R. Christensen
International Gambling Studies, volume 18, issue 2 (2018) pp. 286–309

For any permission-related enquiries please visit:
http://www.tandfonline.com/page/help/permissions

Notes on Contributors

Fiza Arshad Peter Boris Centre for Addiction Research, Department of Psychiatry and Behavioural Neurosciences, McMaster University, Hamilton, Canada.

Iris M. Balodis Department of Psychiatry, Yale University School of Medicine, New Haven, USA; Peter Boris Centre for Addiction Research, Department of Psychiatry and Behavioural Neurosciences, McMaster University, Hamilton, Canada.

Gerhard Bühringer Faculty of Psychology, School of Science, Technische Universität Dresden, Germany; IFT Institut für Therapieforschung, Munich, Germany.

Darren R. Christensen Faculty of Health Sciences, University of Lethbridge, Alberta Gambling Research Institute, Lethbridge, Canada.

Luke Clark Centre for Gambling Research at UBC, Department of Psychology, University of British Columbia, Vancouver, Canada.

Patricia Di Ciano Translational Addiction Research Laboratory, Centre for Addiction and Mental Health (CAM H), Toronto, Canada.

Mira Fauth-Bühler Department of Addictive Behaviour and Addiction Medicine, Central Institute of Mental Health, Medical Faculty Mannheim, University of Heidelberg, Germany; iwp Institute for Economic Psychology, FOM University of Applied Sciences for Economics and Management, Essen, Germany.

Thomas Goschke Faculty of Psychology, School of Science, Technische Universität Dresden, Germany.

Anna E. Goudriaan Department of Psychiatry, Amsterdam Institute for Addiction Research (AIAR), Academic Medical Center, University of Amsterdam, The Netherlands; Arkin Mental Health, The Netherlands.

Falk Kiefer Department of Addictive Behaviour and Addiction Medicine, Central Institute of Mental Health, Medical Faculty Mannheim, University of Heidelberg, Germany.

Anja Kräplin Faculty of Psychology, School of Science, Technische Universität Dresden, Germany.

Bernard Le Foll Addiction Division, Centre for Addiction and Mental Health (CAM H), Toronto, Canada; Departments of Pharmacology and Toxicology, Psychiatry, Family and Community Medicine, Institute of Medical Sciences, University of Toronto, Canada.

NOTES ON CONTRIBUTORS

Tagrid Lemenager Department of Addictive Behaviour and Addiction Medicine, Central Institute of Mental Health, Medical Faculty Mannheim, University of Heidelberg, Germany.

Jakob Linnet Gambling Disorder Clinic, Department of Occupational and Environmental Medicine, Odense University Hospital, Denmark.

Karl Mann Department of Addictive Behaviour and Addiction Medicine, Central Institute of Mental Health, Medical Faculty Mannheim, University of Heidelberg, Germany.

Juan F. Navas Department of Experimental Psychology, University of Granada, Spain; Mind, Brain, and Behaviour Research Centre (CIMCYC), University of Granada, Spain.

Godfrey D. Pearlson Department of Psychiatry, Yale University School of Medicine, New Haven, USA; Institute of Living/Hartford Hospital & Olin Neuropsychiatry Research Center, Hartford, USA; Department of Neuroscience, Yale University School of Medicine, New Haven, USA.

José C. Perales Department of Experimental Psychology, University of Granada, Spain; Mind, Brain, and Behaviour Research Centre (CIMCYC), University of Granada, Spain.

Marc N. Potenza Department of Psychiatry, Yale University School of Medicine, New Haven, USA; Department of Neuroscience, Yale University School of Medicine, New Haven, USA; Child Study Center, Yale University School of Medicine, New Haven, USA; Connecticut Mental Health Center, New Haven, USA; The Connecticut Council on Problem Gambling, Wethersfield, USA.

Cristian M. Ruiz de Lara Department of Experimental Psychology, University of Granada, Spain; Mind, Brain, and Behaviour Research Centre (CIMCYC), University of Granada, Spain.

Stefan Scherbaum Faculty of Psychology, School of Science, Technische Universität Dresden, Germany.

André Schmidt Faculty of Psychology, School of Science, Technische Universität Dresden, Germany.

Guillaume Sescousse Donders Institute for Brain, Cognition and Behaviour, Radboud University, Nijmegen, The Netherlands; Department of Psychiatry, Radboud University Medical Centre, Nijmegen, The Netherlands.

Carles Soriano-Mas Department of Psychiatry, Bellvitge University Hospital-IDIBELL, Barcelona, Spain; CIBERSAM, Carlos III Health Institute, Barcelona, Spain; Department of Psychobiology and Methodology in Health Sciences, Universitat Autònoma de Barcelona, Spain.

Michael C. Stevens Department of Psychiatry, Yale University School of Medicine, New Haven, USA; Institute of Living/Hartford Hospital & Olin Neuropsychiatry Research Center, Hartford, USA.

Tim van Timmeren Department of Psychiatry, Academic Medical Center, University of Amsterdam, The Netherlands; Amsterdam Institute for Addiction Research (AIAR), The Netherlands.

xii NOTES ON CONTRIBUTORS

Ruth J. van Holst Department of Psychiatry, Academic Medical Center, University of Amsterdam, The Netherlands; Amsterdam Institute for Addiction Research (AIAR), The Netherlands; Donders Institute for Cognition, Brain and Behaviour, Radboud University, Nijmegen, The Netherlands.

Sabine Vollstädt-Klein Department of Addictive Behaviour and Addiction Medicine, Central Institute of Mental Health, Medical Faculty Mannheim, University of Heidelberg, Germany.

Patrick D. Worhunsky Department of Psychiatry, Yale University School of Medicine, New Haven, USA.

Paul Zhutovsky Department of Psychiatry, Academic Medical Center, University of Amsterdam, The Netherlands.

Evangelos Zois Department of Addictive Behaviour and Addiction Medicine, Central Institute of Mental Health, Medical Faculty Mannheim, University of Heidelberg, Germany.

INTRODUCTION

The neuroscience and neuropsychology of gambling and gambling addiction

Luke Clark and Anna E. Goudriaan [iD]

ABSTRACT
Neuroscience research on gambling, including neuropsychological, neuroimaging, and psychophysiological experiments, is often regarded as aligned with the 'brain disease model of addictions'. We assert that a bio-psycho-social framework represents the consensus view of disordered gambling, giving equal weighting to biological and psychosocial predisposing factors (and their interactions). Within this framework, we highlight three ways in which neuroscience can inform gambling research - none of which rely on one's endorsement of biological 'causal explanations': i) as a toolbox of objective measures for studying gambling behaviour, ii) as a way of understanding treatment mechanisms, of both psychological and biological treatments, iii) as a way of probing the impact of gambling product features relevant to gambling policy.

We are delighted to introduce this special issue of *International Gambling Studies* dedicated to the neuroscience and neuropsychology of gambling and gambling addiction, featuring a combination of review articles on contemporary topics and original research papers, from leading groups in the field. In some respects, this special issue is published at a curious time, with something of a backlash in progress against biomedical models of addictions. At a major gambling conference in February 2018, the author Johann Hari opined that neuroscience explanations of addictions were akin to examining the plot of Romeo and Juliet in terms of the molecules that were moving in the protagonists' bodies, and that this was, in his view, an inappropriate level of explanation for addictive disorders. Instead, Hari presents a case for the primary (and in his view neglected) role of psychosocial factors including early adversity and social connectedness (Hari, 2015).

Gambling disorder as a biopsychosocial disorder

The 'brain disease model of addictions' has been positioned by some as the dominant school of thought in addiction science over the past 20 years (e.g. Hall, Carter, & Forlini, 2015;

Heyman, 2009). This perception varies across countries but, nevertheless, it has also received robust critique. For example, it is clear from epidemiological research that many individuals suffering from substance addictions must undergo spontaneous recovery without engaging with treatment services, which does not fit easily with a theory based on a chronic, brain-based illness (Heyman, 2009). It has been argued that sustained funding of neuroscience research on addictions has yielded negligible advances in pharmacotherapy (Hall, Carter & Forlini, 2015). Given that substance addictions are characterized by marked neural changes, which are partly the result of chronic consumption, and that these neurotoxic effects are presumably absent in people with gambling problems, these concerns may be even more pertinent to research on disordered gambling.

Much of this debate is about extreme positions that assert a primary role to one set of factors (e.g. biological factors versus psychosocial factors). In our view, this is a fight between two straw men. The majority of gambling researchers, cognitive neuroscientists and mental health professionals working with people with addictions endorse a bio-psycho-social framework. Indeed, we believe this approach has been well established in the gambling field since at least the introduction of the Pathways Model (Blaszczynski & Nower, 2002; see also Sharpe, 2002). The tenets of this framework are: (1) disordered gambling is maintained (in the moment) by psychological processes that include both behavioural mechanisms (e.g. operant conditioning based on variable reward) and cognitive mechanisms (e.g. faulty beliefs about randomness); and (2) individual biological (e.g. heritability) and/or psychosocial factors (e.g. childhood adversity, early gambling exposure) make some individuals undergo the transition from recreational to disordered gambling more easily. The relative ordering of the factors in the name of the approach is meaningless, and we would encourage a roughly equal distribution of research across the three factors.

Can neuroscience and biobehavioural research provide new avenues?

Where does this leave contemporary research on the neuroscience and biobehavioural mechanisms of gambling? We propose three ways in which neuroscience experiments can illuminate gambling research, and, importantly, these three principles are independent of one's perspective on biological 'causal explanations'. The first area of research – and one that is capably evidenced in each of the articles in this special issue – is that neuroscience provides a toolkit of techniques for studying gambling behaviour. This toolkit includes functional and structural brain imaging, electroencephalography, peripheral psychophysiology (e.g. heart rate) and hormone measurements (e.g. cortisol, testosterone), and these techniques each require firm grounding in behavioural analysis (e.g. task-related fMRI [functional magnetic resource imaging]). These tools help to overcome a range of problems with the main alternative technique, self-report, which is introspective, often retrospective, and susceptible to numerous forms of bias including demand characteristics and social desirability. As a concrete example, craving is an important clinical, experiential phenomenon in people with gambling problems (Cornil et al., 2018), but the measurement of craving by self-report alone can be complex, due to the biases mentioned above, as well as high levels of 'alexithymia' (difficulty in recognizing emotion or bodily arousal) in problem gamblers (Noël et al., 2017). As a result, self-reported craving and cue reactivity to addiction-related cues are only moderately correlated. By augmenting self-report measurements with behavioural and brain imaging measures, we are able to see the biobehavioural and neural signature of this state both in terms of brain activation and of brain communication (connectivity), which overlaps with other data on cravings in substance addictions (Goudriaan, de Ruiter, van den Brink, Oosterlaan, & Veltman, 2010; Limbrick-Oldfield et al., 2017). Brain responses to cue reactivity have also been employed as a biomarker for treatment development, such as the opioid antagonist naltrexone (Myrick et al., 2008).

This brings us to a second area of research, concerning new avenues for treatment. In the case of animal models for gambling disorder, new findings from behavioural neuroscience may directly highlight new options for medication development, such as dopamine agents that more selectively bind to D3 and D4 receptors (Di Ciano & Le Foll, 2018). Indeed, the most compelling evidence that biological factors *causally* influence the expression of disordered gambling is the emergence of impulse control disorders in patients with Parkinson's disease, as a side-effect of dopamine agonist medications and especially drugs with a high dopamine D3 affinity (Moore, Glenmullen, & Mattison, 2014). However, a popular misconception is that neuroscience research *only* informs medication development. On the contrary, neuroscience research can also shed light on the mechanism of action of psychological treatments for gambling disorder, and thereby be used to further enhance these forms of treatment. For instance, executive dysfunction associated with diminished prefrontal cortex functioning may compromise a patient's ability to implement aspects of cognitive behavioural therapy, such as the use of strategies to cope with high-risk situations. Cognitive protocols geared at improving executive functions, such as goal management training, have shown promising results in pilot studies in substance use disorders (Valls-Serrano, Caracuel, & Verdejo-Garcia, 2016). Neuroscience research may inform the mechanisms underlying cue exposure therapy, a core component of behavioural therapy for which evidence of effectiveness in substance use disorders remains inconsistent (Mellentin et al., 2017). The investigation of psychophysiology during virtual reality gambling exposure has also illuminated factors (e.g. number of sessions; type of environment; effect of mood) that influence positive clinical response (Bouchard et al., 2017).

The third area of research relates to gambling policy. With the international expansion of gambling, there is a growing need to understand which forms of gambling present higher risks, and which specific structural characteristics of gambling games underpin those risks. As articulated in a recent article by Yücel, Carter, Harrigan, van Holst, and Livingstone (2018), 'The relative influence of one design feature over another is unclear, but the combined effects probably impart a powerful drive towards gambling-related thoughts and behaviour' (p. 20). The challenge that this presents to researchers is hugely complex: do we investigate each design feature in isolation, searching for critical addictive ingredients, or do we focus on the summed effects that arise in real-life gambling situations, such as in-game immersion? A detailed understanding of the neural and behavioural impacts of gambling games, and the relevant dimensions of human individual differences in these effects, will provide a foundation for producing safer gambling products. Implementing this knowledge in the form of responsible gambling practices also benefits from dialogue between gambling researchers, gambling regulators and gambling operators, who can in turn support research through facilitating access to data and realistic gambling products, especially in the context of electronic gaming machines (EGMs) and online gambling.

Conflict of interest

Funding sources

Luke Clark is the director of the Centre for Gambling Research at UBC, which is supported by funding from the Province of British Columbia and the British Columbia Lottery Corporation (BCLC), a Canadian Crown Corporation. He receives funding from the Natural Sciences and Engineering Research Council (Canada). He has received a speaker honorarium from Svenska Spel (Sweden) and an award from the National Center for Responsible Gaming (US). He has not received any further direct or indirect payments from the gambling industry or groups substantially funded by gambling. He has provided paid consultancy to, and received royalties from, Cambridge Cognition Ltd. relating to neurocognitive testing.

Competing interests

The Province of British Columbia government and BCLC had no involvement in the ideas expressed herein. Luke Clark has not received any further direct or indirect payments from the gambling industry or groups substantially funded by gambling. Anna Goudriaan reports no conflicts of interest.

Constraints on publishing

The Province of British Columbia government and BCLC imposed no constraints on publishing.

ORCID

Anna E. Goudriaan ⓘ http://orcid.org/0000-0001-8670-9384

References

Blaszczynski, A., & Nower, L. (2002). A pathways model of problem and pathological gambling. *Addiction, 97*, 487–499.

Bouchard, S., Robillard, G., Giroux, I., Jacques, C., Loranger, C., St-Pierre, M., & ... Goulet, A. (2017). Using virtual reality in the treatment of gambling disorder: The development of a new tool for cognitive behavior therapy. *Frontiers in Psychiatry, 8*, 1–10. doi:10.3389/fpsyt.2017.00027

Cornil, A., Lopez-Fernandez, O., Devos, G., de Timary, P., Goudriaan, A. E., & Billieux, J. (2018). Exploring gambling craving through the elaborated intrusion theory of desire: A mixed methods approach. *International Gambling Studies, 18*(1), 1–21. doi:10.1080/14459795.2017.1368686

Di Ciano, P., & Le Foll, B. (2018). The rodent gambling task as a model for the pre-clinical development of treatments for Gambling Disorder. *International Gambling Studies.* doi: 10.1080/14459795.2018.1448428

Goudriaan, A. E., de Ruiter, M. B., van den Brink, W., Oosterlaan, J., & Veltman, D. J. (2010). Brain activation patterns associated with cue reactivity and craving in abstinent problem gamblers, heavy smokers and healthy controls: An fMRI study. *Addiction Biology, 15*(4), 491–503. doi:10.1111/j.1369-1600.2010.00242.x

Hall, W., Carter, A., & Forlini, C. (2015). The brain disease model of addiction: Is it supported by the evidence and has it delivered on its promises? *The Lancet Psychiatry, 2*(1), 105–110. doi:10.1016/S2215-0366(14)00126-6

Hari, J. (2015). *Chasing the scream: The first and last days of the war on drugs.* New York, NY: Bloomsbury.

Heyman, G. M. (2009). *Addiction: A disorder of choice.* Cambridge, MA: Harvard University Press.

Limbrick-Oldfield, E. H., Mick, I., Cocks, R. E., McGonigle, J., Sharman, S., Goldstone, A. P., ... Clark, L. (2017). Neural substrates of cue reactivity and craving in gambling disorder. *Translational Psychiatry*, (1), e992. Retrieved from doi:10.1038/tp.2016.256

Mellentin, A. I., Skøt, L., Nielsen, B., Schippers, G. M., Nielsen, A. S., Stenager, E., & Juhl, C. (2017). Cue exposure therapy for the treatment of alcohol use disorders: A meta-analytic review. *Clinical Psychology Review, 57*, 195–207. doi:10.1016/j.cpr.2017.07.006

Moore, T. J., Glenmullen, J., & Mattison, D. R. (2014). Reports of pathological gambling, hypersexuality, and compulsive shopping associated with dopamine receptor agonist drugs. *JAMA Internal Medicine, 22314*, 1930–1933. doi:10.1001/jamainternmed.2014.5262

Myrick, H., Anton, R. F., Li, X., Henderson, S., Randall, P. K., & Voronin, K. (2008). Effect of naltrexone and ondansetron on alcohol cue-induced activation of the ventral striatum in alcohol-dependent people. *Archives of General Psychiatry, 65*(4), 466–475. doi:10.1001/archpsyc.65.4.466

Noël, X., Saeremans, M., Kornreich, C., Bechara, A., Jaafari, N., & Fantini-Hauwel, C. (2017). On the processes underlying the relationship between alexithymia and gambling severity. *Journal of Gambling Studies.* doi:10.1007/s10899-017-9715-1

Sharpe, L. (2002). A reformulated cognitive-behavioral model of problem gambling. A biopsychosocial perspective. *Clinical Psychology Review, 22*(1), 1–25.

Valls-Serrano, C., Caracuel, A., & Verdejo-Garcia, A. (2016). Goal management training and mindfulness meditation improve executive functions and transfer to ecological tasks of daily life in polysubstance users enrolled in therapeutic community treatment. *Drug and Alcohol Dependence, 165*, 9–14. doi:10.1016/j.drugalcdep.2016.04.040

Yücel, M., Carter, A., Harrigan, K., van Holst, R. J., & Livingstone, C. (2018). Hooked on gambling: A problem of human or machine design? *The Lancet Psychiatry, 5*(1), 20–21. doi:10.1016/S2215-0366(17)30467-4

Negative interpersonal scenes decrease inhibitory control in healthy individuals but not in gambling disorder patients

Anja Kräplin [iD], Stefan Scherbaum, Gerhard Bühringer [iD], Thomas Goschke and André Schmidt

ABSTRACT
While impaired cognitive control and decision-making are clearly related to gambling disorder (GD), it remains unclear how they are affected by interpersonal problems as contextual cues for gambling. This study tested whether these impairments in GD are specifically present following presentations of negative interpersonal scenes. Inpatients with GD (n = 49) and healthy individuals (n = 29) performed a go/no-go and an intertemporal choice task with randomly presented pictures depicting either neutral scenes or negative interpersonal scenes related to a lack of autonomy (e.g. prison scene) or appreciation (e.g. thumb downwards). The reduction of inhibitory control in the go/no-go task after negative autonomy-related compared to neutral interpersonal scenes was significantly larger in the control compared to the GD group. Within the control group, we also found a reduction of inhibitory control after negative appreciation-related compared to neutral scenes. There were no further significant between- or within-group-effects. Unexpectedly, negative interpersonal scenes decreased inhibitory control in healthy individuals but not in GD patients that may be explained post hoc by differences in stress responses or emotion regulation in reaction to the negative scenes. The effects of interpersonal problems on gambling behaviour in GD cannot directly be explained by cue-induced impairments of inhibitory control or decision-making.

Introduction

Several models of gambling disorder (GD) assume that multiple (neuro)biological, psychological and social variables contribute to the development and maintenance of GD (Blaszczynski & Nower, 2002; Shaffer & Korn, 2002; Sharpe, 2002). However, it is an important unresolved question how putative impairments of cognitive control and decision-making mechanisms interact with motivational processes related to social interactions. The aim of this study was to investigate whether inhibitory control and decision-making processes are particularly impaired in GD patients after being confronted with negative interpersonal scenes.

Neuropsychological research indicates that impaired cognitive control networks and dysfunctional valuation systems are two core mechanisms involved in GD development and maintenance (Clark, 2010; Goschke, 2014; van Holst, van den Brink, Veltman, & Goudriaan, 2010). There is evidence for impaired performance and aberrant brain activity in tasks requiring inhibitory control (Smith, Mattick, Jamadar, & Iredale, 2014; Verdejo-García, Lawrence, & Clark, 2008) or decision-making in GD (MacKillop et al., 2011; Wiehler & Peters, 2015). However, it remains an open research question whether these neuropsychological processes are generally impaired in GD or particularly in disorder-specific contexts (Goschke, 2014).

In addition to this intra-individual neuropsychological perspective, GD models have also highlighted the importance of social environments (Hardoon, Gupta, & Derevensky, 2004; Shaffer & Korn, 2002; Shaffer et al., 2004; Sharpe, 2002) such as parental or peer gambling (Hardoon et al., 2004; Wickwire, Whelan, Meyers, & Murray, 2007; Winters, Stinchfield, Botzet, & Anderson, 2002). Among such, interpersonal problems seem to be particularly strongly associated with GD, partly as antecedent risk factors (Kausch, Rugle, & Rowland, 2006; N. M. Petry & Steinberg, 2005) and partly as consequences of recurrent gambling problems (Shaw, Forbush, Schlinder, Rosenman, & Black, 2007; R. J. Williams, West, & Simpson, 2012). Interpersonal problems are therefore considered as important diagnostic criteria for GD (American Psychiatric Association [APA], 2013). Furthermore, interpersonal problems and conflicts have long been recognized as gambling motives (Ledgerwood & Petry, 2006a; Stewart, Zack, Collins, & Klein, 2008) and one important precondition for relapse in GD and a variety of other addictive disorders (Ledgerwood & Petry, 2006b; Marlatt, 1996; McCormick, 1994).

According to motivational theories, interpersonal problems may thwart basic psychological needs (Baumeister & Leary, 1995; Deci & Ryan, 2000). For instance, according to the self-determination theory, human motivation requires the consideration of the psychological needs for relatedness, autonomy and competence (Deci & Ryan, 2000). Other theories specifically focus on the need for relatedness as one of the most important needs that motivate humans (Baumeister & Leary, 1995). Within this theoretical framework, interpersonal conflicts may thwart these psychological needs so that an addictive participation in gambling or other behaviours can be regarded as one maladaptive strategy to satisfy these needs (Masur, Reinecke, Ziegele, & Quiring, 2014; Neighbors & Larimer, 2004) and to regulate the associated negative emotions (Blaszczynski & Nower, 2002). In healthy individuals, it has been shown that negative emotions and thoughts induce impulsive behaviour, possibly to regulate negative affect by immediate rewards (e.g. Liu, Feng, Chen, & Li, 2013; Selby, Kranzler, Panza, & Fehling, 2016; Tice, Bratslavsky, & Baumeister, 2001). Moreover, previous research has shown that emotional stimuli generally impair inhibitory control by inducing interfering attentional (Verbruggen & De Houwer, 2007) or cognitive processes (e.g. Whitmer & Banich, 2007). In individuals with GD, interpersonal problems are much more frequent and disordered gambling behaviour has been established as important strategy to satisfy interpersonal needs and regulate emotions (Blaszczynski & Nower, 2002; Neighbors & Larimer, 2004). Besides the neuropsychological mechanisms that may underlie the relation of interpersonal problems and impaired inhibitory control and decision-making in healthy individuals, interpersonal problems in GD become contextual gambling cues over time that additionally induce impairments in these processes (Redish, Jensen, & Johnson, 2008). Previous studies have shown that gambling-related cues (e.g. cards, roulette, slot machines) induce altered brain activity in valuation and inhibitory control networks in GD participants (de Greck et al., 2010; Miedl, Büchel, & Peters, 2014), which could explain impaired inhibitory control and decision-making in these gambling contexts (Boyer & Dickerson, 2003; Dixon, Jacobs, & Sanders, 2006; Miedl et al., 2014). Up to now, there are no neuropsychological studies available on the effect of interpersonal cues on inhibitory control and decision-making in GD. Only one neuroimaging study applied videotaped scenarios that included negative interpersonal cues for gambling (e.g. problems at home) and found decreased brain activations in regions related to inhibitory control in GD patients compared to controls (Potenza et al., 2003). However, inhibitory control performance was not assessed. To conclude, there is a strong need to investigate whether interpersonal problems are important cues that induce further impaired inhibitory control and decision-making in GD which, in turn, result in risky gambling behaviour. Results would be important to further develop GD models with regard to interactions between neuropsychological and psychosocial variables and might have implications for cue-induced relapse.

In a first laboratory study addressing this open research question, we hypothesized that negative interpersonal scenes are context factors that impair inhibitory control and decision-making in GD patients to a larger degree as compared to healthy controls. We thereby focused on scenes that represent a lack of autonomy or a lack of appreciation to thwart two important basic psychological needs according to motivational theories, the need for autonomy and the need for relatedness (Baumeister & Leary, 1995; Deci & Ryan, 2000).

Methods

Design and recruitment

We applied a cross-sectional quasi-experimental design with the observed (non-randomized) between factor group (GD patients vs. healthy controls) and the within factor condition (neutral vs. negative interpersonal scenes). The GD group was recruited from a psychosomatic clinic in Germany with inpatient and outpatient treatment for mental disorders including specific sections for substance use and gambling disorders. The healthy control group was recruited from the general community with information flyers in different regions of Germany (non-clinical and non-university setting). The control group was matched as closely as possible to the GD group in terms of age and gender. All participants were informed about the study, their option to withdraw from study participation at any time without any disadvantages, and signed informed consent. After an intense screening, included participants were allocated to the GD group or to the healthy control group. The study protocol was approved by the local Ethics Committee at the Technische Universität Dresden, Germany.

Sample selection and procedure

In the GD group, inclusion criteria were a GD diagnosis according to clinical experts and based on the International Classification of Diseases (ICD)-10 (World Health Organization [WHO], 1992) and additionally based on a positive screening in the German short questionnaire for gambling behaviour (Kurzfragebogen zum Glücksspielverhalten, KFG; J. Petry & Baulig, 1996). The KFG contains 20 items based on the Gamblers Anonymous questions that assess different GD criteria from the *Diagnostic and Statistical Manual of Mental Disorders* (DSM; APA, 2013) on 4-point Likert scales (0–3) with a cut-off of 16 for probable GD. In the control group, participants were included who do not fulfil diagnostic criteria of GD or exceed the KFG cut-off for probable GD. General exclusion criteria in both groups were: (1) age under 18 or over 69; (2) current use of psychotropic substances or medication; (3) conditions that might influence test performance (chronic disorders like mental disability or states like flu); (4) co-morbid substance use disorders according to DSM-IV (with the exception of nicotine use and alcohol use disorder in the GD group), schizophrenia, and bipolar disorder in both groups. Additionally, other axis I disorders according to DSM-IV were exclusion criteria in the control group, whereas they were not excluded but recorded in the GD group (e.g. major depression). Exceptions of the last exclusion criterion had to be made to recruit a sufficiently large sample of GD participants who are typically characterized by high co-morbidity rates (Lorains, Cowlishaw, & Thomas, 2011). Mental disorders in the GD group were clinically diagnosed by psychologists in the inpatient clinic. In the control group, mental disorders were screened with the Symptom Screening Questionnaire (SSQ) of the DIA-X/M-CIDI (Wittchen & Pfister, 1997). Included participants were tested in two settings, the GD group at intake in the clinic and the control group at a psychological outpatient treatment centre. Both groups performed the two-hour test session in a quiet room. The test session comprised several questionnaires and two neuropsychological tasks described below. After the test session, four participants were excluded from the analyses due to insufficient German language skills ($n = 1$), self-reported lack of sleep ($n = 2$), or a glaucoma ($n = 1$).

Instruments

Negative interpersonal scenes

We preselected different scenes with high face validity that were either neutral or represented a lack of autonomy or a lack of appreciation thwarting two important basic psychological needs according to motivational theories (Baumeister & Leary, 1995; Deci & Ryan, 2000). In a pilot study, we tested 180 preselected pictures in a sample of 13 psychologists trained in interpersonal psychotherapy (7 female, age 26–52). We focused on these trained psychologists as they were experts in the construct 'interpersonal needs' and associated interpersonal conflicts. We did not include GD patients to preselect the pictures as they may not be familiar with the constructs of interest and as GD patients are well known to have general difficulties to identify and describe their needs and emotions (e.g. alexithymia; Toneatto, Lecce, & Bagby, 2009). The scenes were individually rated by the psychologists on 7-point Likert scales regarding their content (e.g. how much is the scene related to a lack of appreciation/ autonomy?) and their emotional valence (positive or negative). We then selected 60 scenes that significantly differed from the expected mean value regarding content and valence, even after Bonferroni correction for multiple testing. From these 60 pictures, we included 20 appreciation-related and 20 autonomy-related scenes with the most negative valence ratings in the final picture set (see Figure 1 for examples). For the neutral scenes, we correspondingly selected 20 from the remaining 120 pictures that did not significantly differ from the mean value on all ratings.

Inhibitory control

To assess inhibitory control, we used a go/no-go paradigm from our lab for which basic task effects have already been confirmed in order to facilitate the interpretation of results (Beck et al., 2016). Participants were instructed to react as fast as possible to the letter 'M' (go trials), but to withhold their response to the letter 'W' (no-go trials). No-go stimuli were presented on 20% randomly chosen trials. The task was administered in three conditions: negative autonomy-related, negative appreciation-related, or neutral scenes. The order of conditions was randomly selected. For each condition, 100 trials were presented in 4 blocks with 25 trials. Before each block, five scenes of the corresponding condition were selected at random and presented for two seconds each. After the 5 scenes, one block with 25 trials started. After four blocks of the same condition, participants had a break before the next condition started with four blocks. Within one trial, the letters were presented for 150 milliseconds (ms) at the centre of the screen. The inter-stimulus interval between the letters was 850 ms. Go/no-go data of participants was excluded if the binomial probability that a participant would have obtained that score by chance was > .01 to ensure adherence to the task instruction (Friedman et al., 2008). Three participants had to be excluded, two in the GD group and one in the control group. The dependent measure was the inverse efficiency score (IES; Bruyer & Brysbaert, 2011) calculated as the mean reaction time for correct go trials divided by the proportion of correct no-go trials. In general, participants with lower inhibitory control obtain higher IES scores. Although there has been criticism of the IES (Bruyer & Brysbaert, 2011), it is a valid reflection of the relative weights of speed and accuracy (Bogacz, 2014). To address the criticism, we additionally conduct analyses with reaction times and error rates, to make sure that IES is in line with them. According to our hypothesis, GD patients should display lower inhibitory control, i.e. higher IES scores, especially after negative interpersonal scenes.

Decision-making

To assess decision-making, we also applied an already validated intertemporal choice (ITC) task that has been described in detail in previous studies (e.g. Kräplin et al., 2014). In the current study, the task was administered in three randomized blocks for each of the three

Figure 1. Examples of presented stimuli with interpersonal scenes that are either categorized as neutral, related to a lack of autonomy or to a lack of appreciation. Neutral (From left to right): ©lightpoet/Fotolia, ©Amir Kaljikovic/Fotolia, ©konradbak/Fotolia, ©blas/ Fotolia; Lack of autonomy (From left to right): ©Liv Friss-larse/Fotolia, ©Serhan Sidan/Fotolia, ©Stephan Morrosch/Fotolia, ©Aamo/Fotolia; Lack of appreciation (From left to right): ©olly/Fotolia, ©runzelkorn/Fotolia, ©Peter Atkins/Fotolia, ©Kitty/Fotolia.

scene conditions with breaks between blocks, the length of which was up to the participants. Within each block, participants were instructed to decide in 144 trials between a smaller monetary gain delivered sooner and a larger monetary gain delivered later. The sooner/smaller reward was randomly selected from a pool of items with a mean value of 20 euros and a standard deviation of 2 euros. The value of the later/larger reward was generated by increasing the sooner/smaller reward by 1, 2, 5, 7, 12, 18, 27, 40 or 80%. The time delay for the sooner/smaller reward was either 'now' or in seven days and the later/larger reward was additionally delayed by 1, 2, 3, 5, 7, 9, 12 or 15 days. The scenes within the three blocks were selected at random and presented for two seconds before each trial followed by a blank screen of 300 ms. Varying the amount of money and the delay of time offers the possibility to identify the indifference points of each participant. To estimate the indifference points, we determined the point of inflection of a logistic function fitted to the individual choices (smaller/sooner vs. larger/later) as a function of increasing value differences. The fitting of the logistic regression model was performed using the toolbox StixBox by Anders Holtsberg (http://www.maths.lth.se/matstat/stixbox/). The fit was based on the model log $[p / (1 - p)] = Xb$, where p is the probability that the choice is 1 (sooner option) and not 0 (later option), X represents value differences, and b represents the point estimates for the logistic function. Indifference points lying outside the valid interval [0,1] were replaced by the minimum (0.01) or maximum (0.8) of the manipulated subjective value. In the next step, we fitted for each subject a hyperbolic function to the indifference points over the different intervals and extracted the k parameter of this function (Green & Myerson, 2004). A higher k-value is taken as indicator of an increased discounting of delayed rewards. According to our hypothesis, GD patients should display an increased delay discounting especially after negative interpersonal scenes.

Statistical analyses

We used regression analyses to test our hypotheses regarding the effect of negative interpersonal scenes on inhibitory control and decision-making. It is important to note that our two-by-two design has produced data that do not meet the assumptions of repeated ANOVA (normally distributed outcome with equal variance in all four conditions). Therefore, we applied regression analyses for which requirements regarding data distribution and variance are less strict, as regression models provide additional robust estimates of the standard errors, p-values, and confidence intervals (e.g. robust regression; for an overview see Field & Wilcox, 2017). In addition to other suitable methods, e.g. mixed effects models, robust regression provides the advantage of correcting outliers effects, i.e. that individuals have very different impact on the results (according to the squared errors method), by (nearly) equally weighting them. As robust regression can only be applied for univariate outcomes, we have used specific contrasts (negative interpersonal vs. neutral scenes) within the two-by-two design. The dependent variables of the regression models were the performance differences between trials with either negative appreciation-related or autonomy-related pictures and trials with neutral pictures (e.g. the mean k-value in the negative appreciation-related condition minus the mean k-value in the neutral condition). Group was used as predictor. Since the dependent variables are difference scores (between the negative interpersonal and the neutral conditions), performance in the neutral condition was used as an additional predictor to control for general performance differences between groups that might otherwise bias or mask effects. Furthermore, as education years have been shown to be negatively correlated with performance in inhibitory control and decision-making tasks (e.g. Reimers, Maylor, Stewart, & Chater, 2009; as well as in our sample), we included education years as a factor in the between-group comparisons to control for the significantly lower education levels in the GD group. As results did not differ between the standard and the robust regression methods, we report only results of the standard regression models. Instead of effect sizes, we report 95% confidence intervals (CI) to inform which range of parameters is in line with the data at the given confidence level (Wilkinson & APA Task Force on Statistical Inference, 1999). All statistical analyses were conducted using Stata 14.1 (Stata Corp, 2014).

Results

Participants

Sample characteristics are presented in Table 1. The 49 participants in the GD group were between 20 and 63 years old, predominantly male (84%), and contained a high proportion (96%) of patients with one or several co-morbid mental disorders, mostly tobacco (78%) and alcohol use disorder (37%) and major depression (14%). In the control group, age ranged from 19 to 63 and the proportion of males was 72%. Control participants did not display any gambling problems. They answered the KFG items with 0 (strongly disagree) or 1 (disagree), gambled less than once per week and had no gambling debts. GD patients gambled almost daily before their treatment. Their gambling preferences were 81.3% for land-based gambling machines ($n = 39$), 33.3% for casinos ($n = 16$) and 16.7% for lotto tickets (e.g. lotto 6 out of 49, Toto) ($n = 16$). Groups did not significantly differ in mean age ($t = -0.22, p = 0.82$) or gender proportion ($\chi^2 = 1.42, p = 0.23$). Education was significantly higher in the control group both with respect to years of education ($t = 8.83; p < 0.001$) and education levels ($\chi^2 = 37.61, p < 0.001$). We therefore controlled for education years in the statistical analyses.

Inhibitory control

Descriptive results of the go/no-go task for each of the three conditions are presented in Table 2. In the neutral condition, we found no significant group differences for IES ($\beta = -10.60, p = 0.93$, CI: $-236.39-215.19$), false alarm rates ($\beta = -.02, p = 0.74$,

Table 1. Demographical and clinical characteristics with either means (M) and standard deviations (SD) or numbers (*n*) and percentages for the gambling disorder (GD) group and the control group (CG).

Variables	GD M(SD)	CG M(SD)
n	49	29
Age	37.24 (12.87)	37.88 (11.64)
Education years	13.21 (2.03)	18.43 (3.12)
Gambling disorder severity (KFG)[a]	36.49 (8.32)	0.59 (2.00)
	n (%)	*n* (%)
Male participants	41 (83.7%)	21 (72.4%)

[a]The German short questionnaire for gambling behaviour (Kurzfragebogen zum Glücksspielverhalten, KFG) is a screening for GD severity with 20 items on 4-point Likert scales (0–3) and a cut-off of 16 for GD.

THE NEUROSCIENCE AND NEUROPSYCHOLOGY OF GAMBLING

Table 2. Means (M) and standard deviations (SD) of the study outcomes decision-making and inhibitory control performance for the three conditions (neutral, negative autonomy-related, and negative appreciation-related interpersonal scenes) in the gambling disorder (GD) group and the control group (CG).

Variables per condition	GD M(SD)	CG M(SD)
Inhibitory control		
IES[a] go/no-go task		
Neutral	755.05 (387.51)	647.08 (235.56)
Negative autonomy-related	709.92 (210.10)	739.43 (264.51)
Negative appreciation-related	693.74 (164.43)	665.01 (166.30)
No-go error rates		
Neutral	22.13 (20.26)	18.10 (15.14)
Negative autonomy-related	21.17 (18.60)	25.86 (20.44)
Negative appreciation-related	22.23 (15.70)	21.25 (16.02)
Go reaction times		
Neutral	523.87 (73.40)	496.74 (65.09)
Negative autonomy-related	526.50 (71.75)	493.50 (58.41)
Negative appreciation-related	519.23 (68.86)	497.03 (56.89)
Decision-making		
k-values[b] ITC task		
Neutral	0.07 (0.05)	0.05 (0.07)
Negative autonomy-related	0.07 (0.05)	0.05 (0.09)
Negative appreciation-related	0.07 (0.05)	0.04 (0.04)

Note: IES = Inverse efficiency score, ITC = intertemporal choice.
[a]Higher values indicate lower inhibitory control.
[b]Higher values indicate increased discounting of delayed rewards.

CI: -0.14–0.10), or go reaction times ($\beta = 25.59$, $p = 0.32$, CI: -25.49–76.66, not displayed in the tables).

Testing our hypothesis that negative interpersonal scenes impair inhibitory control, we found a significant effect of group on IES differences between negative autonomy-related scenes and neutral scenes (Table 3). Unexpectedly, the reduction of inhibitory control after negative autonomy-related interpersonal scenes was significantly larger in the control compared to the GD group ($\beta = -139.52$, $p = 0.03$, CI: -264.94–-14.11). Additional analyses (not displayed in the tables) revealed that the effect was driven by higher false alarm rates ($\beta = -.11$, $p = 0.02$, CI: -0.22–0.02) and not by slower go reaction times ($\beta = 13.53$, $p = 0.28$, CI: -11.19–38.24). No such effect was evident for negative appreciation-related scenes (Table 3).

Within group analyses (not displayed in the tables) also indicated that there is a significant within-group difference between IES values after negative autonomy-related compared to neutral scenes in the control group ($\beta = 92.36$, $p = 0.04$, CI: 4.14–180.57) but not in the GD group ($\beta = -=-45.13$, p $=0.38$, CI: -146.73–56.47). The beta-value shows that the control group had higher IES values indicating a lower inhibitory control after negative autonomy-related compared to neutral scenes. This within-group effect was driven by higher false alarm rates ($\beta = 0.08$, $p = 0.01$, CI: 0.03–0.13) and not by slower reaction times ($\beta = -2.10$, $p = 0.81$, CI: -19.81–15.61). Additionally, we found a within-group effect between IES after negative appreciation-related compared to neutral scenes in the control group ($\beta = 42.18$, $p = 0.04$, CI: 0.30–84.06) but not in the GD group ($\beta = -61.31$, $p = 0.17$, CI: -150.41–27.78). Again, the positive beta value indicated lower inhibitory control after negative appreciation-related compared to neutral scenes in the control group. The effect seems to be neither solely due to higher false alarm rates ($\beta = 0.04$, $p = 0.09$, CI: -0.01–0.09) nor to slower reaction times alone ($\beta = -3.24$, $p = 0.66$, CI: -18.21–11.74), but to a combination

Table 3. Results of the regression analyses for hypotheses testing. The outcomes were the effects of the negative interpersonal scenes defined as performance differences between trials with either negative autonomy-related or appreciation-related pictures and those with neutral pictures. The predictors were group (gambling disorder and control group) and performance in the neutral condition. All results were adjusted for group differences in education years.

	Beta	Standard error	t	p-value	95% confidence interval
Negative autonomy-related versus neutral scenes					
Effects on IES (go/no-go task)					
Group	−139.52	62.87	−2.22	0.03	−264.94−−14.11
Education years	−14.68	7.29	−2.02	0.05	−29.21−−0.15
IES neutral condition	−0.72	0.11	−6.58	<0.001	−0.94−−0.50
Effects on *k*-value (ITC task)[a]					
Group	0.17	0.30	0.57	0.57	−0.43−0.78
Education years	−0.01	0.04	−0.15	0.88	−0.09−0.08
k-value neutral condition	−0.52	0.10	−4.95	<0.001	−0.72−−0.31
Negative appreciation-related versus neutral scenes					
Effects on IES (go/no-go task)					
Group	−37.92	43.50	−0.87	0.39	−124.72−48.88
Education years	−6.62	5.97	−1.11	0.27	−18.53−5.30
IES neutral condition	−0.70	0.05	−15.29	<0.001	−0.79−−0.61
Effects on *k*-value (ITC task)[a]					
Group	0.33	0.24	1.38	0.17	−0.15−0.82
Education years	−0.03	0.03	−0.82	0.42	−0.10−0.04
k-value neutral condition	−0.70	0.08	−8.40	<0.001	−0.86−−0.53

Note: IES = Inverse efficiency score, ITC = intertemporal choice.
[a]We report the results of the standardized *k*-values to provide a better scaling of beta values and confidence intervals.

of both. In sum, results revealed lower inhibitory control in the control group after negative interpersonal scenes while there was no effect in the GD group.

Decision-making

Descriptive results of the ITC task can be found in Table 2. Although the GD group had higher *k*-values compared to the control group in the unadjusted regression analyses, we found no group difference in the neutral condition after adjusting for education years ($\beta = 0.02$; $p = 0.95$, CI: −0.67−0.71, not displayed in the tables). It is important to note that we report regression analyses results of the standardized *k*-values to provide a better scaling of beta values and confidence intervals.

Testing our hypothesis that negative interpersonal scenes impair decision-making, the regression analyses revealed no significant group effect regarding the difference of decision-making performance after negative interpersonal compared to neutral scenes (Table 3).

Additional within-group analyses revealed no evidence for differences between the negative autonomy-related (GD: $\beta = 0.04$; $p = 0.71$, CI: −0.18−0.26; CG: $\beta = -0.24$, $p = 0.28$, CI: −0.69−0.21) or appreciation-related conditions and the neutral condition (GD: $\beta = 0.04$, $p = 0.71$, CI: −0.19−0.28; CG: $\beta = -0.26$, $p = 0.28$, CI: −0.74−0.22). In sum, we found no hypothesized effects of negative interpersonal scenes on decision-making in GD.

Discussion

The aim of our study was to contribute to disorder models of GD by combining assumptions from neuropsychological and psychosocial theories. We examined for the first time whether inhibitory control and decision-making in GD are impaired more strongly following the presentation of negative compared to neutral interpersonal scenes. For decision-making, we found no effect of the scenes. Surprisingly, we found that negative interpersonal scenes decreased inhibitory control in healthy individuals but not in GD patients. This is an important finding since reverse results were expected assuming interpersonal problems as important contextual cues for gambling that induce impairments in inhibitory control. To contribute to replication studies that are definitively needed in this new field of research, we propose two post hoc explanations for these unexpected results.

One possible explanation could be different stress responses following negative interpersonal scenes between GD and control participants (Goudriaan, Oosterlaan, de Beurs, & Van den Brink, 2004). While several studies have observed increased heart rate and hypothalamic–pituitary–adrenal axis (HPA) activation in recreational gamblers during gambling-related activities (Wulfert, Franco, Williams, Roland, & Maxson, 2008), the opposite has been observed in individuals with GD. GD seems to be related to an exaggerated sympathetic tone (Meyer et al., 2004) and lower cortisol awakening responses (Wohl, Matheson, Young, & Anisman, 2008) suggesting heightened levels of arousal and stress which may, in the long run, result in allostatic load and in hyporeactivity to stress (Koob & Le Moal, 2001). In line with this assumption, it has been shown that GD is related to a sympathetic and HPA hypoactivation in gambling-related (Paris, Franco, Sodano, Frye, & Wulfert, 2010) and social stress situations (Maniaci, Goudriaan, Cannizzaro, & van Holst, 2018). It may thus be speculated that the negative interpersonal scenes induced a stronger stress response in the control group who therefore displayed impaired prefrontal abilities like cognitive control by high levels of monoamine and glucocorticoid release (Arnsten, 2009; Schwabe, 2013). In contrast, GD patients may have responded with less pronounced stress responses that did not influence task performance. Future studies may use videotaped scenarios as more potent stressors to further test this post hoc hypothesis. For instance, one study using videotaped scenes as stressors revealed decreased brain activations in regions related to inhibitory control in GD patients compared to controls (Potenza et al., 2003). Moreover, our results revealed higher effects of scenes representing a lack of autonomy compared to a lack of appreciation. This emphasizes the importance of the content of interpersonal problems which could be addressed in further studies, for instance, with the presentation of individualized scenarios of interpersonal problems using audiotapes or imagination. However, irrespective of the methods to induce interpersonal distress, there is a high need for future research that additionally assesses physiological and neuroendocrine stress markers to detect whether an altered stress response in GD could probably be an explanation of our results.

A second possible explanation rests on the assumption that the presentation of negative interpersonal scenes may have induced negative affect that has been found to impair self-control in healthy individuals (Tice et al., 2001). One assumed mechanism underlying such impairments are cognitive coping strategies like reappraisal (Tice et al., 2001). These cognitive coping strategies are associated with brain activations in the prefrontal and anterior cingulate cortex (e.g. Drabant, McRae, Manuck, Hariri, & Gross, 2009; Goldin, McRae, Ramel, & Gross, 2008; Ochsner, Bunge, Gross, & Gabrieli, 2002) and may thus have interfered with the recruitment of cognitive control processes in our healthy participants.

In contrast, research has revealed that individuals with GD are characterized by a lack of emotional awareness and maladaptive escape-/avoidance-oriented coping strategies like behavioural distraction (e.g. Getty, Watson, & Frisch, 2000; Ledgerwood & Petry, 2006b; Nower, Derevensky, & Gupta, 2004; Sleczka, Braun, Grüne, Bühringer, & Kraus, 2016; A. D. Williams, Grisham, Erskine, & Cassedy, 2012). Possibly, GD patients used task performance as behavioural distraction strategy after the negative interpersonal scenes and achieved comparable error rates to the neutral condition. This is in line with the assumption that altered emotion regulation and dysfunctional coping skills are important moderators in the relation between impulsivity traits and addictive behaviours (Adams, Kaiser, Lynam, Charnigo, & Milich, 2012; Navas et al., 2017). However, differences in emotion regulation cannot explain the lack of an effect of negative interpersonal scenes on decision-making in our study, whereas previous studies have shown a shift towards immediate rewards after negative emotions and thoughts (e.g. Selby et al., 2016; Tice et al., 2001). One explanation could be that delay discounting has been found to be very stable and has been considered a personality trait (Odum, 2011). Nevertheless, previous research has also shown that state variables like the context can influence discounting in GD over short time periods (Dixon et al., 2006). Possibly, the emotional content of our pictures did not evoke strong enough context effects. Unfortunately, the time schedule in the clinic did not allow assessing the ratings of the picture and the actual mood of the participants to further test the assumptions of our post hoc explanation. Therefore, future studies on this topic need to apply ratings of the valence, arousal and mood induced by the pictures combined with an assessment of habitual coping strategies. Another promising method might be ecological momentary assessments, which so far have shown that negative emotions and rumination induce different kinds of impulsive behaviours in healthy individuals (Selby et al., 2016). In further studies, it will also be important to assess subtypes of gamblers (Milosevic & Ledgerwood, 2010; Navas et al., 2017). One study, for instance, has shown that only gamblers who viewed gambling as a way to enhance positive mood may be characterized by dysfunctional decision-making (Shead, Callan, & Hodgins, 2008). In our sample, highly co-morbid gamblers with a gambling machine preference were assessed who can rather be assigned to the emotional vulnerable subtype who gambles to escape dysphoric moods (Blaszczynski & Nower, 2002; Milosevic & Ledgerwood, 2010; Sharpe, 2002).

Limitations and strength

In this – to our best knowledge – first study on the effects of interpersonal problems on inhibitory control and decision-making, we examined effects of pictures depicting negative interpersonal scenes on performance in well-established laboratory tasks. While this approach has the advantage of high internal validity, its external validity may be lower compared to studies in more naturalistic settings. Although we tested our pictures in a pretest regarding their association with a lack of autonomy or a lack of appreciation as well as regarding their negative valence, we did not assess subjective ratings of the applied pictures in our sample. Therefore, the pictures may not have represented the actual interpersonal problems or may have not been perceived as strongly negative in each individual participant. Moreover, pictures do of course not elicit the same response as real-life interpersonal problems. For the recruitment of the GD patients, we applied a low inclusion threshold to achieve a high generalizability of our GD sample. The disadvantage was that the GD group differed in co-morbidity rates and education levels from the control group. Furthermore, we had no information regarding the income in the GD group due to the data confidentiality regulations in the inpatient clinic. In our analyses, we could not control for differences in co-morbidity rates or income between both groups. This might have biased our conclusions; for instance, regarding emotion regulation differences that are not due to GD but to co-morbid depressive or anxiety disorders. However, we adjusted our analyses regarding the education level. Interestingly, we found no group difference in delay discounting after adjusting for education levels even though previous research yielded consistent evidence for higher delay discounting in GD (MacKillop et al., 2011; Wiehler & Peters, 2015). This highlights the importance of taking into account such confounding variables when comparing naturalistic non-randomized groups. A last limitation regarding our inpatient sample is that our results may not be generalized to the general GD population since it has been shown that only a minority of individuals with GD seek treatment (Slutske, 2006).

Conclusions and future research needs

Interpersonal problems and conflicts have long been recognized as gambling motives (Ledgerwood & Petry, 2006a; Stewart et al., 2008) and as one precondition for relapse (Ledgerwood & Petry, 2006b; Marlatt, 1996). Our study revealed that the effects of interpersonal problems on gambling behaviour in GD may not directly be explained by cue-induced impairments of inhibitory control or decision-making processes. As this was the first study on this topic, replication studies are needed that assess additional outcomes to explain increased gambling or relapse after interpersonal problems. These studies should use more individualized and realistic negative interpersonal stimuli to enhance external validity. To understand the causal role of interpersonal problems in GD, gambling behaviour after the interpersonal stressor could be assessed with experimental slot machine tasks (see, e.g. Devos, Clark, Maurage, Kazimierczuk, & Billieux, 2015), whereby the sample should not include gambling abstinent GD patients. Furthermore, stress responses, negative emotions, and coping strategies need to be assessed to gain a deeper knowledge about the mechanisms involved in increased gambling activities or relapse after interpersonal problems, which in the long run may help to improve clinical assessment and trainings of stress coping and interpersonal skills in GD.

Conflicts of interest

Funding sources

This research was supported by the German Research Foundation (DFG) within the Collaborative Research Centre 'Volition and Cognitive Control' [Grant No. SFB 940/1 2016], [Grant No. SFB 940/2 2017].

Competing interests

Anja Kräplin, Stefan Scherbaum, Thomas Goschke and André Schmidt declare no competing interests. Gerhard Bühringer has received unrestricted gambling research grants from the Bavarian State Ministry of Finance (regulatory authority for and operator of the state gambling monopoly) via the Bavarian State Ministry of Public Health and Care Services, from the German Federal Ministry of Economics and Technology (regulatory authority for parts of the commercial gaming industry), and from public and commercial gambling providers.

Constraints on publishing

The authors declared no constraints on publishing.

Ethical approval

The study protocol was approved by the local Ethics Committee at the Technische Universität Dresden, Germany (reference no. EK 170062012) and was in accordance with the 1964 Helsinki declaration and its later amendments.

Acknowledgements

We wish to thank Dr Michael Höfler for his helpful comments on statistical issues.

ORCID

Anja Kräplin http://orcid.org/0000-0002-1612-3932
Gerhard Bühringer http://orcid.org/0000-0002-5568-1435

References

Adams, Z. W., Kaiser, A. J., Lynam, D. R., Charnigo, R. J., & Milich, R. (2012). Drinking motives as mediators of the impulsivity-substance use relation: Pathways for negative urgency, lack of premeditation, and sensation seeking. *Addictive Behaviors, 37*(7), 848–855. doi:10.1016/j.addbeh.2012.03.016

American Psychiatric Association (APA). (2013). *Diagnostic and statistical manual of mental disorders: DSM-5* (5th ed.). Washington, DC: American Psychiatric Association.

Arnsten, A. F. T. (2009). Stress signalling pathways that impair prefrontal cortex structure and function. *Nature Reviews Neuroscience, 10*(6), 410–422. doi:10.1038/nrn2648

Baumeister, R. F., & Leary, M. R. (1995). The need to belong: Desire for interpersonal attachments as a fundamental human motivation. *Psychological Bulletin, 117*(3), 497–529. doi:10.1037/0033-2909.117.3.497

Beck, S. M., Ruge, H., Schindler, C., Burkart, M., Miller, R., Kirschbaum, C., & Goschke, T. (2016). Effects of Ginkgo biloba extract EGb 761® on cognitive control functions, mental activity of the prefrontal cortex and stress reactivity in elderly adults with subjective memory impairment – a randomized double-blind placebo-controlled trial. *Human Psychopharmacology: Clinical and Experimental, 31*(3), 227–242. doi:10.1002/hup.2534

Blaszczynski, A., & Nower, L. (2002). A pathways model of problem and pathological gambling. *Addiction, 97*(5), 487–499. doi:10.1046/j.1360-0443.2002.00015.x

Bogacz, R. (2014). Speed-accuracy trade-off. In D. Jaeger & R. Jung (Eds.), *Encyclopedia of computational neuroscience* (pp. 1–4). New York, NY: Springer.

Boyer, M., & Dickerson, M. (2003). Attentional bias and addictive behaviour: Automaticity in a gambling-specific modified Stroop task. *Addiction, 98*(1), 61–70. doi:10.1046/j.1360-0443.2003.00219.x

Bruyer, R., & Brysbaert, M. (2011). Combining Speed and Accuracy in Cognitive Psychology: Is the Inverse Efficiency Score (IES) a Better Dependent Variable than the Mean Reaction Time (RT) and the Percentage Of Errors (PE)? *Psychologica Belgica, 51*(1), 5–13. doi:10.5334/pb-51-1-5

Clark, L. (2010). Decision-making during gambling: An integration of cognitive and psychobiological approaches. *Philosophical Transactions of the Royal Society B: Biological Sciences, 365*(1538), 319–330. doi:10.1098/rstb.2009.0147

Deci, E. L., & Ryan, R. M. (2000). The "what" and "why" of goal pursuits: Human needs and the self-determination of behavior. *Psychological Inquiry, 11*(4), 227–268. doi:10.1207/S15327965PLI1104_01

Devos, G., Clark, L., Maurage, P., Kazimierczuk, M., & Billieux, J. (2015). Reduced inhibitory control predicts persistence in laboratory slot machine gambling. *International Gambling Studies, 15*(3), 408–421. doi:10.1080/14459795.2015.1068351

Dixon, M. R., Jacobs, E. A., & Sanders, S. (2006). Contextual Control of Delay Discounting by Pathological Gamblers. *Journal of Applied Behavior Analysis, 39*(4), 413–422. doi:10.1901/jaba.2006.173-05

Drabant, E. M., McRae, K., Manuck, S. B., Hariri, A. R., & Gross, J. J. (2009). Individual differences in typical reappraisal use predict amygdala and prefrontal responses. *Biological Psychiatry, 65*(5), 367–373. doi:10.1016/j.biopsych.2008.09.007

Field, A. P., & Wilcox, R. R. (2017). Robust statistical methods: A primer for clinical psychology and experimental psychopathology researchers. *Behaviour Research and Therapy, 98*(Supplement C), 19–38. doi:10.1016/j.brat.2017.05.013

Friedman, N. P., Miyake, A., Young, S. E., DeFries, J. C., Corley, R. P., & Hewitt, J. K. (2008). Individual differences in executive functions are almost entirely genetic in origin. *Journal of Experimental Psychology: General, 137*(2), 201–225. doi:10.1037/0096-3445.137.2.201

Getty, H. A., Watson, J., & Frisch, G. R. (2000). A comparison of depression and styles of coping in male and female GA members and controls. *Journal of Gambling Studies, 16*(4), 377–391. doi:10.1023/a:1009480106531

Goldin, P. R., McRae, K., Ramel, W., & Gross, J. J. (2008). The neural bases of emotion regulation: Reappraisal and suppression of negative emotion. *Biological Psychiatry, 63*(6), 577–586. doi:10.1016/j.biopsych.2007.05.031

Goschke, T. (2014). Dysfunctions of decision-making and cognitive control as transdiagnostic mechanisms of mental disorders: Advances, gaps, and needs in current research. *International Journal of Methods in Psychiatric Research, 23*(S1), 41–57. doi:10.1002/mpr.1410

Goudriaan, A. E., Oosterlaan, J., de Beurs, E., & Van den Brink, W. (2004). Pathological gambling: A comprehensive review of biobehavioral findings. *Neuroscience & Biobehavioral Reviews, 28*(2), 123–141. doi:10.1016/j.neubiorev.2004.03.001

de Greck, M., Enzi, B., Prösch, U., Gantman, A., Tempelmann, C., & Northoff, G. (2010). Decreased neuronal activity in reward circuitry of pathological gamblers during processing of personal relevant stimuli. *Human Brain Mapping, 31*(11), 1802–1812. doi:10.1002/hbm.20981

Green, L., & Myerson, J. (2004). A Discounting Framework for Choice With Delayed and Probabilistic Rewards. *Psychological Bulletin, 130*(5), 769–792. doi:10.1037/0033-2909.130.5.769

Hardoon, K. K., Gupta, R., & Derevensky, J. L. (2004). Psychosocial variables associated with adolescent gambling. *Psychology of Addictive Behaviors, 18*(2), 170–179. doi:10.1037/0893-164X.18.2.170

van Holst, R. J., van den Brink, W., Veltman, D. J., & Goudriaan, A. E. (2010). Why gamblers fail to win: A review of cognitive and neuroimaging findings in pathological gambling. *Neuroscience & Biobehavioral Reviews, 34*(1), 87–107. doi:10.1016/j.neubiorev.2009.07.007

Kausch, O., Rugle, L., & Rowland, D. Y. (2006). Lifetime Histories of Trauma among Pathological Gamblers. *American Journal on Addictions, 15*(1), 35–43. doi:10.1080/10550490500419045

Koob, G. F., & Le Moal, M. (2001). Drug Addiction, Dysregulation of Reward, and Allostasis. *Neuropsychopharmacology, 24*(2), 97–129. doi:10.1016/S0893-133X(00)00195-0

Kräplin, A., Dshemuchadse, M., Behrendt, S., Scherbaum, S., Goschke, T., & Bühringer, G. (2014). Dysfunctional decision-making in pathological gambling: Pattern specificity and the role of impulsivity. *Psychiatry Research, 215*(3), 675–682. doi:10.1016/j.psychres.2013.12.041

Ledgerwood, D. M., & Petry, N. M. (2006a). Psychological experience of gambling and subtypes of pathological gamblers. *Psychiatry Research, 144*(1), 17–27. doi:10.1016/j.psychres.2005.08.017

Ledgerwood, D. M., & Petry, N. M. (2006b). What do we know about relapse in pathological gambling? *Clinical Psychology Review, 26*(2), 216–228. doi:10.1016/j.cpr.2005.11.008

Liu, L., Feng, T., Chen, J., & Li, H. (2013). The value of emotion: How does episodic prospection modulate delay discounting? *PLoS ONE, 8*(11), e81717. doi:10.1371/journal.pone.0081717

Lorains, F. K., Cowlishaw, S., & Thomas, S. A. (2011). Prevalence of comorbid disorders in problem and pathological gambling: Systematic review and meta-analysis of population surveys. *Addiction, 106*(3), 490–498. doi:10.1111/j.1360-0443.2010.03300.x

MacKillop, J., Amlung, M. T., Few, L. R., Ray, L. A., Sweet, L. H., & Munafò, M. R. (2011). Delayed reward discounting and addictive behavior: A meta-analysis. *Psychopharmacology, 216*(3), 305–321. doi:10.1007/s00213-011-2229-0

Maniaci, G., Goudriaan, A. E., Cannizzaro, C., & van Holst, R. J. (2018). Impulsivity and stress response in pathological gamblers during the Trier Social Stress Test. *Journal of Gambling Studies, 34*(1), 147–160. doi:10.1007/s10899-017-9685-3

Marlatt, G. A. (1996). Taxonomy of high-risk situations for alcohol relapse: Evolution and development of a cognitive-behavioral model. *Addiction, 91*(12s1), 37–49. doi:10.1046/j.1360-0443.91.12s1.15.x

Masur, P. K., Reinecke, L., Ziegele, M., & Quiring, O. (2014). The interplay of intrinsic need satisfaction and Facebook specific motives in explaining addictive behavior on Facebook. *Computers in Human Behavior, 39*, 376–386. doi:10.1016/j.chb.2014.05.047

McCormick, R. A. (1994). The importance of coping skill enhancement in the treatment of the pathological gambler. *Journal of Gambling Studies, 10*(1), 77–86. doi:10.1007/bf02109780

MEYER, G., Schwertfeger, J., Exton, M. S., Janssen, O. E., Knapp, W., Stadler, M. A., & Kruger, T. H. C. (2004). Neuroendocrine response to casino gambling in problem gamblers. *Psychoneuroendocrinology, 29*(10), 1272–1280. doi:10.1016/j.psyneuen.2004.03.005

Miedl, S. F., Büchel, C., & Peters, J. (2014). Cue-Induced Craving Increases Impulsivity via Changes in Striatal Value Signals in Problem Gamblers. *Journal of Neuroscience, 34*(13), 4750–4755. doi:10.1523/jneurosci.5020-13.2014

Milosevic, A., & Ledgerwood, D. M. (2010). The subtyping of pathological gambling: A comprehensive review. *Clinical Psychology Review, 30*(8), 988–998. doi:10.1016/j.cpr.2010.06.013

Navas, J. F., Billieux, J., Perandrés-Gómez, A., López-Torrecillas, F., Cándido, A., & Perales, J. C. (2017). Impulsivity traits and gambling cognitions associated with gambling preferences and clinical status. *International Gambling Studies, 17*(1), 102–124. doi:10.1080/14459795.2016.1275739

Neighbors, C., & Larimer, M. E. (2004). Self-Determination and Problem Gambling Among College Students. *Journal of Social and Clinical Psychology, 23*(4), 565–583. doi:10.1521/jscp.23.4.565.40310

Nower, L., Derevensky, J. L., & Gupta, R. (2004). The Relationship of Impulsivity, Sensation Seeking, Coping, and Substance Use in Youth Gamblers. *Psychology of Addictive Behaviors, 18*(1), 49–55. doi:10.1037/0893-164X.18.1.49

Ochsner, K. N., Bunge, S. A., Gross, J. J., & Gabrieli, J. D. E. (2002). Rethinking feelings: An fMRI Study of the cognitive regulation of emotion. *Journal of Cognitive Neuroscience, 14*(8), 1215–1229. doi:10.1162/089892902760807212

Odum, A. L. (2011). Delay discounting: Trait variable? *Behavioural Processes, 87*(1), 1–9. doi:10.1016/j.beproc.2011.02.007

Paris, J. J., Franco, C., Sodano, R., Frye, C. A., & Wulfert, E. (2010). Gambling pathology is associated with dampened cortisol response among men and women. *Physiology & Behavior, 99*(2), 230–233. doi:10.1016/j.physbeh.2009.04.002

Petry, J., & Baulig, T. (1996). KFG: Kurzfragebogen zum Glücksspielverhalten [German short questionnaire for gambling behavior]. In J. Petry (Ed.), *Psychotherapie der Glücksspielsucht [Psychotherapy of Pathological Gambling]* (pp. 300–302). Weinheim: Psychologie Verlags Union.

Petry, N. M., & Steinberg, K. L. (2005). Childhood maltreatment in male and female treatment-seeking pathological gamblers. *Psychology of Addictive Behaviors, 19*(2), 226–229. doi:10.1037/0893-164X.19.2.226

Potenza, M. N., Steinberg, M. A., Skudlarski, P., Fulbright, R. K., Lacadie, C. M., Wilber, M. K., ... Wexler, B. E. (2003). Gambling urges in pathological gambling. *Archives of General Psychiatry, 60*(8), 828–836. doi:10.1001/archpsyc.60.8.828

Redish, A. D., Jensen, S., & Johnson, A. (2008). A unified framework for addiction: Vulnerabilities in the decision process. *Behavioral and Brain Sciences, 31*, 415–487. doi:10.1017/S0140525X0800472X

Reimers, S., Maylor, E. A., Stewart, N., & Chater, N. (2009). Associations between a one-shot delay discounting measure and age, income, education and real-world impulsive behavior. *Personality and Individual Differences, 47*(8), 973–978. doi:10.1016/j.paid.2009.07.026

Schwabe, L. (2013). Stress and the engagement of multiple memory systems: Integration of animal and human studies. *Hippocampus, 23*(11), 1035–1043. doi:10.1002/hipo.22175

Selby, E. A., Kranzler, A., Panza, E., & Fehling, K. B. (2016). Bidirectional-Compounding effects of rumination and negative emotion in predicting impulsive behavior: Implications for emotional cascades. *Journal of Personality, 84*(2), 139–153. doi:10.1111/jopy.12147

Shaffer, H. J., & Korn, D. A. (2002). Gambling and related mental disorders: A public health analysis. *Annual Review of Public Health, 23*(1), 171–212. doi:10.1146/annurev.publhealth.23.100901.140532

Shaffer, H. J., LaPlante, D. A., LaBrie, R. A., Kidman, R. C., Donato, A. N., & Stanton, M. V. (2004). Toward a syndrome model of addiction: Multiple expressions, common etiology. *Harvard Review of Psychiatry, 12*(6), 367–374. doi:10.1080/10673220490905705

Sharpe, L. (2002). A reformulated cognitive-behavioral model of problem gambling: A biopsychosocial perspective. *Clinical Psychology Review, 22*(1), 1–25. doi:10.1016/S0272-7358(00)00087-8

Shaw, M. C., Forbush, K. T., Schlinder, J., Rosenman, E., & Black, D. W. (2007). The effect of pathological gambling on families, marriages, and children. *CNS Spectrums, 12*(08), 615–622. doi:10.1017/S1092852900021416

Shead, N. W., Callan, M. J., & Hodgins, D. C. (2008). Probability discounting among gamblers: Differences across problem gambling severity and affect-regulation expectancies. *Personality and Individual Differences, 45*(6), 536–541. doi:10.1016/j.paid.2008.06.008

Sleczka, P., Braun, B., Grüne, B., Bühringer, G., & Kraus, L. (2016). Proactive coping and gambling disorder among young men. *Journal of Behavioral Addictions, 5*(4), 639–648. doi:10.1556/2006.5.2016.080

Slutske, W. S. (2006). Natural recovery and treatment-seeking in pathological gambling: Results of two U.S. national surveys. *American Journal of Psychiatry, 163*(2), 297–302. doi:10.1176/appi.ajp.163.2.297

Smith, J. L., Mattick, R. P., Jamadar, S. D., & Iredale, J. M. (2014). Deficits in behavioural inhibition in substance abuse and addiction: A meta-analysis. *Drug and Alcohol Dependence, 145*, 1–33. doi:10.1016/j.drugalcdep.2014.08.009

Stata Corp. (2014). *Stata statistical software: Release 14.0*. College Station, TX: Stata Corp LCC.

Stewart, S. H., Zack, M., Collins, P., & Klein, R. M. (2008). Subtyping pathological gamblers on the basis of affective motivations for gambling: Relations to gambling problems, drinking problems, and affective motivations for drinking. *Psychology of Addictive Behaviors, 22*(2), 257–268. doi:10.1037/0893-164X.22.2.257

Tice, D. M., Bratslavsky, E., & Baumeister, R. F. (2001). Emotional distress regulation takes precedence over impulse control: If you feel bad, do it!. *Journal of Personality and Social Psychology, 80*(1), 53–67. doi:10.1037//0022-3514.80.1.53

Toneatto, T., Lecce, J., & Bagby, M. (2009). Alexithymia and pathological gambling. *Journal of Addictive Diseases, 28*(3), 193–198. doi:10.1080/10550880903014775

Verbruggen, F., & De Houwer, J. (2007). Do emotional stimuli interfere with response inhibition? Evidence from the stop signal paradigm. *Cognition and Emotion, 21*(2), 391–403. doi:10.1080/02699930600625081

Verdejo-García, A., Lawrence, A. J., & Clark, L. (2008). Impulsivity as a vulnerability marker for substance-use disorders: Review of findings from high-risk research, problem gamblers and genetic association studies. *Neuroscience & Biobehavioral Reviews, 32*(4), 777–810. doi:10.1016/j.neubiorev.2007.11.003

Whitmer, A. J., & Banich, M. T. (2007). Inhibition versus switching deficits in different forms of rumination. *Psychological Science, 18*(6), 546–553. doi:10.1111/j.1467-9280.2007.01936.x

Wickwire, E. M., Whelan, J. P., Meyers, A. W., & Murray, D. (2007). Environmental correlates of gambling behavior in urban adolescents. *Journal of Abnormal Child Psychology, 35*(2), 179–190. doi:10.1007/s10802-006-9065-4

Wiehler, A., & Peters, J. (2015). Reward-based decision making in pathological gambling: The roles of risk and delay. *Neuroscience Research, 90*, 3–14. doi:10.1016/j.neures.2014.09.008

Wilkinson, L., & APA Task Force on Statistical Inference., (1999). Statistical methods in psychology journals: Guidelines and explanations. *American Psychologist, 54*, 594–604. doi:10.1037/0003-066X.54.8.594

Williams, A. D., Grisham, J. R., Erskine, A., & Cassedy, E. (2012). Deficits in emotion regulation associated with pathological gambling. *British Journal of Clinical Psychology, 51*(2), 223–238. doi:10.1111/j.2044-8260.2011.02022.x

Williams, R. J., West, B. L., & Simpson, R. I. (2012). *Prevention of problem gambling: A comprehensive review of the evidence, and identified best practices*. Report prepared for the Ontario Problem Gambling Research Centre and the Ontario Ministry of Health and Long Term Care. Retrieved from https://www.uleth.ca/dspace/bitstream/handle/10133/3121/2012-PREVENTION-OPGRC.pdf [23.08.17].

Winters, K. C., Stinchfield, R. D., Botzet, A., & Anderson, N. (2002). A prospective study of youth gambling behaviors. *Psychology of Addictive Behaviors, 16*(1), 3–9. doi:10.1037/0893-164X.16.1.3

Wittchen, H.-U., & Pfister, H. (1997). *DIA-X Interview. Instruktionsmanual zur Durchführung von DIA-X-Interviews [Instruction manual for the DIA-X-Interview]*. Frankfurt: Swets & Zeitlinger.

Wohl, M. J. A., Matheson, K., Young, M. M., & Anisman, H. (2008). Cortisol rise following awakening among problem gamblers: Dissociation from comorbid symptoms of depression and impulsivity. *Journal of Gambling Studies, 24*(1), 79–90. doi:10.1007/s10899-007-9080-6

World Health Organization (WHO). (1992). *The ICD-10 classification of mental and behavioral disorders: Clinical descriptions and diagnostic guidelines*. Geneva: World Health Organization.

Wulfert, E., Franco, C., Williams, K., Roland, B. D., & Maxson, J. H. (2008). The role of money in the excitement of gambling. *Psychology of Addictive Behaviors, 22*(3), 380–390. doi:10.1037/0893-164X.22.3.380

Regional grey matter volume correlates of gambling disorder, gambling-related cognitive distortions, and emotion-driven impulsivity

Cristian M. Ruiz de Lara, Juan F. Navas, Carles Soriano-Mas, Guillaume Sescousse and José C. Perales

ABSTRACT

Reports of regional grey matter volume (GMV) anomalies in patients with gambling disorder (PGD) are inconsistent, which can be attributed to methodological disparity and inattention to individual variability. Voxel-based morphometry was used to compare GMV between 25 PGD and 25 healthy controls. Additionally, the study explored associations of *interpretative bias* (*IB*, the tendency to reinterpret gambling outcomes) and *negative urgency* (*NU*, the tendency to act rashly under negative affect) with GMV in patients. These measures were chosen based on their sound association with gambling disorder in related studies. GMV tests were corrected across the whole brain (using a combination of voxel and cluster-level thresholds for a clusterwise-equivalent $p \leq 0.05$). GMV was smaller in PGD than in controls in the dorsomedial prefrontal cortex. In PGD, a stronger cognitive distortion (higher IB) was associated with reduced GMV in the dorsal anterior cingulate; and patients with higher levels of impulsivity (higher NU) presented reduced GMV in the right ventrolateral prefrontal cortex. These findings are consistent with recent studies exploring individual differences in GD. However, the area discriminating between groups showed no overlap with the ones associated with IB and NU. These traits are thus unlikely to be responsible for between-group GMV differences.

Introduction

Gambling disorder (GD) is characterized by persistent gambling behaviour despite adverse consequences (Hodgins, Stea, & Grant, 2011). In view of its overlap with substance use disorders, a new category has been created in the *Diagnostic and Statistical Manual of*

Mental Disorders (DSM-5; American Psychiatric Association, 2013) for substance-related and addictive disorders, including gambling disorder as the only behavioural addiction currently recognized as such.

Structural magnetic resonance imaging (MRI) studies in substance use disorders have shown that regular drug use causes extensive morphological brain changes (Cousijn et al., 2012; Daumann et al., 2011; Fritz et al., 2014; Tolomeo, Gray, Matthews, Steele, & Baldacchino, 2016), and these alterations are difficult to disentangle from etiological substrates of addiction vulnerability. GD, on the contrary, does not necessarily involve brain exposure to addictive substances. Hence, if samples are carefully selected, comparisons between patients with gambling disorder (PGD) and controls are free of neurotoxic effects, which make GD a valuable model to understand addiction neurobiology.

In spite of this, literature investigating grey matter (GM) alterations in GD is scarce, and results inconsistent. Some studies (Joutsa, Saunavaara, Parkkola, Niemelä, & Kaasinen, 2011; van Holst, de Ruiter, van den Brink, Veltman, & Goudriaan, 2012) found no differences in GM between clinical samples and control groups, whereas others (Grant, Odlaug, & Chamberlain, 2015; Koehler, Hasselmann, Wüstenberg, Heinz, & Romanczuk-Seiferth, 2015; Rahman, Xu, & Potenza, 2014; Zois et al., 2017) found a mixed pattern of increases and decreases in frontal, parietal, and superior medial cortices, the hippocampus, the amygdala and ventral striatum.

These studies vary in methodology, and are not directly comparable. The present study tries to overcome some limitations of previous research by considering a large array of potential confounders (including drug use and psychiatric status) and matching the two groups as closely as possible. Given that most previous studies have used voxel-based morphometry (VBM) to explore regional grey matter volume (GMV), the same measure will be used here, while implementing a number of methodological improvements in order to reliably isolate the specific tissue of interest and better control for false positives[1].

A related question is whether GM alterations in PGD, if they exist, are related to variability among PGD. Gamblers have been classified according to personality traits (e.g. Billieux et al., 2012), clinical features (e.g. Blaszczynski & Nower, 2002) and game modality preferences (e.g. Navas, et al., 2017a). However, structural differences associated with gambling-related traits remain unexplored. The potential association between brain structure and individual differences among PGD is relevant in two domains. First, an overlap between group differences and areas associated with specific personality traits would help to understand how sample selection can account for different results across studies. And second, a lack of correspondence between group differences and regions related to personality traits could be relevant to understand how individual variability is integrated into underlying GD mechanisms to generate individual clinical profiles. Accordingly, this study focuses on traits that (1) have consistently been associated with GD development or complication mechanisms; (2) are easily and reliably measurable with instruments validated for our samples; and (3) can help to establish connections between brain dimensions and behavioural manifestations of GD.

Gambling-related cognitive biases meet these criteria. They are relevant for GD etiology (Clark, Studer, Bruss, Tranel, & Bechara, 2014), and are involved in gambling persistence and severity (Joukhador, Maccallum, & Blaszczynski, 2003; Subramaniam, Chong, Browning, & Thomas, 2017; Xian et al., 2008). With regard to their operationalization, the Gambling-Related Cognitions Scale (GRCS; Raylu & Oei, 2004) has shown good psychometric properties and is clinically informative (Michalczuk, Bowden-Jones, Verdejo-Garcia, & Clark, 2011). The scale covers three cognitive biases (illusions of prediction and control, and interpretative bias), along with subjective expectancies of reward and perceived inability to stop gambling.

In a previous study with a related sample, we identified *interpretative bias* (IB; the ad hoc attribution of gambling successes to ability and losses to bad luck) as the most informative cognitive bias in the GRCS to discriminate both between PGD and healthy control (HC) groups, and between different clinical and behavioural patterns in PGD. Importantly, biased cognitions assessed by IB were highly and independently predictive of gambling severity and clinical status (Del Prete et al., 2017; see also Donati, Ancona, Chiesi, & Primi, 2015; Grall-Bronnec et al., 2012; Navas, Verdejo-García, López-Gómez, Maldonado, & Perales, 2016). In order to avoid multiple testing with different subscales, IB was thus selected a priori as the most promising measure among GRCS cognitions.

Recent research exploring the associations between brain function and gambling-related biases has focused on the *near-miss* effect – the tendency to interpret losses perceptually similar to wins as if they were *almost* wins. Near misses have been shown to maintain motivation to gamble, and to recruit structures also responding to real monetary wins (Clark, Lawrence, Astley-Jones, & Gray, 2009). Functional MRI (fMRI) studies have reported increased striatal response to near-misses in gamblers compared to controls and associations between midbrain and insula activity and/or connectivity during near-misses and gambling severity (Chase & Clark, 2010; Sescousse et al., 2016; van Holst, Chase, & Clark, 2014). Beyond these areas, an fMRI study found that the influence of gambler's fallacy on responses in a card-guessing task correlated with a stronger activation of the lateral prefrontal cortex (lPFC; Xue, Juan, Chang, Lu, & Dong, 2012). Despite these precedents, literature on brain structure associations with individual differences in gambling cognitions is scarce (Clark et al., 2014), and, to our knowledge, there are no previous studies linking trait-like gambling-related cognitions to brain structure.

The second trait meeting our criteria, impulsivity, is actually linked to all addictive processes (Pattij & De Vries, 2013; Perry & Carroll, 2008; Verdejo-García, Lawrence, & Clark, 2008). Among the questionnaires proposed to operationalize impulsivity, the UPPS-P (Whiteside & Lynam, 2001) has been shown to be particularly informative. This model includes five dimensions: negative urgency, positive urgency, sensation seeking, lack of perseverance and lack of premeditation (Cyders & Smith, 2008), with the first three factors representing facets of motivation and affect-driven impulsivity, and the last two corresponding to cognitive impulsivity.

For reasons similar to the ones described above regarding IB, *negative urgency* (henceforth NU, the tendency to act rashly under the influence of strong negative emotions; Whiteside, Lynam, Miller, & Reynolds, 2005) was selected as the best candidate index of impulsivity-related individual variability.

Recent research does support the decisive relevance of NU in GD, with PGD exhibiting particularly high scores in this aspect of impulsivity (Albein-Urios, Martinez-González, Lozano, Clark, & Verdejo-García, 2012; Billieux et al., 2012; MacLaren, Fugelsang, Harrigan, & Dixon, 2011; Michalczuk et al., 2011). A recent integrative meta-analysis (MacLaren et al., 2011) confirms NU as an important vulnerability factor in the etiology of GD. Beyond addictive processes, NU has been observed to be a major determinant of externalizing behaviour (Berg, Latzman, Bliwise, & Lilienfeld, 2015), and a recent theoretical model

(Navas, Billieux, Verdejo-García, & Perales, 2018) suggests its contribution to gambling complications. In neurofunctional terms, available studies link NU in addicted individuals to anomalies in the functioning of cortico-striatal and cortico-amygdalar circuits (e.g. Clark et al., 2012; Contreras-Rodríguez et al., 2016). However, no previous studies have investigated the association of NU with brain structure in PGD.

Summing up, the aims of the present study were to explore potential differences in GMV between PGD and a well-matched group of HC, using a VBM approach; and to analyse the involvement of two specific measures of gambling-related cognitive distortions and affect-driven impulsivity (IB and NU) in individual GM variability.

With regard to the first aim, previous studies seem compatible with a reduction of GMV in PGD in control and regulation structures (Grant et al., 2015; Zois et al., 2017), but concordance is insufficient to make hypotheses about specific anatomical areas. Similarly, studies point to the involvement of insular and dorsal prefrontal cortices in gambling-related cognitive distortions, and of ventral prefrontal cortex, striatum and amygdala in affect-driven impulsivity (e.g. Clark et al., 2012; Contreras-Rodríguez et al., 2016), but no direct structural evidence is available. This makes whole-brain analysis with appropriate control of α-error growth necessary. However, with regard to NU, previous research has found its involvement in psychopathology and externalizing behaviour, adding upon and complicating GD symptomatology (see also Navas et al., 2018). Therefore, our specific hypothesis regarding this impulsivity dimension is that its association with GMV anomalies will extend beyond the areas showing differences between groups, towards areas involved in general-purpose regulatory processes.

Materials and methods

Sample characteristics

Socio-demographic and clinical information for the two groups is shown in Table 1. PGD were recruited at a behavioural addictions rehabilitation centre in Andalusia, Spain (Granadian Association of Rehabilitated Gamblers [AGRAJER]). HC participants were selected using purposive sampling, based on characteristics of PGD regarding age, gender, education level, socio-economic status, intelligence quotient (IQ) and smoking severity. All PGD were men; therefore, only male participants were included in HC group.

Exclusion criteria for both groups were: current or past history of psychiatric disorders or serious neurological condition (including past or current substance abuse), current use of psychoactive medication, IQ below 80 and any contraindication for MRI procedures. Participants who did not meet the study criteria were excluded from further assessments (nine PGD, three HC). PGD were abstinent (as part of their treatment commitment), and none of them reported any relapses throughout the study. Although abstinence is not always a selection criterion in gambling research, it is not uncommon either (de Ruiter et al., 2009; Goudriaan, De Ruiter, Van Den Brink, Oosterlaan, & Veltman, 2010), and it is among the inclusion criteria in other areas of addiction research (Bolla et al., 2004; Eldreth, Matochik, Cadet, & Bolla, 2004; Fu et al., 2008; McBride, Barrett, Kelly, Aw, & Dagher, 2006).

As part of their admission protocol, all PGD underwent a semi-structured interview based on DSM-IV for axis I and II disorders with their therapist, comprising all the necessary information to check for exclusion criteria. GD diagnosis was established by the therapist

THE NEUROSCIENCE AND NEUROPSYCHOLOGY OF GAMBLING

Table 1. Demographic information and clinical characteristics from patients with gambling disorder (PGD) and healthy controls (HC).

	PGD	HC			
	Mean (SD)	Mean (SD)	t (1, 48)	p	BF_{10}
Age	31.68 (8.22)	31.10 (7.06)	0.277	0.783	0.292
Years of education	13.40 (3.49)	13.60 (3.27)	−0.209	0.835	0.288
Monthly income	1,560.00 (689.50)	1,440.00 (744.00)	0.591	0.557	0.326
Handedness*	22(R)/3(L)	21(R)/4(L)	–	0.684	–
WAIS Matrix reasoning	97.40 (12.00)	101.80 (13.38)	−1.224	0.227	0.521
WAIS Vocabulary**	100.21 (13.47)	104.80 (15.71)	−1.096	0.279	0.456
WAIS IQ	98.60 (9.19)	103.30 (11.24)	−1.618	0.112	0.818
Months in treatment	2.00 (1.12)	–	–	–	–
SOGS gambling severity	10.08 (3.45)	0.56 (0.96)	13.287	**<0.001**	2.953·10^{14}
MC excessive gambling	2.56 (0.82)	0.04 (0.200)	14.916	**<0.001**	2.263·10^{16}
MC alcohol misuse	0.72 (1.10)	1.00 (0.91)	−0.979	0.332	0.419
MC substance misuse	0.40 (0.76)	0.44 (0.65)	−0.199	0.843	0.287
Smoking severity**	2.50 (2.73)	2.64 (2.08)	−0.202	0.842	0.290
Dysphoric mood	8.68 (8.33)	6.20 (4.97)	1.277	0.209	0.550
Interpretative bias	17.96 (6.16)	7.00 (4.62)	7.117	**<0.001**	1.726·10^{6}
Negative urgency	2.68 (0.83)	2.20 (0.73)	2.167	**0.035**	1.855

Note: Monthly income is expressed in euros. Smoking severity and dysphoric mood were measured with the Fagerström test and the Beck Depression Inventory. Significant differences are indicated in bold. *χ^2 instead of t-tests was used for handedness. Due to data loss from one participant in PGD group, degrees of freedom for variables marked with ** are (1,47). Abbreviations: R, right-handed; L, left-handed; WAIS, Wechsler intelligence scales; MC, MultiCAGE CAD-4, SOGS, South Oaks Gambling Screen.

on the basis of such an interview, and was confirmed by a score equal to or above 5 in the South Oaks Gambling Screen (SOGS; Lesieur & Blume, 1987). For HC, an equivalent interview was carried out by an experienced clinician, and took place at the beginning of the first assessment session.

The final study sample consisted of 50 participants (25 HC and 25 treatment-seeking PGD) All of them were at least 18 years old and spoke fluent Spanish. Participants were informed about all aspects of the study and were required to sign informed consent prior to participation. The procedure was performed in accordance with the declaration of Helsinki and approved by the Ethics Committee of the University of Granada.

Procedure

Assessment was divided into two sessions, with an average two-week inter-session interval. In the first session, lasting for approximately 1 hour and 30 minutes, participants underwent a number of psychometric and neuropsychological tests. For PGD, this session took place in the facilities of their rehabilitation centre, whereas for HC it took place in the Mind, Brain and Behaviour Research Centre at the University of Granada. This session was composed of four counterbalanced blocks of measurements (including questionnaires and experimental tasks), although only intelligence, impulsivity, gambling-related cognitive biases and gambling severity tests are relevant for the aims of the present study. Full questionnaires were administered, although only interpretative bias (IB) from GRCS, and negative urgency (NU) from UPPS-P were considered for the present analyses. Other measures included in the evaluation protocol with partially overlapping samples have been reported elsewhere (see Megías et al., in press [88% overlap]; Navas et al., 2016 [52%]; Navas et al., 2017b [52%]).

In the second session, participants underwent an MRI session in the Mind, Brain and Behaviour Research Centre. The whole MRI protocol consisted of anatomical T1-weighted, resting-state fMRI, and diffusion tensor Imaging sequences. Concerning the aims of the present study, only structural data will be considered. In the same session, they also underwent EEG recording during a learning task that is also unrelated to the aims of the present study (reported in Megías et al., in press). Participants were compensated with approximately 12€/hour for their participation.

Psychometric instruments

The *Gambling-Related Cognition Scale* (GRCS; Spanish version, Del Prete et al., 2017) is a self-report measure of gambling-related distorted cognitions. It comprises 23 items, structured in 5 subscales assessing cognitive biases associated with gambling (gambling expectancies, illusion of control, predictive control, inability to stop gambling and IB). For all subscales, a higher score indicates a stronger distorted/exaggerated cognition. Only the IB subscale was used in the present study.

UPPS-P Impulsive Behavior Scale. The Spanish short version of the UPPS-P scale (Cándido, Orduña, Perales, Verdejo-García, & Billieux, 2012) is based on Whiteside and Lynam's (2001) model of impulsivity, and assesses five facets of impulsivity, namely, sensation seeking, lack of premeditation, lack of perseverance, NU and positive urgency. For all subscales, a higher score means higher impulsivity. Only the NU subscale was used in the present study.

The *Wechsler Adult Intelligence Scale*, Fourth Edition (WAIS-IV; Wechsler, 2008) was used to assess intelligence. A composite IQ was calculated from the vocabulary and matrix reasoning subtests, according to standard instructions.

The *South Oaks Gambling Screen* (SOGS; Spanish version, Echeburúa, Báez, Fernández-Montalvo, & Páez, 1994) is the most commonly used and internationally validated gambling severity scale. This 20-item questionnaire is based on DSM-III diagnostic criteria for pathological gambling, and assesses core symptoms and frequent negative consequences of problem gambling.

MultiCAGE CAD-4 (Pedrero Pérez et al., 2007). This is a quick clinical screening tool for alcohol abuse, illegal drug abuse, excessive gambling, excessive Internet surfing, excessive video gaming, hypersexuality, compulsive money spending/shopping, and eating disorders. Each subscale is composed of four yes/no items, checking for subjectively informed craving; relatives', friends' or other acquaintances' complaints about the behaviour under assessment; guilt or shame feelings/lack of acknowledgment; and self-reported compensatory behaviours. Only excessive gambling, drug abuse and alcohol abuse subscales were used here.

The *Fagerström Test for Nicotine Dependence* (Spanish version; Becoña & Vázquez, 1998) was used to assess smoking severity. The test consists of six items evaluating smoking frequency and quantity, compulsion and dependence.

Beck Depression Inventory II (BDI-II, Spanish version; Sanz, Perdigón, & Vázquez, 2003) is a self-report measure of dysphoric mood experienced in the week prior to the evaluation and is composed of 4-point scale items. No participants met criteria for depressive disorder.

MRI acquisition protocol

MRI data were collected using a Siemens Magnetom TrioTim Syngo MR B17 3T scanner equipped with a 32-channel head coil, located at the Mind, Brain and Behaviour Research Centre (University of Granada). A high-resolution T1-weighted isotropic image using a 3-dimensional magnetization prepared rapid acquisition gradient echo (3D–MPRAGE) sequence was acquired with the following specifications: TR, 2300 milliseconds; TE, 3.1 milliseconds; inversion time (IT), 900 milliseconds; FA, 9°; spatial resolution, 0.8 x 0.8 x 0.8 millimetres; imaging matrix, 256 x 256 pixels; number of slices, 208, field-of-view (FoV), 256 mm.

MRI preprocessing – voxel-based morphometry (VBM) analysis

Structural images from each participant were visually inspected to discard subjects with low quality or motion artefacts. Reoriented images were segmented into grey matter (GM), white matter (WM) and cerebrospinal fluid (CSF) in native space using unified segmentation (New Segmentation Algorithm) in SPM8. The resulting GM tissue maps were imported into DARTEL (Diffeomorphic Anatomical Registration Using Exponentiated Lie Algebra) registration algorithm (Ashburner, 2007) to generate GM tissue maps resliced to an isotropic 1 x 1 x 1 mm voxel size. DARTEL procedure has been shown to improve spatial accuracy by creating a study-specific GM template from the participants' maps, and calculating individual nonlinear transformations to this template. The group's GM template was built after six iterations by averaging participants' GM maps. Followed by the preliminary affine registration of GM templates to tissue probability maps from Montreal Neurological Institute (MNI, http://www.mcgill.ca/neuro/), GM segments were warped nonlinearly to MNI space and scaled using Jacobian determinants of the deformations to restore tissue volume changes after normalization process. This process accounts for the participant's original brain volume and permits to make inferences on regional volume differences. Finally, normalized and modulated GM maps were smoothed using a 10 mm full-width-at-half-maximum (FWHM) Gaussian kernel. The decision was made in accordance with previous studies (Pujol et al., 2004; de Wit et al., 2014), and to maintain a balance between the 12 mm standard recommendation for VBM analysis (Ashburner & Friston, 2000; Friston et al., 2004) and the 10 mm-Gaussian kernel that has been shown to increase the signal to noise ratio, and correct potential errors on spatial normalization (Radua et al., 2014).

Statistical analyses

Group matching and correlational analyses

Two-tailed Welch's t-tests (implemented on JASP Statistical Package; Love et al., 2015) were used to assess group differences in relevant potential confounders. Complementarily, bilateral Bayesian t-tests with default settings as implemented in JASP software [Cauchy prior width = 0.707, prior $P(H_1) = P(H_0) = 0.50$] were performed in order to evaluate relative evidence for the alternative hypothesis versus the null hypothesis. Pearson correlations were used to explore IB and NU associations with clinically relevant indices (SOGS severity, MultiCAGE subscores and BDI dysphoric mood score).

Significance criterion for group matching t-tests was set a $p \leq 0.05$. Ten r coefficients were tested in correlational analyses. Given there were specific directional predictions for correlations of NU with BDI, MultiCAGE scores and SOGS, as well as for the correlation between IB and SOGS, the Bonferroni-corrected significance criterion for these analyses was set at $p \leq 0.005$ (one-tailed).

Grey matter volume analyses

Total intracranial volume (TIV) was calculated by summing up the native space volumes of GM, WM and CSF maps in MATLAB. GM segments generated in VBM-DARTEL processes were used to assess regional volume differences between PGD and HC. The modulated, normalized and smoothed images were used to conduct the statistical analyses. Age and TIV were entered as covariates of no interest in all GMV analyses (Good et al., 2001). Absolute masking was used at an estimated optimal threshold of 0.2 to maximize statistical sensitivity by restricting the analysis to GM tissue and overcome potential inaccuracies in the GM-WM edge definition (Ridgway et al., 2009). A combination of voxel- and cluster-level thresholds was used to reach a clusterwise criterion equivalent to $p \leq .05$. The statistical threshold at the voxel-level was $p \leq 0.001$, and the cluster extent threshold for each analysis was determined using AlphaSim function implemented in DPABI software (Data Processing & Analysis for – Resting State – Brain Imaging, http://rfmri.org/dpabi). Cluster extent was determined by 1000 Monte-Carlo iterations that control for type I and type II errors. AlphaSim function has been shown to be a reliable method to correct for multiple comparisons, when implemented with adequate parameters (Bennett, Wolford, & Miller, 2009; Lieberman, Berkman, & Wager, 2009; Lieberman & Cunningham, 2009; Nichols, 2012; Vul, Harris, Winkielman, & Pashler, 2009) as, for example, with smoothness estimation based on the standardized residuals, instead using the smoothing kernel applied to the data (Bennett et al., 2009; Nichols, 2012). AlphaSim input parameters included a cluster connection radius of 18 mm, and the smoothness was estimated directly from the statistical image with full width at half maximum (FWHM) of FWHMx = 15.023; FWHMy = 14.599; FWHMz = 14.810. We used the brain mask generated from the statistical analysis, with a volume of 397470 voxels. The minimum cluster size determined by AlphaSim function to be considered significant was 416 voxels. Cluster extent was further adjusted to account for non-isotropic smoothness of structural images, as described by Hayasaka, Phan, Liberzon, Worsley, and Nichols (2004).

In order to explore potential GMV differences between PGD and HC, GM maps were submitted to a voxel-wise whole-brain two-sample comparison in SPM8 to examine the main effect of group.

To investigate the relationships between the traits of interest and GMV (in the PGD group), GM individual segments from the PGD group were submitted to two voxel-wise whole-brain multiple regression models in SPM8, using IB and NU scores as main independent variables.

Regression analyses were complemented with follow-up tests. These analyses were carried out to visualize how high- and low-NU gamblers (and high- and low-IB gamblers) differed from controls in GMV (that is, to visualize whether high scores in IB/NU made gamblers more similar or dissimilar to controls in GMV in areas previously identified to correlate with such traits). Given that these analyses are mostly illustrative and partially redundant with regression analyses, they are reported in Appendix 1 (Supplemental Material). In these

THE NEUROSCIENCE AND NEUROPSYCHOLOGY OF GAMBLING   31

post hoc analyses, planned comparisons between pairs when exploring the main effect of group were considered significant at $p \leq 0.05$.

Results

Group matching and correlational analyses

Welch's t-tests yielded no significant differences between groups in any of the potentially confounding variables (see Table 1). As expected, groups differed in gambling measures (SOGS and MultiCAGE), IB and NU. Bayes factors provided substantial evidence in favour of the null hypothesis ($BF_{10} < 1/3$) for age, education years, monthly income, drug misuse and nicotine dependence; and just anecdotal evidence in favour of the null hypothesis ($1 > BF_{10} > 1/3$) for IQ measures, MultiCAGE alcohol misuse subscore and BDI. For none of the potential confounders under consideration the Bayes factor (either anecdotally or substantially) supported the existence of differences between groups, which indicates a good global matching. Additionally, Bayes factors strongly supported the existence of differences between groups in SOGS and MultiCAGE gambling subscores, and IB. Although the difference between groups in NU was statistically significant according to the Welch's t-test, the Bayes factor for this measure only provided anecdotal evidence of a difference between groups.

Additionally, global volume measures were estimated for HC (mean ± SD GMV: 0.75 ± 0.04 l; mean ± SD WM volume: 0.55 ± 0.03 l; mean ± SD TIV: 1.68 ± 0.09 l) and PGD (mean ± SD GMV: 0.74 ± 0.05 l; mean ± SD WM volume: 0.55 ± 0.04 l; mean ± SD TIV: 1.67 ± 0.11 l). Analyses revealed no significant global differences between groups in GMV [$t(48) = -0.46, p = 0.32$], WM volume [$t(48) = -0.38; p = 0.35$] or TIV [$t(48) = -0.49; p = 0.31$].

Analyses of correlations of IB and NU with clinical measures (SOGS severity, MultiCAGE gambling, alcohol and drug subscores, and BDI dysphoric mood score) yielded a small set of significant associations. NU was associated with BDI and MultiCAGE gambling subscore (Pearson's $r = 0.52, p < 0.005$, and $r = 0.56, p < 0.005$, one-tailed). IB correlated with total SOGS severity ($r = 0.50, p = 0.005$, one-tailed). NU did not significantly correlate with IB, SOGS or non-gambling MultiCAGE subscores; nor did IB with any MultiCAGE or BDI scores (min. $p = 0.125$, one-tailed).

VBM analysis

Group differences

Compared to HC, PGD showed a significant decrease in GMV in the dorsomedial prefrontal cortex (dmPFC) (peak x, y, z MNI coordinates = 6, 42, 42; T-value = 3.94; cluster size = 491; Figure 1). Figure A2.1 in Appendix 2 (Supplemental Material) depicts the full T-map for this contrast (and peak coordinates). The full set of T-values can be downloaded from the University of Granada Open Repository: http://hdl.handle.net/10481/48216.

Multiple regressions

In the first regression analysis in PGD, GMV in dorsal anterior cingulate cortex (dACC) from a cluster covering both hemispheres correlated negatively with IB scores (peak x,

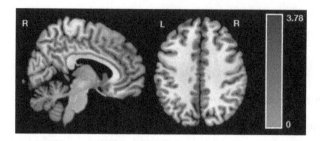

Figure 1. Region showing a significant reduction in grey matter volume in patients with gambling disorder, compared with healthy controls, after controlling for age and total intracranial volume.

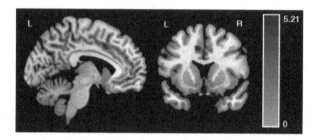

Figure 2. Brain region showing a significant negative association between grey matter volume and interpretative bias scores in patients with gambling disorder, after controlling for age and total intracranial volume.

y, z MNI coordinates = −12, 11, 42; T-value = 5.21; cluster size = 589, Figure 2; see also Appendix 1 in Supplemental Material). Figure A2.2 in Appendix 2 (Supplemental Material) depicts the full T-map for this contrast (and peak coordinates). The full set of T-values can be downloaded from the University of Granada Open Repository. http://hdl.handle.net/10481/48216.

In the second regression analysis in PGD, GMV in the right ventro-lateral prefrontal cortex (vlPFC) (i.e. right middle frontal gyrus extending to right orbital gyrus) correlated negatively with NU (peak x, y, z MNI coordinates = 45, 54, −2; T-value = 5.07; cluster size = 1222; Figure 3, see also Appendix 1 in Supplemental Material). Figure A2.3 in Appendix 2 (Supplemental Material) depicts the full T-map for this contrast (and peak coordinates). The full set of T-values can be downloaded from the University of Granada Open Repository: http://hdl.handle.net/10481/48216.

Discussion

In the present study, a voxel-based morphometry (VBM) approach was used to explore regional grey matter volume (GMV) differences between patients with gambling disorder (PGD) and healthy controls (HC). In addition, we examined potential relationships between regional GMV and two gambling disorder-related traits, identified by previous research to be key markers of clinical status and prognosis: the interpretative bias (IB) and negative urgency (NU).

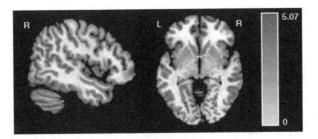

Figure 3. Brain region showing a significant negative association between grey matter volume and negative urgency scores in patients with gambling disorder, after controlling for age and total intracranial volume.

Indeed, associations between these constructs and clinical measures corroborated their clinical significance. NU correlated with BDI dysphoric mood and MultiCAGE gambling scores, whereas IB correlated with SOGS severity scores. NU did not significantly correlate with SOGS severity. However, as we have argued elsewhere (Navas et al., 2018), NU is more directly related to GDP subtyping and the assessment of complications and co-morbidity risk than to severity of symptoms as measured by the SOGS[2]

With regard to structural measures, dmPFC regional GMV was reduced in PGD, compared to HC. Additionally, in PGD, IB and NU scores were associated with reduced volumes in dACC and right vlPFC, respectively.

Our finding from between-groups contrast is consistent with results reported by Zois et al. (2017). This study investigated GM differences between a sample of PGD without substance use disorder co-morbidities, two groups of PGD with substance abuse co-morbidities (alcohol and poly-substance abuse) and a group of controls (including regular gamblers, and participants diagnosed with specific phobias). These results suggest, first, an association between GD and GMV reduction in the same area from prefrontal cortex (dmPFC), and, second, that the association occurs independently from substance abuse.

A brief critical revision of studies investigating GM anomalies in GD is presented in Appendix 3 (Supplemental Material). In brief, some studies have failed to detect differences between groups, or have found differences in areas not directly related to the ones identified here (Joutsa et al., 2011; Rahman et al., 2014; van Holst et al., 2012); and some others report differences in the opposite direction (Fuentes et al., 2015; Koehler et al., 2015). From the studies reporting prefrontal GM reductions (Grant et al., 2015; Zois et al., 2017), Zois et al.'s report is actually the one most directly comparable to ours (if we consider the contrast between pure PGD and controls). Discrepancies with other studies are probably attributable to sample size, the presence of other conditions such as SUD and depression, and methodological aspects (i.e. whole brain versus region of interest analysis or even corrected versus uncorrected results; Zois et al., 2017, p. 868). Socio-demographic and community sampling differences are also likely to influence the observed inconsistencies.

The dmPFC is known to participate in a number of different functions (Bechara & Damasio, 2005), which makes difficult to infer its precise link with GD. Tentatively, the observed reduction in dmPFC GMV could compromise its normal functioning in reward-based decision-making (Gläscher et al., 2012). dmPFC activation has been observed to mediate the relationship between impulsivity and reward-related dopaminergic release in left NAcc (Weiland et al., 2014), and a network including dmPFC shows increased activity during the representation of the magnitude of potential rewards when individuals decide which gamble to play to maximize benefits (Rogers et al., 2004). These activations have been more consistently observed in decision-making tasks under ambiguity (where uncertainty can be resolved by learning from feedback) than under risk (where probabilities are known beforehand; Hsu, Bhatt, Adolphs, Tranel, & Camerer, 2005). The involvement of dmPFC in emotional processes associated with risk-taking (Coombes, Corcos, Pavuluri, & Vaillancourt, 2012; Hsu et al., 2005; Phan et al., 2004; Xue et al., 2009;) could also be relevant for its potential role in gambling behaviour.

As noted earlier, neurotoxic effects are absent in PGD without drug abuse co-morbidities and, in contrast with some previous studies, the observed between-group structural differences are not attributable to detrimental effects of drugs. Still, structural neuroadaptions caused by gambling-related practice and learning cannot be discarded. This possibility is compatible with the fact that the structural anomalies reported here are less extensive than the ones reported in drug-addicted individuals (see, for example, Gonçalves, Baptista, & Silva, 2014). Consequently, structural differences between PGD and controls could either precede GD onset (and thus be potential vulnerability markers), or be caused by gambling-related behaviour during the course of the disorder. Longitudinal studies are needed to check for the existence of structural differences prior to GD onset and to track neural changes occurring during GD course.

With regard to heterogeneity in our sample of PGD, dACC GMV showed a negative association with a measure of biased gambling-related attributions (IB). We did not observe, however, the relationships with the insula and dlPFC that were suggested by previous fMRI and lesion studies.

Recent models link the dACC to the expected value of exerting control, motivation of effortful behaviour, and learning flexibility (see Shenhav, Cohen, & Botvinick, 2016). However, the pattern of PGD individual differences in GMV was such that high IB PGD showed reduced dACC GMV compared to low bias PGD, which made the former visually *more* similar to controls than the latter. The specific pattern makes our results on individual differences in this cognitive bias quite difficult to interpret. In a study with a mostly overlapping sample (Megías et al., in press), we observed a similar trend in individuals' response to uncertainty. As a group, PGD showed an abnormal electroencephalographic response to uncertain outcomes. However, the sign of the relation between the magnitude of such anomaly and gambling-related cognitive biases (including the IB) was opposite to the hypothesized direction. Patients with stronger biases showed a *less* abnormal response to uncertainty (which made them similar to controls). Relatedly, in a study with a different sample (Perales, Navas, Ruiz de Lara, Maldonado, & Catena, 2017), we observed that PGD were less accurate than controls in learning observational contingencies in a causal learning task. However, gamblers with strong gambling-related biases (as measured by the GRCS scale, and including the IB) were *more* accurate at discriminating the programmed contingencies, and also more similar to controls, than gamblers with weaker gambling-related biases.

Thus, whatever the role of dACC in gambling is, it is plausible that cognitive biases characterize a subgroup of patients in which certain neuropsychological functions are preserved.

Specifically, Navas et al. (2017a, 2018) have recently proposed that certain cognitive biases associated with strategic gambling require intact executive control or even overexertion of control, in relation to other gamblers and controls.

Our findings on the relationship between vlPFC and NU in PGD were more in line with our expectations. In PGD, regional GMV in vlPFC decreased as the NU level in gamblers increased. Post hoc analysis revealed that, although PGD as a group did not show reduced GMV in this area relative to HC, high-NU PGD exhibited lower GM vlPFC volume than low NU patients and controls (see Appendix 1). The section from right vlPFC identified to correlate with NU is reliably linked to inhibitory control, an essential ability to optimize adaptive decision-making and effectively adjust actions to an uncertain world. Indeed, fMRI studies have consistently show activation of right vlPFC in inhibitory tasks including Stop-Signal, Stroop and Go/No-Go tasks (Aron, Robbins, & Poldrack, 2014). Specifically, right vlPFC has been consistently linked to regulation of negative emotions (Kim & Hamann, 2007; Ochsner et al., 2004; Wager, Davidson, Hughes, Lindquist, & Ochsner, 2008).

NU, namely the proneness to lose control of behaviour under intense negative emotions (Cyders & Smith, 2008), has been previously associated with failure on inhibitory control (Billieux, Gay, Rochat, & Van der Linden, 2010). More specifically, recent models stress the importance of the vlPFC in inhibitory modulation of negative emotions (Etkin, Büchel, & Gross, 2015). In this view, urgent behaviours occur because these regulatory mechanisms fail to modulate the emotion that triggers them (e.g. frustration or craving; Navas et al., 2018; Wager et al., 2008).

This type of emotion regulation failure could play a crucial role in GD. However, the relation between NU and psychopathology seems to go beyond GD. In general, impulsive behaviour is common to diverse neuropsychiatric disorders (Albein-Urios et al., 2013; Bøen et al., 2015; Dawe & Loxton, 2004; Egan, Dawson, & Wymbs, 2017; Fischer, Settles, Collins, Gunn, & Smith, 2012; Grant, Odlaug, & Chamberlain, 2016; MacLaren et al., 2011; Verdejo-García et al., 2008). NU (and particularly its *feelings-trigger-action* component; Johnson, Carver, & Joormann, 2013; Johnson, Tharp, Peckham, Carver, & Haase, 2017) has been proposed to be an important factor of a shared endophenotype contributing to an array of externalizing disorders, including GD, other additive processes, conduct problems and aggression (see also Castellanos-Ryan et al., 2014). This is consistent with previous data showing that NU is not only related to gambling severity, but also, and even more consistently, to clinical complications and poor prognosis (Grant et al., 2016; MacLaren et al., 2011; Savvidou et al., 2017; Steward et al., 2017; Torres et al., 2013; Yan, Zhang, Lan, Li, & Sui, 2016). Although associations between NU and drug use in our sample were precluded by the stringent selection of pure, strictly abstinent PGD, the association of NU with poorer mood and current, treatment-resistant symptoms in the clinical group reinforces the role of NU as a complication factor.

The relative unspecificity of NU in GD accounts for the fact that PGD tend to differ in this trait from controls, but not necessarily from other groups of addicted individuals (Torres et al., 2013). Similarly, it accounts for the discrepancy between the area associated with NU in PGD and the region yielding differences between PGD and controls. Most likely, NU is relevant for GD assessment, but neither specific nor necessary for its diagnosis.

Strengths and limitations

In this work, we tried to overcome the methodological shortcomings of previous research. Samples were selected to ensure comparability and avoid confounding. Presence of frequently co-morbid conditions and use of psychoactive medication were evaluated a priori, and purposive sampling for HC was performed based on socio-demographic and clinical information from PGD. Additionally, age was entered, along TIV, as covariate of no interest in GMV analyses.

First, we used VBM settings recommended by Radua et al. (2014), to optimize sensitivity [large smoothing kernels (FWHM = 10 mm) and voxel-based spatial statistics]. Brain image segmentation was performed using unified segmentation, which has shown higher sensitivity and specificity than other software packages (FSL and Brainsuite; Kazemi & Noorizadeh, 2014). Complementarily, the DARTEL registration procedure has been shown to increase spatial accuracy by using a participant-based template (Ashburner, 2007).

Second, with regard to false positive control, AlphaSim correction for multiple comparisons was computed with a voxel-wise threshold of $p < 0.001$, and further adjusted using Hayasaka et al.'s (2004) method, to account for non-isotropic smoothness.

And finally, selection of variables of interest (IB and NU) was done in a strictly a priori manner, without considering other dimensions from the questionnaires and based on previous works with samples from the same socio-demographic background.

Despite these considerations, results must be interpreted in light of a number of limitations. First, the cross-sectional nature of the study precludes drawing sound conclusions about causal direction of results. Second, our samples consisted of male participants, and generalization of results to females is not ensured. Third, GD diagnosis was based on DSM-IV criteria for pathological gambling. And fourth, although samples are larger than usual in GD neurobiological research, it is also true that they could be considered not large enough to overcome some recent critiques to neuroimaging research (Button et al., 2013). Small sample size, combined with strict post hoc alpha-error correction for whole-brain analyses could have rendered the present study underpowered; that is, insensitive to small-to-medium size effects (especially for within-sample regressions and comparisons). In other words, reported effects are probably strong, but weaker effects could have remained undetected.

Final remarks

In contrast with the recent flourishing of functional MRI research in GD, structural literature has been sparse and the results inconsistent. In the present study, we used a reliable morphometric approach to study structural brain differences between PGD and HC, and potential associations of GM structure with individual variation in two traits involved in GD development and putative complications.

Results suggest that maladaptive GD traits (i.e. distorted attributions and recall of gambling outcomes, and the tendency towards rash action under negative emotions) are associated with diminished GMV in dACC and vlPFC, respectively. Further, results suggest that GD, despite not entailing the consumption of toxic substances, is associated with structural brain alterations in dmPFC. The functions attributed to these areas by previous research are definitely relevant for gambling behaviour. All these areas are involved in executive cognition, and are functionally interconnected, but do not overlap between them, which could

THE NEUROSCIENCE AND NEUROPSYCHOLOGY OF GAMBLING

be indicating that the processes that are crucial for clinical status and the ones underlying patients' heterogeneity are dissociable.

Authors' contributions

CMRL drafted the original manuscript. CMRL and CSM performed voxel-based morphometry analyses. CMRL, JCP and JFN carried out behavioural data analyses. JFN was responsible for data collection (behavioural assessments and magnetic resonance imaging). CMRL, JFN, CSM, GS, and JCP participated in results interpretation and discussion, and in successive revisions of the original manuscript. JCP is the principal investigator of the research project (G-Brain).

Conflicts of interest

Funding

Research described in this article was supported by the Spanish Government (Ministerio de Economía y Competitividad, Secretaría de Estado de Invetigación, Desarrollo e Innovación; Convocatoria 2013 de Proyectos I+D de Excelencia), under project reference no. PSI2013-45055-P (G-Brain). CMRL is funded by an individual grant linked to this project (PSI2013-45055-P). JCP is member of a RETICS (RD12/0028/0017) group, funded by the Spanish Ministerio de Sanidad y Consumo. JFN has been awarded with an individual research grant (Ministerio de Educación, Cultura y Deporte, Programa FPU, grant no. FPU13/00669). CS-M is supported by a Miguel Servet contract from the Carlos III Health Institute (CPII16/00048).

Competing interests

CMRL, JFN, CS-M, GS declare that they have no competing interest. JCP is regional assistant editor of *International Gambling Studies*.

Constraints on publishing

The authors reported no constraints on publishing.

Ethical approval

The procedure performed in this study involving human participants was approved by the Ethics Committee of the University of Granada as part of the PSI2013-45055-P research project, and was in accordance with the 1964 Helsinki declaration and its later amendments.

Notes

1. Specifically, we used the Unified Segmentation algorithm as implemented in SPM to isolate tissue probability maps (which has shown higher sensitivity and specificity than other packages; Kazemi & Noorizadeh, 2014), and applied processing parameters shown to improve sensitivity and spatial accuracy (Radua, Canales-Rodríguez, Pomarol-Clotet, & Salvador, 2014). Generating a study template from participants' tissue probability maps using DARTEL

also improves spatial accuracy, and the use of a 0.2 absolute threshold mask further ensures the restriction of analysis to GM tissue (Ashburner, 2007). Finally, we applied a multiple-comparison correction method with a significance threshold of $p < 0.001$ at the voxel level, to avoid false positive results.

2. In addition, we did find a significant association between NU and the MC gambling subscore. In contrast to SOGS, MC is highly sensitive to present-day symptoms and, specifically, to the current occurrence of cravings. Therefore, the lower correlation of NU with SOGS relative to MC gambling severity scores can be accounted for by differential sensitivity to separate aspects or timings of GD manifestations.

Acknowledgements

We thank Warren Tierney for his assistance in revising the English version of this article.

References

Albein-Urios, N., Martinez-González, J. M., Lozano, Ó., Clark, L., & Verdejo-García, A. (2012). Comparison of impulsivity and working memory in cocaine addiction and pathological gambling: Implications for cocaine-induced neurotoxicity. *Drug and Alcohol Dependence, 126*, 1–6.

Albein-Urios, N., Martínez-González, J. M., Lozano, Ó., Moreno-López, L., Soriano-Mas, C., & Verdejo-Garcia, A. (2013). Negative urgency, disinhibition and reduced temporal pole gray matter characterize the comorbidity of cocaine dependence and personality disorders. *Drug and Alcohol Dependence, 132*, 231–237.

American Psychiatric Association. (2013). *Diagnostic and Statistical Manual of Mental Disorders, Fifth Edition (DSM-5)*. American Psychiatric Pub, Washington, DC: APA.

Aron, A. R., Robbins, T. W., & Poldrack, R. A. (2014). Inhibition and the right inferior frontal cortex: One decade on. *Trends in Cognitive Sciences, 18*, 177–185.

Ashburner, J. (2007). A fast diffeomorphic image registration algorithm. *NeuroImage, 38*, 95–113.

Ashburner, J., & Friston, K. J. (2000). Voxel-based morphometry – The methods. *NeuroImage, 11*, 805–821.

Bechara, A., & Damasio, A. R. (2005). The somatic marker hypothesis: A neural theory of economic decision. *Games and Economic Behavior, 52*, 336–372.

Becoña, E., & Vázquez, F. L. (1998). The Fagerström test for nicotine dependence in a Spanish sample. *Psychological Reports, 83*, 1455–1458.

Bennett, C. M., Wolford, G. L., & Miller, M. B. (2009). The principled control of false positives in neuroimaging. *Social Cognitive and Affective Neuroscience, 4*, 417–422.

Berg, J. M., Latzman, R. D., Bliwise, N. G., & Lilienfeld, S. O. (2015). Parsing the heterogeneity of impulsivity: A meta-analytic review of the behavioral implications of the UPPS for psychopathology. *Psychological Assessment, 27*, 1129–1146.

Billieux, J., Gay, P., Rochat, L., & Van der Linden, M. (2010). The role of urgency and its underlying psychological mechanisms in problematic behaviours. *Behaviour Research and Therapy, 48*, 1085–1096.

Billieux, J., Lagrange, G., Van der Linden, M., Lançon, C., Adida, M., & Jeanningros, R. (2012). Investigation of impulsivity in a sample of treatment-seeking pathological gamblers: A multidimensional perspective. *Psychiatry Research, 198*, 291–296.

Blaszczynski, A., & Nower, L. (2002). A model of problem and pathological gambling. *Addiction, 97*, 487–499.

Bøen, E., Hummelen, B., Elvsåshagen, T., Boye, B., Andersson, S., Karterud, S., & Malt, U. F. (2015). Different impulsivity profiles in borderline personality disorder and bipolar II disorder. *Journal of Affective Disorders, 170*, 104–111.

Bolla, K., Ernst, M., Kiehl, K., Mouratidis, M., Eldreth, D., Contoreggi, C., … Funderburk, F. (2004). Prefrontal cortical dysfunction in abstinent cocaine abusers. *The Journal of Neuropsychiatry and Clinical Neurosciences, 16*, 456–464.

Button, K. S., Ioannidis, J. P., Mokrysz, C., Nosek, B. A., Flint, J., Robinson, E. S., & Munafò, M. R. (2013). Power failure: Why small sample size undermines the reliability of neuroscience. *Nature Reviews Neuroscience, 14*, 365–376.

Cándido, A., Orduña, E., Perales, J. C., Verdejo-García, A., & Billieux, J. (2012). Validation of a short Spanish version of the UPPS-P impulsive behaviour scale. *Trastornos Adictivos, 14*, 73–78.

Castellanos-Ryan, N., Struve, M., Whelan, R., Banaschewski, T., Barker, G. J., Bokde, A. L., … The IMAGEN Consortium. (2014). Neural and cognitive correlates of the common and specific variance across externalizing problems in young adolescence. *American Journal of Psychiatry, 171*, 1310–1319.

Chase, H. W., & Clark, L. (2010). Gambling severity predicts midbrain response to near-miss outcomes. *Journal of Neuroscience, 30*, 6180–6187.

Clark, L., Lawrence, A. J., Astley-Jones, F., & Gray, N. (2009). Gambling near-misses enhance motivation to gamble and recruit win-related brain circuitry. *Neuron, 61*, 481–490.

Clark, L., Stokes, P. R., Wu, K., Michalczuk, R., Benecke, A., Watson, B. J., … Lingford-Hughes, A. R. (2012). Striatal dopamine D(2)/D(3) receptor binding in pathological gambling is correlated with mood-related impulsivity. *NeuroImage, 63*, 40–46.

Clark, L., Studer, B., Bruss, J., Tranel, D., & Bechara, A. (2014). Damage to insula abolishes cognitive distortions during simulated gambling. *Proceedings of the National Academy of Sciences, 111*, 6098–6103.

Contreras-Rodríguez, O., Albein-Urios, N., Vilar-López, R., Perales, J. C., Martínez-Gonzalez, J. M., Fernández-Serrano, M. J., ... Verdejo-García, A. (2016). Increased corticolimbic connectivity in cocaine dependence versus pathological gambling is associated with drug severity and emotion-related impulsivity. *Addiction Biology, 21*, 709–718.

Coombes, S. A., Corcos, D. M., Pavuluri, M. N., & Vaillancourt, D. E. (2012). Maintaining force control despite changes in emotional context engages dorsomedial prefrontal and premotor cortex. *Cerebral Cortex, 22*, 616–627.

Cousijn, J., Wiers, R. W., Ridderinkhof, K. R., van den Brink, W., Veltman, D. J., & Goudriaan, A. E. (2012). Grey matter alterations associated with cannabis use: Results of a VBM study in heavy cannabis users and healthy controls. *NeuroImage, 59*, 3845–3851.

Cyders, M. A., & Smith, G. T. (2008). Emotion-based dispositions to rash action: Positive and negative urgency. *Psychological Bulletin, 134*, 807–828.

Daumann, J., Koester, P., Becker, B., Wagner, D., Imperati, D., Gouzoulis-Mayfrank, E., & Tittgemeyer, M. (2011). Medial prefrontal gray matter volume reductions in users of amphetamine-type stimulants revealed by combined tract-based spatial statistics and voxel-based morphometry. *NeuroImage, 54*, 794–801.

Dawe, S., & Loxton, N. J. (2004). The role of impulsivity in the development of substance use and eating disorders. *Neuroscience & Biobehavioral Reviews, 28*, 343–351.

de Ruiter, M. B., Veltman, D. J., Goudriaan, A. E., Oosterlaan, J., Sjoerds, Z., & van den Brink, W. (2009). Response perseveration and ventral prefrontal sensitivity to reward and punishment in male problem gamblers and smokers. *Neuropsychopharmacology, 34*, 1027–1038.

Del Prete, F., Steward, T., Navas, J. F., Fernández-Aranda, F., Jiménez-Murcia, S., Oei, T. P., & Perales, J. C. (2017). The role of affect-driven impulsivity in gambling cognitions: A convenience-sample study with a Spanish version of the Gambling-Related Cognitions Scale. *Journal of Behavioral Addictions, 6*, 51–63.

De Wit, S. J., Alonso, P., Schweren, L., Mataix-Cols, D., Lochner, C., Menchón, J. M., ... Hoexter, M. Q. (2014). Multicenter voxel-based morphometry mega-analysis of structural brain scans in obsessive-compulsive disorder. *American Journal of Psychiatry, 171*, 340–349.

Donati, M. A., Ancona, F., Chiesi, F., & Primi, C. (2015). Psychometric properties of the Gambling Related Cognitions Scale (GRCS) in young Italian gamblers. *Addictive Behaviors, 45*, 1–7.

Echeburúa, E., Báez, C., Fernández-Montalvo, J., & Páez, D. (1994). Cuestionario de juego patológico de South Oaks (SOGS): Validación española [The South Oaks Gambling Screen (SOGS): Spanish validation]. *Análisis y Modificación de Conducta, 20*, 769–791.

Egan, T. E., Dawson, A. E., & Wymbs, B. T. (2017). Substance use in undergraduate students with histories of Attention-Deficit/Hyperactivity Disorder (ADHD): The role of impulsivity. *Substance Use & Misuse, 52*, 1375–1386.

Eldreth, D. A., Matochik, J. A., Cadet, J. L., & Bolla, K. I. (2004). Abnormal brain activity in prefrontal brain regions in abstinent marijuana users. *NeuroImage, 23*, 914–920.

Etkin, A., Büchel, C., & Gross, J. J. (2015). The neural bases of emotion regulation. *Nature Reviews Neuroscience, 16*, 693–700.

Fischer, S., Settles, R., Collins, B., Gunn, R., & Smith, G. T. (2012). The role of negative urgency and expectancies in problem drinking and disordered eating: Testing a model of comorbidity in pathological and at-risk samples. *Psychology of Addictive Behaviors, 26*, 112–123.

Friston, K. J., Frith, C. D., Dolan, R. J., Price, C. J., Zeki, S., Ashburner, J. T., & Penny, W. D. (Eds.). (2004). *Human brain function*. San Diego, CA: Academic Press.

Fritz, H. C., Wittfeld, K., Schmidt, C. O., Domin, M., Grabe, H. J., Hegenscheid, K., ... Lotze, M. (2014). Current smoking and reduced gray matter volume-a voxel-based morphometry study. *Neuropsychopharmacology, 39*, 2594–2600.

Fu, L. P., Bi, G. H., Zou, Z. T., Wang, Y., Ye, E. M., Ma, L., ... Yang, Z. (2008). Impaired response inhibition function in abstinent heroin dependents: An fMRI study. *Neuroscience Letters, 438*, 322–326.

Fuentes, D., Rzezak, P., Pereira, F. R., Malloy-Diniz, L. F., Santos, L. C., Duran, F. L., ... Gorenstein, C. (2015). Mapping brain volumetric abnormalities in never-treated pathological gamblers. *Psychiatry Research: Neuroimaging, 232*, 208–213.

Gläscher, J., Adolphs, R., Damasio, H., Bechara, A., Rudrauf, D., Calamia, M., … Tranel, D. (2012). Lesion mapping of cognitive control and value-based decision making in the prefrontal cortex. *Proceedings of the National Academy of Sciences, 109*, 14681–14686.

Gonçalves, J., Baptista, S., & Silva, A. P. (2014). Psychostimulants and brain dysfunction: A review of the relevant neurotoxic effects. *Neuropharmacology, 87*, 135–149.

Good, C. D., Johnsrude, I. S., Ashburner, J., Henson, R. N., Friston, K. J., & Frackowiak, R. S. (2001). A voxel-based morphometric study of ageing in 465 normal adult human brains. *NeuroImage, 14*, 21–36.

Goudriaan, A. E., De Ruiter, M. B., Van Den Brink, W., Oosterlaan, J., & Veltman, D. J. (2010). Brain activation patterns associated with cue reactivity and craving in abstinent problem gamblers, heavy smokers and healthy controls: An fMRI study. *Addiction Biology, 15*, 491–503.

Grall-Bronnec, M., Bouju, G., Sébille-Rivain, V., Gorwood, P., Boutin, C., Vénisse, J. L., & Hardouin, J. B. (2012). A French adaptation of the Gambling-Related Cognitions Scale (GRCS): A useful tool for assessment of irrational thoughts among gamblers. *Journal of Gambling Issues, 27*, 1–21.

Grant, J. E., Odlaug, B. L., & Chamberlain, S. R. (2015). Reduced cortical thickness in gambling disorder: A morphometric MRI study. *European Archives of Psychiatry and Clinical Neuroscience, 265*, 655–661.

Grant, J. E., Odlaug, B. L., & Chamberlain, S. R. (2016). Neural and psychological underpinnings of gambling disorder: A review. *Progress in Neuro-Psychopharmacology and Biological Psychiatry, 65*, 188–193.

Hayasaka, S., Phan, K. L., Liberzon, I., Worsley, K. J., & Nichols, T. E. (2004). Nonstationary cluster-size inference with random field and permutation methods. *NeuroImage, 22*, 676–687.

Hodgins, D. C., Stea, J. N., & Grant, J. E. (2011). Gambling disorders. *The Lancet, 378*, 1874–1884.

Hsu, M., Bhatt, M., Adolphs, R., Tranel, D., & Camerer, C. F. (2005). Neural systems responding to degrees of uncertainty in human decision-making. *Science, 310*, 1680–1683.

Johnson, S. L., Carver, C. S., & Joormann, J. (2013). Impulsive responses to emotion as a transdiagnostic vulnerability to internalizing and externalizing symptoms. *Journal of Affective Disorders, 150*, 872–878.

Johnson, S. L., Tharp, J. A., Peckham, A. D., Carver, C. S., & Haase, C. M. (2017). A path model of different forms of impulsivity with externalizing and internalizing psychopathology: Towards greater specificity. *British Journal of Clinical Psychology, 56*, 235–252.

Joukhador, J., Maccallum, F., & Blaszczynski, A. (2003). Differences in cognitive distortions between problem and social gamblers. *Psychological Reports, 92*, 1203–1214.

Joutsa, J., Saunavaara, J., Parkkola, R., Niemelä, S., & Kaasinen, V. (2011). Extensive abnormality of brain white matter integrity in pathological gambling. *Psychiatry Research: Neuroimaging, 194*, 340–346.

Kazemi, K., & Noorizadeh, N. (2014). Quantitative comparison of SPM, FSL, and Brainsuite for brain MR Image segmentation. *Journal of Biomedical Physics & Engineering, 4*, 13–26.

Kim, S. H., & Hamann, S. (2007). Neural correlates of positive and negative emotion regulation. *Journal of Cognitive Neuroscience, 19*, 776–798.

Koehler, S., Hasselmann, E., Wüstenberg, T., Heinz, A., & Romanczuk-Seiferth, N. (2015). Higher volume of ventral striatum and right prefrontal cortex in pathological gambling. *Brain Structure and Function, 220*, 469–477.

Lesieur, H. R., & Blume, S. B. (1987). The South Oaks Gambling Screen (SOGS): A new instrument for the identification of pathological gamblers. *American Journal of Psychiatry, 144*, 1184–1188.

Lieberman, M. D., Berkman, E. T., & Wager, T. D. (2009). Correlations in social neuroscience aren't voodoo: Commentary on Vul et al. (2009). *Perspectives on Psychological Science, 4*, 299–307.

Lieberman, M. D., & Cunningham, W. A. (2009). Type I and Type II error concerns in fMRI research: Re-balancing the scale. *Social Cognitive and Affective Neuroscience, 4*, 423–428.

Love, J., Selker, R., Verhagen, J., Marsman, M., Gronau, Q. F., Jamil, T., … Matzke, D. (2015). Software to sharpen your stats. *APS Observer, 28*(3), 27–29.

MacLaren, V. V., Fugelsang, J. A., Harrigan, K. A., & Dixon, M. J. (2011). The personality of pathological gamblers: A meta-analysis. *Clinical Psychology Review, 31*, 1057–1067.

McBride, D., Barrett, S. P., Kelly, J. T., Aw, A., & Dagher, A. (2006). Effects of expectancy and abstinence on the neural response to smoking cues in cigarette smokers: An fMRI Study. *Neuropsychopharmacology, 31*, 2728–2738.

Megías, A., Navas, J. F., Perandrés-Gómez, A., Maldonado, A., Catena, A., & Perales, J. C. (in press). Electroencephalographic evidence of abnormal anticipatory uncertainty processing in gambling disorder patients. *Journal of Gambling Studies*. https://link.springer.com/article/10.1007/s10899-017-9693-3

Michalczuk, R., Bowden-Jones, H., Verdejo-Garcia, A., & Clark, L. (2011). Impulsivity and cognitive distortions in pathological gamblers attending the UK National Problem Gambling Clinic: A preliminary report. *Psychological Medicine, 41*, 2625–2635.

Navas, J. F., Verdejo-García, A., López-Gómez, M., Maldonado, A., & Perales, J. C. (2016). Gambling with rose-tinted glasses on: use of emotion-regulation strategies correlates with dysfunctional cognitions in gambling disorder patients. *Journal of Behavioral Addictions, 5*, 271–281.

Navas, J. F., Billieux, J., Perandrés-Gómez, A., López-Torrecillas, F., Cándido, A., & Perales, J. C. (2017a). Impulsivity traits and gambling cognitions associated with gambling preferences and clinical status. *International Gambling Studies, 17*, 102–124.

Navas, J. F., Contreras-Rodríguez, O., Verdejo-Román, J., Perandrés-Gómez, A., Albein-Urios, N., Verdejo-García, A., & Perales, J. C. (2017b). Trait and neurobiological underpinnings of negative emotion regulation in gambling disorder. *Addiction, 112*, 1086–1094.

Navas, J. F., Billieux, J., Verdejo-García, A., & Perales, J. C. (2018). A neurocognitive approach to core components of gambling disorder: Implications for assessment, treatment and policy. In H. Bowden-Jones, C. Dickson, C. Dunand, & O. Simon (Eds.), *Harm reduction for problem gambling: A public health approach*. (Accepted). Routledge (due by June, 2018).

Nichols, T. E. (2012). Multiple testing corrections, nonparametric methods, and random field theory. *NeuroImage, 62*, 811–815.

Ochsner, K. N., Ray, R. D., Cooper, J. C., Robertson, E. R., Chopra, S., Gabrieli, J. D., & Gross, J. J. (2004). For better or for worse: Neural systems supporting the cognitive down-and up-regulation of negative emotion. *NeuroImage, 23*, 483–499.

Pattij, T., & De Vries, T. J. (2013). The role of impulsivity in relapse vulnerability. *Current Opinion in Neurobiology, 23*, 700–705.

Pedrero Pérez, E. J., Rodríguez Monje, M. T., Gallardo Alonso, F., Fernández Girón, M., Pérez López, M., & Chicharro Romero, J. (2007). Validación de un instrumento para la detección de trastornos de control de impulsos y adicciones: El MULTICAGE CAD-4 [Validation of a tool for screening of impulse control disorders and addiction: MULTICAGE CAD-4]. *Trastornos Adictivos, 9*, 269–278.

Perales, J. C., Navas, J. F., Ruiz de Lara, C. M., Maldonado, A., & Catena, A. (2017). Causal learning in gambling disorder: Beyond the illusion of control. *Journal of Gambling Studies, 33*, 705–717.

Perry, J. L., & Carroll, M. E. (2008). The role of impulsive behavior in drug abuse. *Psychopharmacology, 200*, 1–26.

Phan, K. L., Taylor, S. F., Welsh, R. C., Ho, S. H., Britton, J. C., & Liberzon, I. (2004). Neural correlates of individual ratings of emotional salience: A trial-related fMRI study. *NeuroImage, 21*, 768–780.

Pujol, J., Soriano-Mas, C., Alonso, P., Cardoner, N., Menchón, J. M., Deus, J., & Vallejo, J. (2004). Mapping structural brain alterations in obsessive-compulsive disorder. *Archives of General Psychiatry, 61*, 720–730.

Radua, J., Canales-Rodríguez, E. J., Pomarol-Clotet, E., & Salvador, R. (2014). Validity of modulation and optimal settings for advanced voxel-based morphometry. *NeuroImage, 86*, 81–90.

Rahman, A. S., Xu, J., & Potenza, M. N. (2014). Hippocampal and amygdalar volumetric differences in pathological gambling: A preliminary study of the associations with the behavioral inhibition system. *Neuropsychopharmacology, 39*, 738–745.

Raylu, N., & Oei, T. P. (2004). The Gambling Related Cognitions Scale (GRCS): Development, confirmatory factor validation and psychometric properties. *Addiction, 99*, 757–769.

Ridgway, G. R., Omar, R., Ourselin, S., Hill, D. L., Warren, J. D., & Fox, N. C. (2009). Issues with threshold masking in voxel-based morphometry of atrophied brains. *NeuroImage, 44*, 99–111.

Rogers, R. D., Ramnani, N., Mackay, C., Wilson, J. L., Jezzard, P., Carter, C. S., & Smith, S. M. (2004). Distinct portions of anterior cingulate cortex and medial prefrontal cortex are activated by reward processing in separable phases of decision-making cognition. *Biological Psychiatry, 55*, 594–602.

Sanz, J., Perdigón, A. L., & Vázquez, C. (2003). Adaptación española del Inventario para la Depresión de Beck-II (BDI-II): 2. Propiedades psicométricas en población general [Spanish adaptation of the Beck Depression Inventory-II (BDI-II): 2. Psychometric features in the general population]. *Clínica y Salud, 14*, 249–280.

Savvidou, L. G., Fagundo, A. B., Fernández-Aranda, F., Granero, R., Claes, L., Mallorquí-Baqué, N., … Jiménez-Murcia, S. (2017). Is gambling disorder associated with impulsivity traits measured by the UPPS-P and is this association moderated by sex and age? *Comprehensive Psychiatry, 72*, 106–113.

Sescousse, G., Janssen, L. K., Hashemi, M. M., Timmer, M. H., Geurts, D. E., ter Huurne, N. P., … Cools, R. (2016). Amplified striatal responses to near-miss outcomes in pathological gamblers. *Neuropsychopharmacology, 41*, 2614–2623.

Shenhav, A., Cohen, J. D., & Botvinick, M. M. (2016). Dorsal anterior cingulate cortex and the value of control. *Nature Neuroscience, 19*, 1286–1291.

Steward, T., Mestre-Bach, G., Fernández-Aranda, F., Granero, R., Perales, J. C., Navas, J. F., … Jiménez-Murcia, S. (2017). Delay discounting and impulsivity traits in young and older gambling disorder patients. *Addictive Behaviors, 71*, 96–103.

Subramaniam, M., Chong, S. A., Browning, C., & Thomas, S. (2017). Cognitive distortions among older adult gamblers in an Asian context. *PLoS One, 12*, e0178036.

Tolomeo, S., Gray, S., Matthews, K., Steele, J. D., & Baldacchino, A. (2016). Multifaceted impairments in impulsivity and brain structural abnormalities in opioid dependence and abstinence. *Psychological Medicine, 46*, 2841–2853.

Torres, A., Catena, A., Megías, A., Maldonado, A., Cándido, A., Verdejo-García, A., & Perales, J. C. (2013). Emotional and non-emotional pathways to impulsive behavior and addiction. *Frontiers in Human Neuroscience, 7*, 43.

van Holst, R. J., Chase, H. W., & Clark, L. (2014). Striatal connectivity changes following gambling wins and near-misses: Associations with gambling severity. *NeuroImage: Clinical, 5*, 232–239.

van Holst, R. J., de Ruiter, M. B., van den Brink, W., Veltman, D. J., & Goudriaan, A. E. (2012). A voxel-based morphometry study comparing problem gamblers, alcohol abusers, and healthy controls. *Drug and Alcohol Dependence, 124*, 142–148.

Verdejo-García, A., Lawrence, A. J., & Clark, L. (2008). Impulsivity as a vulnerability marker for substance-use disorders: Review of findings from high-risk research, problem gamblers and genetic association studies. *Neuroscience and Biobehavioral Reviews, 32*, 777–810.

Vul, E., Harris, C., Winkielman, P., & Pashler, H. (2009). Puzzlingly high correlations in fMRI studies of emotion, personality, and social cognition. *Perspectives on Psychological Science, 4*, 274–290.

Wager, T. D., Davidson, M. L., Hughes, B. L., Lindquist, M. A., & Ochsner, K. N. (2008). Prefrontal-subcortical pathways mediating successful emotion regulation. *Neuron, 59*, 1037–1050.

Wechsler, D. (2008). *Wechsler adult intelligence scale adult intelligence scale*. San Antonio, TX: NCS Pearson.

Weiland, B. J., Heitzeg, M. M., Zald, D., Cummiford, C., Love, T., Zucker, R. A., & Zubieta, J. K. (2014). Relationship between impulsivity, prefrontal anticipatory activation, and striatal dopamine release during rewarded task performance. *Psychiatry Research: Neuroimaging, 223*, 244–252.

Whiteside, S. P., & Lynam, D. R. (2001). The Five Factor Model and impulsivity: Using a structural model of personality to understand impulsivity. *Personality and Individual Differences, 30*, 669–689.

Whiteside, S. P., Lynam, D. R., Miller, J. D., & Reynolds, S. K. (2005). Validation of the UPPS impulsive behaviour scale: A four-factor model of impulsivity. *European Journal of Personality, 19*, 559–574.

Xian, H., Shah, K. R., Phillips, S. M., Scherrer, J. F., Volberg, R., & Eisen, S. A. (2008). The association of cognitive distortions with problem and pathological gambling in adult male twins. *Psychiatry Research, 160*, 300–307.

Xue, G., Juan, C. H., Chang, C. F., Lu, Z. L., & Dong, Q. (2012). Lateral prefrontal cortex contributes to maladaptive decisions. *Proceedings of the National Academy of Sciences, 109*, 4401–4406.

Xue, G., Lu, Z., Levin, I. P., Weller, J. A., Li, X., & Bechara, A. (2009). Functional dissociations of risk and reward processing in the medial prefrontal cortex. *Cerebral Cortex, 19*, 1019–1027.

Yan, W. S., Zhang, R. R., Lan, Y., Li, Y. H., & Sui, N. (2016). Comparison of impulsivity in non-problem, at-risk and problem gamblers. *Scientific Reports, 6*, 39233.

Zois, E., Kiefer, F., Lemenager, T., Vollstädt-Klein, S., Mann, K., & Fauth-Bühler, M. (2017). Frontal cortex gray matter volume alterations in pathological gambling occur independently from substance use disorder. *Addiction Biology, 22*, 864–872.

The Rat Gambling Task as a model for the preclinical development of treatments for gambling disorder

Patricia Di Ciano and Bernard Le Foll

ABSTRACT

Gambling is a harmless pastime for many, but for some it can become problematic with serious social and financial consequences. To date, no pharmacological treatments for gambling disorder have been approved. Progress in this regard is undoubtedly hampered by the lack of established preclinical models that allow for the screening of the potential efficacy of new approaches. The Rat Gambling Task (rGT), based on the Iowa Gambling Task in humans, is a model of some of the decision-making processes involved in gambling. The purpose of the present review is to summarize the literature to date on the use of the rGT for preclinical testing of pharmacological agents. First, the rGT is described and compared to the IGT. Next, validity is examined to establish the rGT as a viable model for preclinical evaluation of new drugs. Finally, the available data on the effects of pharmacological challenges on the rGT are reviewed focusing on dopamine, norepinephrine, serotonin and opioid systems. It is concluded that the rGT may provide a viable preclinical model for new drug development for the treatment of gambling.

Gambling is ubiquitous, and it is estimated that about 4 out of 5 people have gambled in their lifetime, with about 10% in one US survey having gambled more than 1000 times in their life (Kessler et al., 2008). For some, this gambling becomes problematic, with the lifetime prevalence of pathological gambling being between about 0.42% to 0.6% in the US (Kessler et al., 2008; Petry, Stinson, & Grant, 2005). Gambling disorder (GD) is the first behavioral disorder to be classified as an addictive disorder in the *Diagnostic and Statistical Manual of Mental Disorders* (DSM5); in the DSM-5, gambling has been described as having the diagnostic features of 'risking something of value in the hopes of obtaining something of greater value'.

To date, there are no approved pharmacological treatments for GD. Part of the difficulty in developing treatment approaches for GD is undoubtedly the paucity of preclinical models suitable for the preliminary evaluation of efficacy. Being a behavioural disorder with features similar to those of substance use, GD poses a challenge for preclinical models. Unlike with substance use, GD has no pharmacologically induced state that produces withdrawal or dependence. All manifestations must be produced through behavioural manipulations. Therefore, most models have focused on one modality of the 'gaming', i.e. slot machines (Cocker & Winstanley, 2015) or a feature of gambling such as 'chasing losses' with the loss-chasing task (Barrus, Cherkasova, & Winstanley, 2016; Cocker & Winstanley, 2015).

One model, the Rat Gambling Task (rGT; Zeeb, Robbins, & Winstanley, 2009), models some of the decision-making in gambling. In this review, we will summarize the main features of this model, followed by a discussion of its validity. We will then review the literature on the effects of pharmacological manipulations on the rGT. This will be compared to analogous studies in humans, where they exist. In the present review, the main focus was on pharmacological interventions in the rat version of the rGT. Search terms entered into PubMed included 'rGT' (19 April 2017) and 'Iowa Gambling Task' (8 March 2017 and 19 April 2017). Papers were selected if they included pharmacological manipulations of the rGT. Papers were read carefully and any manuscripts referenced that did not turn up in the literature search were also included in the present review.

The Rat Gambling Task

The Iowa Gambling Task (IGT; Bechara, Damasio, Damasio, & Anderson, 1994) is a card game designed to capture decision-making under uncertainty, of the type that generally underlies gambling. In the IGT, human participants are given a choice of four decks of cards. Each deck is differently 'stacked' such that some decks produce large rewards (earning money) with high penalties (losing money). In the IGT, the advantageous strategy is for the player to learn to select the decks with lower monetary gain, as they also produce lower punishments, and thus, in the long-term, yield the greatest reward. Thus, the participant must learn to resist the 'tempting' option of high reward. The IGT has generated a great deal of research over the years and there has been interest in modelling this task in animals. A number of rodent versions of the IGT have been developed (de Visser et al., 2011). Of these, the rat gambling task (rGT; Zeeb et al., 2009) has risen to prominence over the past years. It is the only rodent version of the IGT that allows for repeated pharmacological testing and is thus the focus of this review.

In the rat version of the rGT Zeeb et al., 2009), the IGT is modelled through the use of a modified 5-Choice Serial Reaction Time Task (Robbins, 2002). The behavioural equipment is a five-hole operant conditioning chamber with five response options in an array (of which only the outer four are active). On the opposite side of the wall is a food hopper with a traylight (see Figure 1). When lit, rats can make a response in the food hopper to initiate a trial. After initiation, a 5-s inter-trial interval (ITI) is started, after which the lights in the 4 response holes are illuminated. A response in one of the holes results in delivery of the preset amount of reward or a preset 'punishing' time-out. The amount of reward (1–4 food pellets) or punishing time-outs (5–40 s) vary such that the response with the highest reward also has the greatest punishing time-outs. The task for the rat is to learn which of the holes yields the greatest number of rewards overall (99–411) during the 30-min session. As with the IGT, the hole with relatively few rewards also produces the greatest number of rewards per session (see Figure 1). Similarly to the IGT, the rat must learn to inhibit the

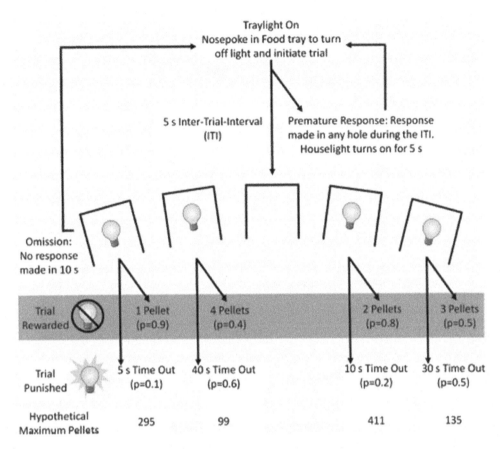

Figure 1. Schematic showing the trial structure of the rGT. The task began with illumination of the tray light. A nose-poke response in the food tray extinguished the tray light and initiated a new trial. After an inter-trial-interval (ITI) of 5 s, 4 stimulus lights were turned on in holes 1, 2, 4, and 5, and the animal was required to respond in one of these holes within 10 s. This response was then rewarded or punished depending on the reinforcement schedule for that option (indicated by the probability of a win or loss in brackets for each option). If the animal was rewarded, the stimulus lights were extinguished and the animal received the corresponding number of pellets in the now-illuminated food tray. A response at the food tray then started a new trial. If the animal was punished, the stimulus light in the corresponding hole flashed at a frequency of 0.5 Hz for the duration of the punishing timeout and all other lights were extinguished. At the end of the punishment period, the tray light was turned on and the animal could initiate a new trial. Failure to respond at the illuminated holes resulted in an omission, whereas a response during the ITI was classified as a premature response and punished by a 5-s timeout during which the house light was turned on. The maximum number of pellets that could be obtained if an animal chose one option exclusively is given in the 'Hypothetical Maximum Pellets'. Taken (with permission) from: Zeeb & Winstanley (2011).

'tempting' response to obtain the largest number of food rewards in order to maximize the long-term gain.

The variable of primary interest is the percent choice of each response option (P1–P4; Figure 1). Most rats will learn to make most responses on the P2 option, the choice with the greatest pay-off over the session (see Figure 2). However, some animals will chose the disadvantageous options (P3 or P4) more than the advantageous ones (P1 and P2; see section below on face validity) (Gueye, Trigo, Vemuri, Makriyannis, & Le Foll, 2016). Other

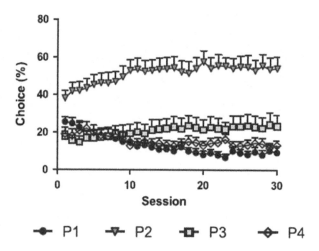

Figure 2. Mean ± SEM percent choice of P1, P2, P3 or P4 during acquisition of the rodent gambling task in rats previously trained saline pre-treatment during adolescence. Taken (with permission) from Pushparaj et al. (2015).

response measures can also be taken: (1) omissions are scored as trials in which a rodent initiates a trial in the food hopper but does not make a response in the array; (2) premature responses occur when the rodent makes a response in the array before the end of the 5-s ITI (these are punished by a 5-s time-out); (3) perseverative responses in the array after rewarded or punished trials can also be recorded; and (4) the latency to make a response in the array after initiating a trial (response latency) or the latency to collect a reward after making a response in the array (collect latency).

What is interesting about the rGT is that a certain percentage of rodents persist in selecting the disadvantageous (P3 and P4) options more than the advantageous options (P1 and P2) (Di Ciano & Le Foll, 2016; Di Ciano et al., 2015; Gueye et al., 2016), which is evident from the start of acquisition (Figure 3). To reflect the differences in baseline performance, some reports have separated rats into different 'optimal' or 'suboptimal' ('risk-preferring') groups and compared the effects of treatment on these different groups (Di Ciano & Le Foll, 2016; Pushparaj et al., 2015). To separate rats into these groups, rats that select the advantageous option more at baseline are placed in the 'optimal' groups, whereas those that select the disadvantageous option more at baseline are grouped as 'suboptimal'.

Validity of the rGT

Although the ability to measure multiple dimensions is a strength of the rGT, it remains to be determined to what extent the rGT is actually a measure of gambling per se. It is a challenge even for the most creative theorist to propose that rats are actually 'gambling'. Instead, the rGT is a model of the IGT, and thus it measures the same underlying construct as the IGT, i.e. decision-making in a laboratory setting. In psychiatry, it is not uncommon for an animal model to measure a single feature of a disorder (e.g. relapse is modelled by the 'reinstatement' model; Epstein & Preston, 2003). The utility of an animal model lies in its face, construct and predictive validity, each of which will be considered below for the rGT.

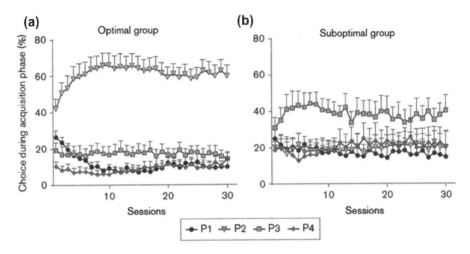

Figure 3. Mean ± SEM percent choice of P1, P2, P3 and P4 during acquisition of the rat gambling task in optimal (left panel) rats and suboptimal rats (right panel). Acquisition of the various choices was different in the 2 groups of rats. Taken with permission from Gueye et al. (2016).

It should be noted that the validity of the rGT has been considered elsewhere (de Visser et al., 2011; Winstanley & Clark, 2016) and is therefore only summarized briefly below.

Face validity of the rGT

An animal model is said to have good face validity if it essentially captures the superficial nature of the procedure that is modelled. In this sense, the rGT has good face validity because it essentially parallels the IGT. That is, in both the IGT and rGT, there is a choice of four options, each associated with its unique set of rewards and punishments. In both, the task is to learn these contingencies. The ultimate aim of the task is to learn to inhibit the 'tempting' response options that produce high reward, as these also produce high rates of punishment. In both the IGT and rGT, the preference develops over time and the participant generally learns to select the advantageous responses over the disadvantageous responses (Pushparaj et al., 2015; Zeeb & Winstanley, 2013).

One difference between the rGT and the IGT is certainly the amount of training required. In the rGT, rats are given extended training (for about a month prior to treatments), whereas in the IGT this is not the case. Thus, the IGT likely measures decision-making under uncertainty, whereas in the rGT, the contingencies are known. Thus, the rGT more realistically reflects decision-making under risk, and not under uncertainty. These differences are of note and may impact the face validity of the rGT.

Construct validity

The IGT was originally developed to measure the effects of prefrontal lesions on decision-making (Bechara et al., 1994). Humans with damage to the ventromedial prefrontal cortex (which includes the orbitofrontal cortex) and the amygdala perform poorly on the

IGT, selecting the disadvantageous options more than the advantageous ones (Bechara & Damasio, 2002). This is paralleled in rodents in that functional disconnection of the baso-lateral amygdala from the orbitofrontal cortex (OFC) impaired the acquisition of the rGT (Zeeb & Winstanley, 2013). However, once established, inactivation of the OFC had no effect on performance of the rGT (Zeeb, Baarendse, Vanderschuren, & Winstanley, 2015). Thus, it appears that the rGT has construct validity.

Although it measures decision-making, the rGT has evolved to become a measure of gambling behaviours. Thus, the exact nature of the impairment on the IGT observed in people with GD needs to be considered and whether it has parallels to the rGT. In an early study of the decision-making impairments evident in GD, Cavedini, Riboldi, Keller, D'Annucci, and Bellodi (2002) reported that people with GD selected the disadvantageous decks more than the advantageous ones (Cavedini et al., 2002). Further, this impairment developed over the learning session, with the selection of disadvantageous decks emerging over the session. This directly parallels the observation made in rats that a subset of animals will persist in selecting the suboptimal choices in the rGT. These observations from both the human and preclinical literature were additionally supported by a recent meta-analysis of 17 studies that investigated impairments in the IGT in people with GD (Kovács, Richman, Janka, Maraz, & Andó, 2017). In this study, it was found that people with GD display less advantageous decision-making than healthy controls. Thus, there is good consilience between the rGT and IGT.

There are also parallels between the IGT and rGT in terms of the brain substrates the mediate these tasks. As mentioned above, disconnection of the OFC and basolateral amyg-dala impaired acquisition of the rGT (Zeeb & Winstanley, 2013). In humans, an functional magnetic resonance imaging (fMRI) study has shown that the OFC and ventromedial prefrontal cortex are activated during performance of the IGT in healthy controls (Li, Lu, D'Argembeau, Ng, & Bechara, 2010), while another found that activation of the ventral prefrontal cortex was lower in those in GD as compared to health controls during gambling tasks (Potenza, Leung et al., 2003; Potenza, Steinberg et al., 2003; Reuter et al., 2005). Thus, the rGT appears to have good construct validity.

Some consideration of the construct validity of the human IGT in terms of its ability to model decision-making is warranted at this point, as there is some debate as to whether the IGT is a valid model of decision-making. In a review of this topic (Buelow & Suhr, 2009), it was concluded that the IGT has good construct validity for measuring the decision-making impairment following damage to the prefrontal cortex. However, it was concluded that a number of issues remain to be determined. For example, the reliability of the IGT has not yet been established, nor is it clear if there is good consilience between the IGT and other decision-making tasks. Further, the exact nature of the decision-making measured by the IGT is still an open question. Buelow and Suhr (2009) argued that the IGT measures 'hot' but not 'cold' decision-making, an assertion that has been both supported (Toplak, Sorge, Benoit, West, & Stanovich, 2010) and challenged (Gansler, Jerram, Vannorsdall, & Schretlen, 2011). In this view, 'cold' decision-making involves the rational and cognitive determinants of making a decision, such as knowledge of the risk/benefit ratio, the ability to retrieve them from memory and the ability to hold them in memory. By comparison, 'hot' decision-making involves the affective and emotional responses to decision-making.

It should also be mentioned that a number of different rodent versions of the IGT have been developed (de Visser et al., 2011). Although they have all been shown to have validity to various degrees, one issue common to all of them is the modelling of rewards with food pellets and the use of this to model the concept of loss, which for humans is a financial loss. That is, it is hard to take sugar pellets away from rats once they have been consumed, whereas in the human IGT, earned winnings can be deducted as a punishment. In the rGT that is the focus of the present review, punishment is modelled by a delay. Although this results in some decrease in the number of reinforcements earned, it does not model loss in the same way as the human IGT (Bechara, 2004; Pushparaj et al., 2015).

Predictive validity

Predictive validity of a model lies in its ability to predict scores on some other criterion. For example, a model with good predictive validity would be able to predict the real-world efficacy of treatments. One way to test the predictive validity is to assess the impact of pharmacological treatments on the model. If there is good consilience between the findings in the animal model and the therapeutic efficacy, then the model is said to have good predictive validity.

To date, few treatments have been shown to have efficacy in treating GD in humans (Hloch et al.). Based on case reports, disulfiram has shown promise (Müller, Banas, Heinz, & Hein, 2011; Mutschler et al., 2010). Disulfiram is a dopamine (DA) beta hydroxylase (DBH) inhibitor, which inhibits the synthesis of norepinephrine (NE) from DA (Bourdélat-Parks et al., 2005; Goldstein & Nakajima, 1967; Karamanakos, Pappas, Stephanou, & Marselos, 2001; Musacchio, Goldstein, Anagnoste, Poch, & Kopin, 1966; Schroeder et al., 2010). Indeed, administration of disulfiram increased DA, and decreased NE, in the striatum at doses that were effective in the rGT (Di Ciano et al., 2018). In clinical trials, few pharmacological treatment approaches have been used successfully with the exception perhaps of opioid antagonists such as naltrexone (Grant, Odlaug, & Schreiber, 2014; Grant, Won Kim, & Potenza, 2003) or nalmefene (Grant, Odlaug, Potenza, Hollander, & Kim, 2010; Grant et al., 2006). Disulfiram (Di Ciano et al., 2018) or naltrexone (Di Ciano & Le Foll, 2016) have both been administered to rats prior to performance on the rGT. In both studies, only choice responding was dose-dependently affected by the treatments; all other measures were intact. When rats were divided into subgroups based on whether they made the optimal or suboptimal choice more, it was found that disulfiram or naltrexone only affected responding in the suboptimal group. That is, both treatments increased the number of advantageous choices made in the suboptimal group, with no effect on the performance of the optimal group performance. These studies are further considered below in sections on norepinephrine (disulfiram study) and opioids (naltrexone study). Thus, the rGT appears to have good predictive validity.

Reliability

Reliability is a necessary but not sufficient aspect of validity and should be considered here. Reliability refers to the degree to which a measurement is accurate, and is generally measured as the extent to which repeated tests produce the same result. In this regard, one consistent observation is the finding that rats choose the P2 option more than the other options

(Barrus & Winstanley, 2016; Gueye et al., 2016; Silveira, Malcolm, Shoaib, & Winstanley, 2015; Silveira, Murch, Clark, & Winstanley, 2016; Tremblay & Winstanley, 2016; Zeeb et al., 2009). What is less clear is the proportion of responses on the other options. In some studies, rats make more P3 options than P4 or P1 options (Barrus & Winstanley, 2016; Gueye et al., 2016; Tremblay & Winstanley, 2016), while in others this is not the case (Baarendse, Winstanley, & Vanderschuren, 2013; Silveira et al., 2015, 2016; Zeeb et al., 2009). It may be that heterogeneity within cohorts in terms of the proportion of optimal and suboptimal rats may influence these results, since suboptimal rats make more P3 and P4 options than optimal rats (Di Ciano & Le Foll, 2016; Di Ciano et al., 2018; Gueye et al., 2016)

The rGT is also reliable in terms of the baseline characteristics of optimal and suboptimal rats. That is, the suboptimal, or 'risk-preferring', group have been found to make more premature responses, complete fewer trials (due to the longer punishing time outs), made fewer omissions and were faster to choose between the options (Barrus, Hosking, Zeeb, Tremblay, & Winstanley, 2015; Ferland & Winstanley, 2016). In other papers, suboptimal rats made more premature responses (Di Ciano et al., 2018) and fewer trials (Di Ciano & Le Foll, 2016; Di Ciano et al., 2018). Thus, it appears that the suboptimal/'risk-preferring' rats are generally more impulsive. One interesting finding is that rats that chose the P4 option more at baseline were more susceptible, as compared to controls, to increase their choice of the P4 option following training in a learned helplessness model (Nobrega, Hedayatmofidi, & Lobo, 2016). Learned helplessness is an animal model of depression which subjects the animal to inescapable shock. Thus, it appears that exposure to stressful events may predispose animals to make more risky choices on the rGT.

Perhaps the strongest evidence of reliability in the rGT is the consistency of effects following administration of amphetamine to rats (see summary below). That is, following administration of amphetamine, rats in all (see Table 1) but one (Tremblay & Winstanley, 2016) study made more P1 responses and fewer P2 responses. What is less clear is the effects of amphetamine on ancillary responding, as these varied by study (see below and Table 1). In sum, it appears that choice responding is a reliable measure of the rGT, while other behaviours measured may be susceptible to individual differences; the nature of these are yet to be clarified.

Dopamine receptor interventions and rodent gambling tasks

DA is of clear importance in substance use disorders (Di Chiara, 1999), and also in gambling (Linnet, Møller, Peterson, Gjedde, & Doudet, 2011; Reuter et al., 2005; Zack & Poulos, 2007). DA has five main receptor subtypes, D_1–D_5, which can be classed as 'D1-like' (D_1, D_5) and 'D2-like' (D_2, D_3, D_4). The D2-like have received particular attention with respect to the development of treatment strategies for addictive disorders. The D_2 and D_3 receptor subtypes share homology (Sibley & Monsma, 1992), but antagonism of the D_2 receptor is believed to result in the debilitating side effects seen after treatment with dopamine antagonists (Achat-Mendes et al., 2010; Millan et al., 2000). Thus, efforts have been focused on developing agents that are selective for the D_3 as opposed to the D_2 (Heidbreder et al., 2005). This is especially germane given the putative role of the D_3 receptor in substance abuse, especially that controlled by conditioned environmental cues (Pilla et al., 1999). By comparison, the D_4 receptor has been of interest for a number of years

Table 1. Summary of studies conducted on the effects of pharmacological interventions on the rGT/mIGT.

Drug	Mechanism	P1	P2	P3	P4	Adv	Dis	Trial	Prem	Om	PP	RP	Ch	Coll	Ref
DOPAMINE RECEPTOR AGONISTS															
SKF 81,297	D_1 agonist	−	−	−	−			−	−	−	−	↓	−	−	(Zeeb et al., 2009)
Bromocriptine	D_2/D_3 agonist	−	−	−	−			−	−	−	−	−	−	↑	(Zeeb et al., 2009)
Quinpriole	D_2/D_3 agonist	−	−	−	−			↓	↓	↑	↓	↓	↑	↑	(Zeeb et al., 2009)
PD 128,907	D_3 agonist					−		−	−	−	−	−	−	−	(Di Ciano et al., 2015)
PD128907	D_3 agonist							−	↑↓	↑	−	−	↑	↑	(Barrus et al., 2016)
PD128907	D_3 agonist	−	−	↑C	−			−	−	−	−	−	−	−	(Barrus et al., 2016)
PD-168077	D_4 agonist	−	−	−	−			−	−	−	−	−	−	−	(Barrus et al., 2016)
PD 168077	D_4 agonist					↓*		−	−	−	−	−	−	↓	(Di Ciano et al., 2015)
DOPAMINE RECEPTOR ANTAGONISTS															
SCH 23,390	D_1 antagonist	−	−	−	−			↓	↓	↑	↓	−	↑	−	(Zeeb et al., 2009)
Eticlopride	D_2 antagonist		↑	↓	↓			↑	−	−	−	−	−	↓	(Zeeb et al., 2009)
Eticlopride	D_2 antagonist	−	−	−	−			−	↓	↑	−	−	↑	−	(Barrus et al., 2016)
L-741626	D_2 antagonist					−		−	−	−	−	−	−	−	(Di Ciano et al., 2015)
SB-277011-A	D_3 antagonist					−		−	−	−	−	−	−	−	(Di Ciano et al., 2015)
SB-277011-A	D_3 antagonist	−	−	−	−			−	−	−	−	−	−	−	(Barrus et al., 2016)
SB-277011-A	D_3 antagonist	−	−	↓C	−			−	−	−	−	−	−	−	(Barrus et al., 2016)
L-745870	D_4 antagonist					−		↑	−	−	−	−	−	↑	(Di Ciano et al., 2015)
A-38193	D_4 antagonist	−	−	−	−			−	−	−	−	−	−	−	(Barrus et al., 2016)
DOPAMINE REUPTAKE INHIBITORS															
GBR 12909	DA reuptake inhibitor	−	−	−	−	−	−		↑	−					(Baarendse et al., 2013)
COMBINATIONS OF NEUROTRANSMITTERS															
Amphetamine	DA agonist	↑	↓					↓	−	−			−	−	(Silveira et al., 2015)
Amphetamine	DA agonist	↑	↓		↑			↓	↑	−	↑	↑	−	↓	(Zeeb et al., 2009)
Ampetamine	DA agonist	↑	↓		↑			↓	↑	−	−	−	−	−	(Zeeb et al., 2013).
Amphetamine	DA agonist	↑	↓	−	−			↓	−	↑	↓	↑	−	−	(Silveira et al., 2016)
Amphetamine	DA agonist	↑	↓	−	−			−	↑	−	−	−	↑	−	(Barrus & Winstanley, 2016)
Amphetamine	DA agonist	↑	↓	−	−	−			↑	−					(Baarendse et al., 2013)
Amphetamine	DA agonist	−	−	−	−			−	↑	−			−	−	(Tremblay & Winstanley, 2016)
GBR12909 and atomoxetine	DA and NE reuptake inhibitor	↑	↓	↑	↑	↓	↑		↑	↑					(Baarendse et al., 2013)
GBR12909 and citalopram	DA and serotonin reuptake inhibitor	↑	↓	−	−	−	−		↑	−					(Baarendse et al., 2013)

(Continued)

Table 1. (*Continued*).

Drug	Mechanism	P1	P2	P3	P4	Adv	Dis	Trial	Prem	Om	PP	RP	Ch	Coll	Ref
Atomoxetine and citalopram	NE and serotonin reuptake inhibitor	↑	–	–	–	–	–	–	↓	↑	–	–	–	–	(Baarendse et al., 2013)
Buspirone (3 mg/kg, i.p.)	D_2/D_3, D_4 antagonist, 5-HT$_{1A}$ partial agonist	–	↑	–	–	↓	↓	↓	↓	↑	–	–	↑	–	(Di Ciano et al., 2017)
NOREPINEPHRINE															
Atomoxetine	NE reuptake inhibitor	→	–	–	→	–	–	→	→	↓	→	–	–	–	(Baarendse et al., 2013)
Atomoxetine	NE reuptake inhibitor	–	→	–	–	–	–	→	→	–	↑	–	↓	–	(Silveira et al., 2016)
Disulfiram	DBH inhibitor	–	–	–	–	↑SO	–	–	–	–	↑	–	–	–	(Di Ciano et al., 2018)
SEROTONIN															
WAY100635	5-HT$_{1A}$ antagonist	↓	↓	–	–			→	→	→	–	–	↓	–	(Zeeb et al., 2009)
8-OH-DPAT	5-HT$_{1A}$ Agonist	←	→	←	–			→	→	–	–	–	–	–	(Zeeb et al., 2009)
Citalopram	Serotonin reuptake inhibitor	–	–	–	–	–	–	–	–	–	–	–	↑	↑	(Baarendse et al., 2013)
CANNABINOIDS															
WIN 55,212-2	CB1 agonist	–	–	–	–	↑SO	↓SO	–	–	↑O	–	–	↑SO	–	(Gueye et al., 2016)
URB 597	FAAH inhibitor	–	–	–	–	–	–	–	–	–	–	–	–	–	(Gueye et al., 2016)
AM 4113	CB1 antagonist	–	–	–	–	–	–	–	–	–	–	–	–	–	(Gueye et al., 2016)
AM 630	CB2 antagonist	–	–	–	–	–	–	–	–	–	–	–	–	–	(Gueye et al., 2016)
ACETYLCHOLINE															
Oxotremorine	Ach agonist	–	–	–	–			→	⇄	–	–	–	←	–	(Silveira et al., 2015)
Scopolamine	Muscarinic antagonist	←	–	–	–			→	→	↑	–	–	←	←	(Silveira et al., 2015)
Nicotine	Nicotinic agonist	–	–	–	–			→	–	–	–	–	←	←	(Silveira et al., 2015)
Mecamylamine	Nicotinic antagonist	–	–	–	–			→	–	↑	–	–	→	←	(Silveira et al., 2015)
ANTICONVULSANTS															
Valproate	Anticonvulsant	–	–	–	–	–	–	–	–	–	–	–	–	–	(Tremblay & Winstanley, 2016)
Lamotrigine	Anticonvulsant	–	–	–	–	–	–	–	–	–	–	–	–	–	(Tremblay & Winstanley, 2016)
Carbamazepine	Aniticonvulsant	–	–	–	–	–	–	–	→	–	–	–	↑	–	(Tremblay & Winstanley, 2016)
OPIOIDS															
naltrexone	Opioid antagonist	↑SO	–	–	–	↑SO	–	–	–	–	–	–	–	–	(Di Ciano & Le Foll, 2016)

Notes:

Greyed cells indicate studies that did not measure that variable. ↑↓ indicates studies with inverted-U or U-shaped dose-response functions. Adv: Advantageous responses; Dis: Disadvantageous responses; Prem: Premature responses; Om: Omissions; PP: punishment perseverations; Ch: Choice latencies; Coll: Collect latencies; RP: reward perseverations; DA: dopamine; 5-HT: serotonin; NE: norepinephrine; DBH: dopamine beta hydroxylase; CB1/CB2: cannabinoid type 1 and 2 receptors; FAAH: fatty acid amide hydrolase; Ach: Acetylcholine; SO: suboptimal group only; O: optimal group only. *Small effect; C: cued version of the task.

(Di Ciano, Grandy, & Le Foll, 2014), but due to the relative lack of selective pharmacological agents, studies of the role of the D_4 receptor in addictive disorders have not been abundant.

One consistent finding in the literature is that people with substance use disorders have lowered D_2 receptor levels as compared to healthy controls (Fehr et al., 2008; Martinez et al., 2005; Volkow et al., 1993). By contrast, it has been demonstrated that D_3 receptor levels are increased in the brains of those with substance use disorders (Boileau et al., 2012). These divergent findings speak to the importance of investigating the role of the various DA receptor subtypes in addictive disorders. Interestingly, in a study of those with GD, no differences in basal levels of D_2 (Linnet et al., 2012) or D_3 (Boileau et al., 2009) receptors was found compared to healthy controls. However, the degree of severity of the GD was correlated with the availability of D_3 receptors (Boileau et al., 2009). Thus, it seems that D_3 receptors are involved to some capacity in GD.

An interesting genetic association study with parallels between humans and rodents provided evidence for an involvement of DA D_3 receptors in the rGT (Lobo et al., 2015). In this study, human participants who had at least two of the DSM diagnostic criteria for GD were genotyped and it was found that GD was significantly associated with polymorphisms of the D_3 receptors (rs167771) and *CAMK2D* (rs3815072). When these genes were analysed in rats it was found that performance on the rGT was significantly correlated with only the D_3 receptor genes. In this study, impulsive behaviour was quantified as the percent of P4 choices divided by the percent of P2 choices. Strong correlations between DA D_3 mRNA density and impulsive choice were found in some brain areas. The finding of a significant correlation of performance on the rGT with a DA D_3 receptor genotype is compelling evidence of involvement of this receptor in some aspect of the rGT.

In keeping with this, one study found that D_3 receptors were involved in a cued version of the rGT (Barrus & Winstanley, 2016). In this version of the rGT, cues accompanied the delivery of rewards, and these cues increased in complexity with the number of rewards delivered. Like the uncued rGT, rats learned the task and ultimately selected the advantageous options more than the disadvantageous ones; in the cued task, however, P2 was selected less frequently, and P3 more often, than in the uncued version. Thus, cues have a deleterious effect on performance of the rGT, consistent with results from heroin addicts engaged in the IGT in the presence of cues (Wang et al., 2012). Administration of the D_3 agonist, PD128907, to rats, increased choice of P3 in the cued group. By comparison, the D_3 antagonist SB-277011-A had the reciprocal effect of decreasing the choice of P3 option in the cued group. There were no effects in the uncued group. Thus, D_3 antagonists improve performance, consistent with theories that D_3 antagonists provide a viable therapeutic option for addictive disorders (Heidbreder, 2005), especially under the control of environmental cues (Lefoll, Goldberg, & Sokoloff, 2005). These findings suggest that D_3 receptors are selectively involved in the rGT in the presence of conditioned environmental cues. For a summary of the effects of pharmacological manipulations on the rGT, see Table 1.

Further studies have found that selective D_2, D_3 or D_4 agents were without a marked effect in the rGT in the absence of cues. In one report, the D_4 antagonist, A-381393, and the D_4 agonist, PD-168077, were both without effect on the rGT (Barrus & Winstanley, 2016), on either choice responses or any other behavioural measure. In another study (Di Ciano et al., 2015), the same D_4 agonist had a significant but very small effect of decreasing advantageous responding and also decreased collect latencies; a D_4 antagonist had the opposite effect on collect latencies. In respect of the effects of D_3 agents, one study found that the D_3 agonist PD128907 had dose-dependent effects on premature responding in the rGT; choice latency, collection latency and omissions were also increased (Barrus & Winstanley, 2016). However, this effect was not replicated in another study with the same D_3 agonist, in which no effects of PD128907 were revealed (Di Ciano et al., 2015). In both studies, the D_3 antagonist, SB-277011-A, was without effect (Barrus & Winstanley, 2016; Di Ciano et al., 2015).

In other studies, the D_2 antagonist eticlopride improved performance on the rGT by increasing the P2 option and decreasing the P3 and P4 options. Reward latencies were also reduced and the number of trials increased (Zeeb et al., 2009). However, this was not replicated in a subsequent study by the same group, where premature responses and omissions were decreased and increased, respectively and choice latencies were increased (Barrus & Winstanley, 2016), or in another study with the D_2 antagonist L641626 where no effects were revealed (Di Ciano et al., 2015). It should be mentioned that the less selective DA agonists, quinpirole or bromocriptine, had no effect on choice responding, but they both increased reward latencies, while quinpirole additionally decreased perseverative responding and increased omissions while also decreasing premature responses and the number of trials completed (Zeeb et al., 2009). Together, it seems that there are inconsistent findings from the various studies. The exact role of D_2 receptors in the rGT awaits further experimentation.

It should be mentioned that the D_1 agonist, SKF 81297, was without effect on the rGT, with the exception of decreasing reward latencies; a D_1 antagonist, SCH 23390, decreased the number of trials and premature responses, increased omissions and decreased perseverative responding while also increasing choice latencies, with no effect on choice (Zeeb et al., 2009). Together, these findings are consistent with motoric effects.

The effects of DA agents in combination with other neurotransmitter receptor agents

In comparison to the effects of selective DA receptor agents, it seems that dopaminergic compounds that are not selective for a certain DA receptor subtype are effective in altering performance on the rGT. That is, amphetamine has been found to increase P1 choices and decrease P2 choices in a number of studies (Baarendse et al., 2013; Barrus & Winstanley, 2016; van Enkhuizen, Geyer, & Young, 2013; Silveira et al., 2015, 2016; Zeeb et al., 2009; Zeeb, Wong, & Winstanley, 2013). Despite the fact that one study did not replicate these findings (Tremblay & Winstanley, 2016), these seem to be consistent effects. P1 and P2 are both advantageous options, and, indeed, when these are collapsed as advantageous responses, no effects of amphetamine are seen (Baarendse et al., 2013). What is less clear, however, is the effects of amphetamine on other measures. For example, in the original report (Zeeb et al., 2009), amphetamine increased premature responding, decreased reward latencies and increased perseverative responding. Other studies have not replicated these findings (Barrus & Winstanley, 2016; Silveira et al., 2015, 2016; van Enkhuizen et al., 2013).

Buspirone is an anxiolytic that has been shown to have affinity for the D_2, D_3 and D_4 receptors. Studied initially as a serotonin partial agonist, its affinity for DA receptors lead to efforts to repurpose buspirone for the indications of addictive disorders (Le Foll & Boileau, 2013; Newman et al., 2012). In a study of its effects on the rGT (Di Ciano et al., 2017) it was found that buspirone was non-selective at high doses (10 mg/kg), impacting all measures on the rGT. At a lower dose range (3 mg/kg), buspirone impaired all measures on the rGT except perseverations. By comparison, also at 3 mg/kg, only omissions were increased on the control task the 5-Choice Serial Reaction Time Task, suggesting that buspirone did not simply impair motor performance. At 3 mg/kg, buspirone occupied the D_3 receptor but not the D_2 receptor, as quantified with [^{3}H]-(+)-PHNO; at the higher dose of 10 mg/kg, it occupied both receptors. Thus, it is tempting to speculate that buspirone had effects on the rGT at 3 mg/kg due to actions at the D_3 receptor. However, given the null findings of the effects of D_3 agents on the rGT, it seems more likely that buspirone was acting to affect performance on the rGT through non-selective means. Buspirone is also a partial agonist at serotonin (5-HT$_{1A}$) receptors, and thus it must be considered that buspirone's effects are due to actions at serotonin. As considered in more detail below in the section on serotonin, 8-OH-DPAT (a 5-HT$_{1A}$ agonist), increased P1 responses (Zeeb et al., 2009), while a serotonin reuptake inhibitor, citalopram, had no effects on choice responding (Baarendse et al., 2013). Thus, it seems more likely that buspirone affected performance on the rGT through an interaction at a number of receptors. However, future investigations into the effects of 5-HT$_{1A}$ partial agonists is warranted

Consistent with mediation by a combination of DA receptors, the rGT has also been shown to be mediated by a combination of reuptake inhibitors (van Enkhuizen et al., 2013, 2014). That is, Baarendse et al. (2013) found that GBR12909 (a DA reuptake inhibitor) did not impact choice responding when collapsed into advantageous or disadvantageous responses (Baarendse et al., 2013). GBR12909 or atomoxetine (a norepinephrine reuptake inhibitor) did increase and decrease premature responses, respectively, suggesting opposite effect on impulsivity (DA reuptake inhibiters increase it). However, when atomoxetine and GBR12909 were combined, advantageous responses decreased and premature responses were increased. GBR 12909 and citalopram, combined, increased premature responses and the combination of atomoxetine and citalopram decreased premature responses. Similarly, all combinations of reuptake inhibitors increased P1 and decreased P2, while the combination of GBR12909 and atomoxetine also increased P3 and P4. Atomoxetine combined with either GBR12909 or citalopram increased errors of omission. Thus, it appears that choice behaviour may be under the control of numerous neurotransmitter systems, especially the DA and NE system combined.

Consistent with this, disulfiram also affected performance on the rGT. Specifically, disulfiram increased the number of advantageous responses made by rats that performed suboptimally at baseline (that is, they chose more disadvantageous responses at baseline). No other measures were impacted by disulfiram. What is interesting is the selective impact of disulfiram on only choice responding in a subgroup of rats that have a similar predisposition to disadvantageous responses as those with GD (Linnet, Rojskjaer, Nygaard, & Maher, 2006). Thus, targeting a combination of DA and NE may be especially helpful in developing novel treatment strategies.

Norepinephrine

Norepinephrine has had a recent surge in interest due to a revival of hypotheses that it may be involved in substance use disorders. Indeed, blockade of alpha1-adrenergic receptors with prazosin reduced the intake of cocaine, heroin and ethanol in animals (Colombo et al., 2014; Forget et al., 2010; Gaval-Cruz & Weinshenker, 2009; Greenwell, Walker, Cottone, Zorrilla, & Koob, 2009; Schroeder et al., 2010; Schroeder, Epps, Grice, & Weinshenker,

2013; Walker, Rasmussen, Raskind, & Koob, 2008; Wee, Mandyam, Lekic, & Koob, 2008); Zhang & Kosten, 2005). It has also been shown to be involved in animal models of relapse (Forget et al., 2010; Zhang & Kosten, 2005). In humans, gamblers have increased plasma levels of NE (Meyer et al., 2004; Roy et al., 1988), and have deficits in NE receptor sensitivity (Pallanti et al., 2010).

In humans, administration of a NE reuptake inhibitor, reboxetine, decreased choices on a disadvantageous deck and increased choices on an advantageous deck, but this did not reach statistical significance (O'Carroll & Papps, 2003). The authors argue that the lack of statistical significance was not due to power issues and instead reflects the lack of involvement of NE in the IGT. By comparison, clonidine, the α_2 noradrenergic antagonist, improved performance on the IGT in abstinent heroin addicts, but had no effect in healthy controls (Zhang et al., 2012). Thus, noradrenergic manipulations may be effective in the IGT in some circumstances.

In one study, atomoxetine, a NE reuptake inhibitor, was found to affect performance on the rGT (Silveira et al., 2016). Administration of atomoxetine during adolescence did not impair the acquisition of the rGT but it did decrease the number of P2 choices when rats were challenged with atomoxetine in adulthood. This effect was apparent in both the rats treated with atomoxetine or saline during adolescence and was paralleled by a (non-significant) increase in P3 responses. Atomoxetine also decreased premature responses and the number of perseverations made during the punishing time outs. Choice latencies were also observed to increase. At some doses the number of trials was decreased. Together, the results of this study seem to suggest that atomoxetine impairs choice responding (decrease in the P2 option). In another study (Baarendse et al., 2013), atomoxetine decreased P1 and P4 choices at one dose, and also decreased premature responses and increased errors of omission. Taken together, there is some evidence from premature responses and per-severations that NE reuptake inhibitors, which increase NE levels (Bymaster et al., 2002), may improve performance on the rGT. This should be tempered somewhat, however, by the findings of decreased responding for the P2 option in the Silveira et al. (2016) study.

Serotonin

Serotonin is a neurotransmitter believed to be important in decision-making and thus seems likely to be involved in some way in the gambling process. Specifically, serotonin may inhibit actions when punishments may occur (Cools, Nakamura, & Daw, 2011). Indeed, in gamblers, peripheral measures of serotonin are decreased (Marazziti et al., 2008; Pallanti, Bernardi, Quercioli, DeCaria, & Hollander, 2006). However, treatment of GD with selective serotonin reuptake inhibitors has yielded equivocal findings. That is, fluvoxamine, par-oxetine, citalopram, escitalopram and sertraline have been found to be effective in some studies but not others (reviewed in Hloch, Mladenka, Dosedel, Adriani, & Zoratto, 2017). In this context it is relevant to note a co-morbidity between GD and depressive disorders (Kim, Grant, Eckert, Faris, & Hartman, 2006; Lorains, Cowlishaw, & Thomas, 2011); there is a debate as to whether GD precedes depressive disorders, and this speaks to the fact that treatment of depressive disorders with selective serotonin reuptake inhibitors likely does not worsen GD.

One study investigated the effects of agonism of serotonin by administration of 5-hydrox-ytryptophan (5-HTP) to human participants prior to performance of the IGT. In this study, participants took 5-HTP twice in the hours prior to performance on the task. It was found that task performance was lower in the 5-HTP group as compared to the placebo, but only in the first half of the trials. During this time, the 5-HTP group selected more cards from one of the disadvantageous decks and fewer cards from one of the advantageous decks. The authors interpret the deficit in the first half of the task acquisition as due to impaired decision-making under ambiguity, when the task performance is reflected by subconscious processes. By comparison, task performance in the second half, under risk, was intact in the 5-HTP group as compared to the placebo group (Gendle & Golding, 2010).

Consistent with the equivocal effects found in human IGT studies, one study in rats found that citalopram, a serotonin reuptake inhibitor, did not have any effect on advantageous responses (Baarendse et al., 2013) or any other measure of the rGT. In a human IGT study, subtle effects were found in humans, but were observed only during the first half of acquisition (Gendle & Golding, 2010). Perhaps effects would have been observed in the rGT if the task had been analysed by trial blocks, as in the case with the human study (Baarendse et al., 2013). It may be possible that the effects of serotonin on the rGT may be attributed also to actions at selective receptor subtypes, albeit these effects may not be specific. Study of antagonism or agonism of 5-HT_{1A} receptors with the agonist 8-OH-DPAT or the antagonist WAY100635 revealed effects on the rGT (Zeeb et al., 2009). 8-OH-DPAT increased P1 and P3 options while decreasing the P2 option, an effect that was blocked by administration by WAY100635. WAY100635 did not alter behaviour on its own. The authors interpret the effects of 8-OH-DPAT as an increased sensitivity to punishment magnitude, not probability. In addition, 8-OH-DPAT decreased the number of trials, premature responses, omissions and increased latencies. Together, these findings suggest that 8-OH-DPAT altered motor behaviour.

Opioids

The opioids are of interest in gambling due to their promise as novel pharmacological treatments for GD. As discussed briefly above, few pharmacological treatments have had any success in treating GD with the exception of opioid antagonists. For example, in clinical trials, participants who received naltrexone demonstrated greater improvements in ratings of gambling symptoms and urges, as compared to those receiving placebo (Grant, Kim, & Hartman, 2008; Kim, Grant, Adson, & Shin, 2001; Marazziti et al., 2009), whereas in another study naltrexone reduced the urge to gamble (Kim & Grant, 2001). Similarly, following treatment with nalmefene, another opioid antagonist, ratings of gambling symptoms were reduced as compared to placebo controls (Grant et al., 2006), a finding supported by a controlled multi-centre trial using the same primary outcome measure (Grant et al., 2010). A meta-analysis of the effects of antidepressants and mood stabilizers on gambling revealed that the results may vary based on co-morbidity (Pallesen et al., 2007), and naltrexone was found to be better than these (Rosenberg, Dinur, & Dannon, 2013). The importance of opioid antagonists in treating GD is underscored by the number of clinical trials currently underway, as reported in clinical trials.gov (NCT1528007, NCT01057862, NCT00053677, NCT00132119, NCT00326807, NCT02537197, NCT03223896, NCT01052831; retrieved 3 November 2017).

There is one study examining the effects of opioid antagonists on the rGT (Di Ciano & Le Foll, 2016). In this study, rats were divided into 'optimal' versus 'suboptimal' groups prior to analysis of the effects of naltrexone. It was found that naltrexone increased the number of advantageous responses in the suboptimal group, with no effects on the optimal groups. There were no effects on any other measures. That is, naltrexone selectively improved behaviour in a group of rats with suboptimal performance at baseline. These results may have a parallel in a human study that investigated the relationship between demographic variables and response to treatment with opiate antagonists (Grant, Kim, Hollander, & Potenza, 2008). In this study, the best predictor of response to treatment was a positive family history of alcohol use disorder. By contrast, age, gender, race, education, marital status, or ratings on various emotional scales did not predict the success of treatment. Thus, in both animals and humans, there appear to be subgroups that may respond differentially to treatment with opiate antagonists. To the extent that the suboptimal group in rats reflects suboptimal decision-making in gambling, these findings suggest that naltrexone may be an effective treatment for GD in people with suboptimal decision-making. Further studies may be warranted.

Other treatments

Two other studies of a single investigation of each of cannabinoid (Gueye et al., 2016) and cholinergic agents (Silveira et al., 2015) have been conducted.

To date, there is one study that looked at the effect of cannabinoid ligands on the rGT (Gueye et al., 2016). In this study, both agonists and antagonists of the endocannabinoid system were studied. The CB_1 agonist, WIN 55,212-2, was studied, as was the CB_1 antagonist, AM4113. The non-selective agonist, URB 597, which is a FAAH inhibitor, was also studied, as was the CB_2 antagonist, AM630. In this study, rats were subdivided into optimal and suboptimal groups; at acquisition and baseline, the optimal group showed more choices of the advantageous (P1 and P2) responses as compared to the suboptimal group. Administration of the CB1 agonist increased advantageous choices, and decreased disadvantageous choices, in the suboptimal group, thus improving performance, with no effects in the optimal group. The other cannabinoid ligands had no effect on choice strategy. Similarly, only the CB_1 agonist increased latencies in the suboptimal group. In the optimal group, however, the CB_1 agonist dose-dependently increased punished perseveration. No effects on premature responding were seen. In sum, the effects of cannabinoid ligands on the rGT were modest, with some efficacy in improving performance after administration of the CB_1 agonist, but only in the phenotype at risk for developing GD.

Acetylcholine muscarinic agents

The non-selective cholinergic agonist, oxotremorine, did not affect choice behaviour, in contrast to the effect of the muscarinic antagonist, scopolamine, to increase choice of the P1 option (with a non-significant decrease in choice of the P2 option). Thus, it appears that the cholinergic antagonist impaired decision-making. Other measurements were, however, impaired by the agonist: premature responding was bidirectionally altered, choice latency was increased, with a slight increase in omissions that did not reach significance. In sum, it seems that the muscarinic agonist may have had motivatonal effects on the rats. By comparison, the muscarinic antagonist scopolamine decreased premature responding, increased omissions, and decreased the number of trials as well as collect and choice latencies. The authors interpret the effect of scopolamine on choice as a decision-making impairment.

Acetylcholine nicotinic agents

Following administration of the cholinergic agonist, nicotine, only the number of trials decreased and latencies increased. By comparison, the nicotinic antagonist, mecamylamine, also decreased the number of trials completed and increased collect latencies, but also increased omissions; no effects on premature responding were seen. Thus, it appears that the effects of nicotinic agents were primarily on motor output. It is noteworthy that no effects on decision-making were seen.

Summary and conclusions

In sum, the rGT provides an animal model that can evaluate many facets of problematic gambling: choice, motivation, impulsivity, perseverative responding and even motor deficits. Analysis of the human and rodent literature suggests good consilience between findings, and the rGT clearly has good predictive validity. Findings emerging from the rGT seem to suggest that the DA receptors may mediate the task through interactions with other neurotransmitter systems (except in the case of the cued version, where D_3 receptors are implicated). For example, DA reuptake inhibitors in combination with serotonin or norepinephrine reuptake inhibitors affected performance on the rGT. Cholinergic and cannabinoid manipulations had subtle effects on the rGT. The only manipulations that seemed selective for choice responding were those of the norepinephrine system and also naltrexone (an opioid antagonist). Further evaluation of these mechanisms is warranted.

Conflicts of interest

Funding sources

Bernard Le Foll receives salary support from the Centre for Addiction and Mental Health.

Competing interests

The authors declare no competing interests.

Constraints on publishing

The authors declare no constraints on publishing.

References

Achat-Mendes, C., Grundt, P., Cao, J., Platt, D. M., Newman, A. H., & Spealman, R. D. (2010). Dopamine D3 and D2 receptor mechanisms in the abuse-related behavioral effects of cocaine: Studies with preferential antagonists in squirrel monkeys. [Research Support, N.I.H., Extramural Research Support, N.I.H., Intramural]. *Journal of Pharmacology and Experimental Therapeutics, 334*(2), 556–565. doi:10.1124/jpet.110.167619. Retrieved from http://www.ncbi.nlm.nih.gov/pubmed/20494958

Baarendse, P. J., Winstanley, C. A., & Vanderschuren, L. J. (2013). Simultaneous blockade of dopamine and noradrenaline reuptake promotes disadvantageous decision making in a rat gambling task. *Psychopharmacology, 225*(3), 719–731. doi:10.1007/s00213-012-2857-z. Retrieved from http://www.ncbi.nlm.nih.gov/pubmed/22968659

Barrus, M. M., & Winstanley, C. A. (2016). Dopamine D3 receptors modulate the ability of win-paired cues to increase risky choice in a rat gambling task. *Journal of Neuroscience, 36*(3), 785–794. doi:10.1523/JNEUROSCI.2225-15.2016. Retrieved from http://www.ncbi.nlm.nih.gov/pubmed/26791209

Barrus, M. M., Hosking, J. G., Zeeb, F. D., Tremblay, M., & Winstanley, C. A. (2015). Disadvantageous decision-making on a rodent gambling task is associated with increased motor impulsivity in a population of male rats. *J Psychiatry Neurosci, 40*(2), 108–117. Retrieved from https://www.ncbi.nlm.nih.gov/pubmed/25703645

Barrus, M. M., Cherkasova, M., & Winstanley, C. A. (2016). Skewed by cues? The motivational role of audiovisual stimuli in modelling substance use and gambling disorders. *Curr Top Behav Neurosci, 27*, 507–529. doi:10.1007/7854_2015_393. Retrieved from https://www.ncbi.nlm.nih.gov/pubmed/26531068

Bechara, A. (2004). Disturbances of emotion regulation after focal brain lesions. *Int Rev Neurobiol, 62*, 159–193. doi:10.1016/S0074-7742(04)62006-X. Retrieved from https://www.ncbi.nlm.nih.gov/pubmed/15530572

Bechara, A., & Damasio, H. (2002). Decision-making and addiction (part I): Impaired activation of somatic states in substance dependent individuals when pondering decisions with negative future consequences. *Neuropsychologia, 40*(10), 1675–1689. Retrieved from https://www.ncbi.nlm.nih.gov/pubmed/11992656

Bechara, A., Damasio, A. R., Damasio, H., & Anderson, S. W. (1994). Insensitivity to future consequences following damage to human prefrontal cortex. [Research Support, Non-U.S. Gov't Research Support, U.S. Gov't, P.H.S.]. *Cognition, 50*(1-3), 7–15. Retrieved from http://www.ncbi.nlm.nih.gov/pubmed/8039375

Boileau, I., Guttman, M., Rusjan, P., Adams J. R., Houle, S., Tong J., . . . O. Hornykiewicz (2009). Decreased binding of the D3 dopamine receptor-preferring ligand [11C]-(+)-PHNO in drug-naive Parkinson's disease. [Comparative Study Research Support, Non-U.S. Gov't]. *Brain, 132*(5), 1366–1375. doi:10.1093/brain/awn337. Retrieved from http://www.ncbi.nlm.nih.gov/pubmed/19153147

Boileau, I., Payer, D., Houle, S., Behzadi, A., Rusjan, P. M., Tong, J., & Wilkins, D. (2012). Higher binding of the dopamine D3 receptor-preferring ligand [11C]-(+)-propyl-hexahydro-naphtho-oxazin in methamphetamine polydrug users: A positron emission tomography study. [Comparative Study Research Support, N.I.H., Extramural Research Support, Non-U.S. Gov't]. *Journal of Neuroscience, 32*(4), 1353–1359. doi:10.1523/JNEUROSCI.4371-11.2012. Retrieved from http://www.ncbi.nlm.nih.gov/pubmed/22279219

Bourdélat-Parks, B. N., Anderson, G. M., Donaldson, Z. R., Weiss, J. M., Bonsall, R. W., Emery, M. S., & Liles, Cameron L. (2005). Effects of dopamine beta-hydroxylase genotype and disulfiram inhibition on catecholamine homeostasis in mice. [Research Support, Non-U.S. Gov't]. *Psychopharmacology, 183*(1), 72–80. doi:10.1007/s00213-005-0139-8. Retrieved from http://www.ncbi.nlm.nih.gov/pubmed/16163519

Buelow, M. T., & Suhr, J. A. (2009). Construct validity of the iowa gambling task. *Neuropsychology Review, 19*(1), 102–114. doi:10.1007/s11065-009-9083-4. Retrieved from https://www.ncbi.nlm.nih.gov/pubmed/19194801

Bymaster, F. P., Katner, J. S., Nelson, D. L., Hemrick-Luecke, S. K., Threlkeld, P. G., Heiligenstein, J. H., & Perry, K. W. (2002). Atomoxetine increases extracellular levels of norepinephrine and dopamine in prefrontal cortex of rat a potential mechanism for efficacy in attention deficit/hyperactivity disorder. *Neuropsychopharmacology, 27*(5), 699–711. doi:10.1016/S0893-133X(02)00346-9. Retrieved from https://www.ncbi.nlm.nih.gov/pubmed/12431845

Cavedini, P., Riboldi, G., Keller, R., D'Annucci, A., & Bellodi, L. (2002). Frontal lobe dysfunction in pathological gambling patients. *Biological Psychiatry, 51*(4), 334–341. Retrieved from https://www.ncbi.nlm.nih.gov/pubmed/11958785

Cocker, P. J., & Winstanley, C. A. (2015). Irrational beliefs, biases and gambling: Exploring the role of animal models in elucidating vulnerabilities for the development of pathological gambling. *Behavioural Brain Research, 279*, 259–273. doi:10.1016/j.bbr.2014.10.043. Retrieved from https://www.ncbi.nlm.nih.gov/pubmed/25446745

Colombo, G., Maccioni, P., Vargiolu, D., Loi, B., Lobina, C., Zaru, A., & Carai, Mauro A. M. (2014). The dopamine beta-hydroxylase inhibitor, nepicastat, reduces different alcohol-related behaviors in rats. *Alcoholism: Clinical and Experimental Research, 38*(9), 2345–2353. doi:10.1111/acer.12520. Retrieved from http://www.ncbi.nlm.nih.gov/pubmed/25257286

Cools, R., Nakamura, K., & Daw, N. D. (2011). Serotonin and dopamine: Unifying affective, activational and decision functions. *Neuropsychopharmacology, 36*(1), 98–113. doi:10.1038/npp.2010.121. Retrieved from https://www.ncbi.nlm.nih.gov/pubmed/20736991

Di Chiara, G. (1999). Drug addiction as dopamine-dependent associative learning disorder. *European Journal of Pharmacology, 375*(1-3), 13–30.

Di Ciano, P., & Le Foll, B. (2016). Evaluating the impact of naltrexone on the rat gambling task to test its predictive validity for gambling disorder. *PLOS ONE, 11*(5), e0155604. doi:10.1371/journal.pone.0155604. Retrieved from https://www.ncbi.nlm.nih.gov/pubmed/27191857

Di Ciano, P., Grandy, D. K., & Le Foll, B. (2014). Dopamine D4 receptors in psychostimulant addiction. *Adv Pharmacol, 69*, 301–321. doi:10.1016/B978-0-12-420118-7.00008-1. Retrieved from http://www.ncbi.nlm.nih.gov/pubmed/24484981

Di Ciano, P., Pushparaj, A., Kim, A., Hatch, J., Masood, T., Ramzi, A., & Khaled, Maram A. T. M. (2015). The impact of selective dopamine D2, D3 and D4 Ligands on the rat gambling task. *PLOS ONE, 10*(9), e0136267. doi:10.1371/journal.pone.0136267. Retrieved from http://www.ncbi.nlm.nih.gov/pubmed/26352802

Di Ciano, P., Manvich D. F., Pushparaj A., Gappasov A., Hess E. J., Weinshenker D., & le Foll B. (2018). Effects of disulfiram on choice behavior in a rodent gambling task: Association with catecholamine levels. *Psychopharmacology, 235*(1), 23–35.

Di Ciano, P., McCormick P., Stefan C., Wong E., Kim A., Remington G., & le Foll B. (2017). The effects of buspirone on occupancy of dopamine receptors and the rat gambling task. *Psychopharmacology, 234*(22), 3309–3320.

van Enkhuizen, J., Geyer, M. A., & Young, J. W. (2013). Differential effects of dopamine transporter inhibitors in the rodent Iowa gambling task: Relevance to mania. *Psychopharmacology, 225*(3), 661–674. doi:10.1007/s00213-012-2854-2. Retrieved from https://www.ncbi.nlm.nih.gov/pubmed/22945515

van Enkhuizen, J., Henry, B. L., Minassian, A., Perry, W., Milienne-Petiot, M., Higa, K. K., & Geyer, Mark A. (2014). Reduced dopamine transporter functioning induces high-reward risk-preference consistent with bipolar disorder. *Neuropsychopharmacology, 39*(13), 3112–3122. doi:10.1038/npp.2014.170. Retrieved from https://www.ncbi.nlm.nih.gov/pubmed/25005251

Epstein, D. H., & Preston, K. L. (2003). The reinstatement model and relapse prevention: A clinical perspective. *Psychopharmacology, 168*(1-2), 31–41. Retrieved from http://www.ncbi.nlm.nih.gov/entrez/query.fcgi?cmd=Retrieve&db=PubMed&dopt=Citation&list_uids=12721778

Fehr, C., Yakushev, I., Hohmann, N., Buchholz, H. G., Landvogt, C., Deckers, H., … Eberhardt, Alexandra. (2008). Association of low striatal dopamine d2 receptor availability with nicotine dependence similar to that seen with other drugs of abuse. *American Journal of Psychiatry, 165*(4), 507–514. Retrieved from http://www.ncbi.nlm.nih.gov/entrez/query.fcgi?cmd=Retrieve&db=PubMed&dopt=Citation&list_uids=18316420

Ferland, J. N., & Winstanley, C. A. (2016). Risk-preferring rats make worse decisions and show increased incubation of craving after cocaine self-administration. *Addict Bioldoi*, doi:10.1111/adb.12388. Retrieved from https://www.ncbi.nlm.nih.gov/pubmed/27002211

Forget, B., Wertheim, C., Mascia, P., Pushparaj, A., Goldberg, S. R., & Le Foll, B. (2010). Noradrenergic alpha1 receptors as a novel target for the treatment of nicotine addiction. *Neuropsychopharmacology, 35*(8), 1751–1760. Retrieved from http://www.ncbi.nlm.nih.gov/entrez/query.fcgi?cmd=Retrieve&db=PubMed&dopt=Citation&list_uids=20357760

Gansler, D. A., Jerram, M. W., Vannorsdall, T. D., & Schretlen, D. J. (2011). Does the Iowa gambling task measure executive function? *Archives of Clinical Neuropsychology, 26*(8), 706–717. doi:10.1093/arclin/acr082. Retrieved from https://www.ncbi.nlm.nih.gov/pubmed/22015855

Gaval-Cruz, M., & Weinshenker, D. (2009). mechanisms of disulfiram-induced cocaine abstinence: Antabuse and cocaine relapse. [Research Support, N.I.H., Extramural Review]. *Molecular Interventions, 9*(4), 175–187. doi:10.1124/mi.9.4.6. Retrieved from http://www.ncbi.nlm.nih.gov/pubmed/19720750

Gendle, M. H., & Golding, A. C. (2010). Oral administration of 5-hydroxytryptophan (5-HTP) impairs decision making under ambiguity but not under risk: Evidence from the Iowa Gambling Task. *Human Psychopharmacology: Clinical and Experimental, 25*(6), 491–499. doi:10.1002/hup.1139. Retrieved from https://www.ncbi.nlm.nih.gov/pubmed/20737522

Goldstein, M., & Nakajima, K. (1967). The effect of disulfiram on catecholamine levels in the brain. *J Pharmacol Exp Ther, 157*(1), 96–102. Retrieved from http://www.ncbi.nlm.nih.gov/pubmed/6029496

Grant, J. E., Won Kim, S. W., & Potenza, M. N. (2003). Advances in the pharmacological treatment of pathological gambling. [Review]. *Journal of Gambling Studies, 19*(1), 85–109. Retrieved from http://www.ncbi.nlm.nih.gov/pubmed/12635541

Grant, J. E., Potenza, M. N., Hollander, E., Cunningham-Williams, R., Nurminen, T., Smits, G., & Kallio, A. (2006). Multicenter investigation of the opioid antagonist nalmefene in the treatment of pathological gambling. [Comparative Study Multicenter Study Randomized Controlled Trial Research Support, Non-U.S. Gov't]. *American Journal of Psychiatry, 163*(2), 303–312. doi:10.1176/appi.ajp.163.2.303. Retrieved from http://www.ncbi.nlm.nih.gov/pubmed/16449486

Grant, J. E., Kim, S. W., & Hartman, B. K. (2008). A double-blind, placebo-controlled study of the opiate antagonist naltrexone in the treatment of pathological gambling urges. [Randomized Controlled Trial Research Support, N.I.H., Extramural]. *The Journal of Clinical Psychiatry, 69*(5), 783–789. Retrieved from http://www.ncbi.nlm.nih.gov/pubmed/18384246

Grant, J. E., Kim, S. W., Hollander, E., & Potenza, M. N. (2008). Predicting response to opiate antagonists and placebo in the treatment of pathological gambling. *Psychopharmacology, 200*(4), 521–527. doi:10.1007/s00213-008-1235-3. Retrieved from https://www.ncbi.nlm.nih.gov/pubmed/18581096

Grant, J. E., Odlaug, B. L., Potenza, M. N., Hollander, E., & Kim, S. W. (2010). Nalmefene in the treatment of pathological gambling: Multicentre, double-blind, placebo-controlled study. [Multicenter Study Randomized Controlled Trial Research Support, Non-U.S. Gov't]. *British Journal of Psychiatry, 197*(04), 330–331. doi:10.1192/bjp.bp.110.078105. Retrieved from http://www.ncbi.nlm.nih.gov/pubmed/20884959

Grant, J. E., Odlaug, B. L., & Schreiber, L. R. (2014). Pharmacological treatments in pathological gambling. *British Journal of Clinical Pharmacology, 77*(2), 375–381. doi:10.1111/j.1365-2125.2012.04457.x. Retrieved from http://www.ncbi.nlm.nih.gov/pubmed/22979951

Greenwell, T. N., Walker, B. M., Cottone, P., Zorrilla, E. P., & Koob, G. F. (2009). The alpha1 adrenergic receptor antagonist prazosin reduces heroin self-administration in rats with extended access to heroin administration. [Research Support, N.I.H., Extramural Research Support, Non-U.S. Gov't]. *Pharmacology Biochemistry and Behavior, 91*(3), 295–302. doi:10.1016/j.pbb.2008.07.012. Retrieved from http://www.ncbi.nlm.nih.gov/pubmed/18703080

Gueye, A. B., Trigo, J. M., Vemuri, K. V., Makriyannis, A., & Le Foll, B. (2016). Effects of various cannabinoid ligands on choice behaviour in a rat model of gambling. *Behavioural Pharmacology, 27*(2-3 Spec Issue), pp. 258–269. doi:10.1097/FBP.0000000000000222. Retrieved from https://www.ncbi.nlm.nih.gov/pubmed/26905189

Heidbreder, C. (2005). Novel pharmacotherapeutic targets for the management of drug addiction. *European Journal of Pharmacology, 526*(1-3), 101–112. Retrieved from http://www.ncbi.nlm.nih. gov/entrez/query.fcgi?cmd=Retrieve&db=PubMed&dopt=Citation&list_uids=16253234

Heidbreder, C. A., Gardner, E. L., Xi, Z. X., Thanos, P. K., Mugnaini, M., Hagan, J. J., & Ashby, C. R. Jr. (2005). The role of central dopamine D(3) receptors in drug addiction: A review of pharmacological evidence. *Brain Research Reviews, 49*(1), 77–105. Retrieved from http://www.ncbi.nlm.nih.gov/ entrez/query.fcgi?cmd=Retrieve&db=PubMed&dopt=Citation&list_uids=15960988

Hloch, K., Mladenka, P., Dosedel, M., Adriani, W., & Zoratto, F. (2017). The current clinical knowledge on the treatment of gambling disorder: A summary. *Synapse.* doi:10.1002/syn.21976. Retrieved from https://www.ncbi.nlm.nih.gov/pubmed/28420033

Karamanakos, P. N., Pappas, P., Stephanou, P., & Marselos, M. (2001). Differentiation of disulfiram effects on central catecholamines and hepatic ethanol metabolism. *Pharmacology and Toxicology, 88*(2), 106–110. doi:pto880208 [pii]. Retrieved from http://www.ncbi.nlm.nih.gov/entrez/query. fcgi?cmd=Retrieve&db=PubMed&dopt=Citation&list_uids=11169169

Kessler, R. C., Hwang, I., LaBrie, R., Petukhova, M., Sampson, N. A., Winters, K. C., & Shaffer, H. J. (2008). DSM-IV pathological gambling in the national comorbidity survey replication. *Psychol Med, 38*(9), 1351–1360. doi:10.1017/S0033291708002900. Retrieved from https://www.ncbi.nlm. nih.gov/pubmed/18257941

Kim, S. W., & Grant, J. E. (2001). An open naltrexone treatment study in pathological gambling disorder. *International Clinical Psychopharmacology, 16*(5), 285–289. Retrieved from http://www. ncbi.nlm.nih.gov/pubmed/11552772

Kim, S. W., Grant, J. E., Adson, D. E., & Shin, Y. C. (2001). Double-blind naltrexone and placebo comparison study in the treatment of pathological gambling. [Clinical Trial Comparative Study Randomized Controlled Trial Research Support, Non-U.S. Gov't]. *Biological Psychiatry, 49*(11), 914–921. Retrieved from http://www.ncbi.nlm.nih.gov/pubmed/11377409

Kim, S. W., Grant, J. E., Eckert, E. D., Faris, P. L., & Hartman, B. K. (2006). Pathological gambling and mood disorders: Clinical associations and treatment implications. *Journal of Affective Disorders, 92*(1), 109–116. doi:10.1016/j.jad.2005.12.040. Retrieved from https://www.ncbi.nlm.nih.gov/ pubmed/16443282

Kovács, I., Richman, M. J., Janka, Z., Maraz, A., & Andó, B. (2017). Decision making measured by the Iowa Gambling Task in alcohol use disorder and gambling disorder: A systematic review and meta-analysis. *Drug and Alcohol Dependence, 181*, 152–161. doi:10.1016/j.drugalcdep.2017.09.023. Retrieved from https://www.ncbi.nlm.nih.gov/pubmed/29055269

Le Foll, B., & Boileau, I. (2013). Repurposing buspirone for drug addiction treatment. *The International Journal of Neuropsychopharmacology, 16*(2), 251–253. doi:10.1017/S1461145712000995. Retrieved from https://www.ncbi.nlm.nih.gov/pubmed/23174122

Lefoll, B., Goldberg, S. R., & Sokoloff, P. (2005). The dopamine D3 receptor and drug dependence: Effects on reward or beyond? *Neuropharmacology, 49*(4), 525–541. Retrieved from http://www.ncbi. nlm.nih.gov/entrez/query.fcgi?cmd=Retrieve&db=PubMed&dopt=Citation&list_uids=15963538

Li, X., Lu, Z. L., D'Argembeau, A., Ng, M., & Bechara, A. (2010). The Iowa gambling task in fMRI images. *Hum Brain Mapp, 31*(3), 410–423. doi:10.1002/hbm.20875. Retrieved from https://www. ncbi.nlm.nih.gov/pubmed/19777556

Linnet, J., Rojskjaer, S., Nygaard, J., & Maher, B. A. (2006). Episodic chasing in pathological gamblers using the Iowa gambling task. [Research Support, Non-U.S. Gov't]. *Scandinavian Journal of Psychology, 47*(1), 43–49. doi:10.1111/j.1467-9450.2006.00491.x. Retrieved from http://www.ncbi. nlm.nih.gov/pubmed/16433661

Linnet, J., Møller, A., Peterson, E., Gjedde, A., & Doudet, D. (2011). Inverse association between dopaminergic neurotransmission and Iowa Gambling Task performance in pathological gamblers and healthy controls. *Scandinavian Journal of Psychology, 52*(1), 28–34. doi:10.1111/j.1467-9450.2010.00837.x. Retrieved from https://www.ncbi.nlm.nih.gov/pubmed/20704689

Linnet, J., Mouridsen, K., Peterson, E., Møller, A., Doudet, D. J., & Gjedde, A. (2012). Striatal dopamine release codes uncertainty in pathological gambling. *Psychiatry Research: Neuroimaging, 204*(1), 55–60. doi:10.1016/j.pscychresns.2012.04.012. Retrieved from https://www.ncbi.nlm.nih.gov/ pubmed/22889563

Lobo, D. S., Aleksandrova, L., Knight, J., Casey, D. M., el-Guebaly, N., Nobrega, J. N., & Kennedy, J. L. (2015). Addiction-related genes in gambling disorders: New insights from parallel human and pre-clinical models. *Molecular Psychiatry, 20*(8), 1002–1010. doi:10.1038/mp.2014.113. Retrieved from https://www.ncbi.nlm.nih.gov/pubmed/25266122

Lorains, F. K., Cowlishaw, S., & Thomas, S. A. (2011). Prevalence of comorbid disorders in problem and pathological gambling: Systematic review and meta-analysis of population surveys. *Addiction, 106*(3), 490–498. doi:10.1111/j.1360-0443.2010.03300.x. Retrieved from https://www.ncbi.nlm.nih.gov/pubmed/21210880

Marazziti, D., Golia, F., Picchetti, M., Pioli, E., Mannari, P., Lenzi, F., ... Conversano, Ciro (2008). Decreased density of the platelet serotonin transporter in pathological gamblers. *Neuropsychobiology, 57*(1-2), 38–43. doi:10.1159/000129665. Retrieved from https://www.ncbi.nlm.nih.gov/pubmed/18451636

Marazziti, D., Baroni, S., Masala, I., Giannaccini, G., Betti, L., Palego, L., & Dell'Osso, Mario Catena (2009). [(3)H]-YM-09151-2 binding sites in human brain postmortem. *Neurochemistry International, 55*(7), 643–647. doi:10.1016/j.neuint.2009.06.005. Retrieved from https://www.ncbi.nlm.nih.gov/pubmed/19540292

Martinez, D., Gil, R., Slifstein, M., Hwang, D. R., Huang, Y., Perez, A., & Kegeles, Lawrence. (2005). Alcohol dependence is associated with blunted dopamine transmission in the ventral striatum. *Biological Psychiatry, 58*(10), 779–786. doi:10.1016/j.biopsych.2005.04.044. Retrieved from http://www.ncbi.nlm.nih.gov/pubmed/16018986

Meyer, G., Schwertfeger, J., Exton, M. S., Janssen, O. E., Knapp, W., Stadler, M. A., & Kruger, T. H. (2004). Neuroendocrine response to casino gambling in problem gamblers. [Clinical Trial Comparative Study Research Support, Non-U.S. Gov't]. *Psychoneuroendocrinology, 29*(10), 1272–1280. doi:10.1016/j.psyneuen.2004.03.005. Retrieved from http://www.ncbi.nlm.nih.gov/pubmed/15288706

Millan, M. J., Dekeyne, A., Rivet, J. M., Dubuffet, T., Lavielle, G., & Brocco, M. (2000). S33084, a novel, potent, selective, and competitive antagonist at dopamine D(3)-receptors: II. Functional and behavioral profile compared with GR218,231 and L741,626. [Comparative Study]. *J Pharmacol Exp Ther, 293*(3), 1063–1073. Retrieved from http://www.ncbi.nlm.nih.gov/pubmed/10869411

Müller, C. A., Banas, R., Heinz, A., & Hein, J. (2011). Treatment of pathological gambling with disulfiram: A report of 2 cases. [Case Reports Letter]. *Pharmacopsychiatry, 44*(2), 81–83. doi:10.1055/s-0031-1271683. Retrieved from http://www.ncbi.nlm.nih.gov/pubmed/21328196

Musacchio, J. M., Goldstein, M., Anagnoste, B., Poch, G., & Kopin, I. J. (1966). Inhibition of dopamine-beta-hydroxylase by disulfiram *in vivo*. *J Pharmacol Exp Ther, 152*(1), 56–61. Retrieved from http://www.ncbi.nlm.nih.gov/entrez/query.fcgi?cmd=Retrieve&db=PubMed&dopt=Citation&list_uids=5937402

Mutschler, J., Buhler, M., Grosshans, M., Diehl, A., Mann, K., & Kiefer, F. (2010). Disulfiram, an option for the treatment of pathological gambling? [Case Reports Research Support, Non-U.S. Gov't]. *Alcohol and Alcoholism, 45*(2), 214–216. doi:10.1093/alcalc/agp093. Retrieved from http://www.ncbi.nlm.nih.gov/pubmed/20083479

Newman, A. H., Blaylock, B. L., Nader, M. A., Bergman, J., Sibley, D. R., & Skolnick, P. (2012). Medication discovery for addiction: Translating the dopamine D3 receptor hypothesis. [Research Support, N.I.H., Extramural Research Support, N.I.H., Intramural Review]. *Biochemical Pharmacology, 84*(7), 882–890. doi:10.1016/j.bcp.2012.06.023. Retrieved from http://www.ncbi.nlm.nih.gov/pubmed/22781742

Nobrega, J. N., Hedayatmofidi, P. S., & Lobo, D. S. (2016). Strong interactions between learned helplessness and risky decision-making in a rat gambling model. *Scientific Reports, 6*, 1177. doi:10.1038/srep37304. Retrieved from https://www.ncbi.nlm.nih.gov/pubmed/27857171

O'Carroll, R. E., & Papps, B. P. (2003). Decision making in humans: The effect of manipulating the central noradrenergic system. *Journal of Neurology, Neurosurgery & Psychiatry, 74*(3), 376–378. Retrieved from https://www.ncbi.nlm.nih.gov/pubmed/12588933

Pallanti, S., Bernardi, S., Quercioli, L., DeCaria, C., & Hollander, E. (2006). Serotonin dysfunction in pathological gamblers: Increased prolactin response to Oral m-CPP versus placebo. *CNS Spectrums, 11*(12), 956–965. Retrieved from https://www.ncbi.nlm.nih.gov/pubmed/17146409

Pallanti, S., Bernardi, S., Allen, A., Chaplin, W., Watner, D., DeCaria, C. M., & Hollander, E. (2010). Noradrenergic function in pathological gambling: Blunted growth hormone response to clonidine. *Journal of Psychopharmacology, 24*(6), 847–853. doi:10.1177/0269881108099419 [pii]. Retrieved from http://www.ncbi.nlm.nih.gov/entrez/query.fcgi?cmd=Retrieve&db=PubMed&dopt=Citation&list_uids=19028836

Pallesen, S., Molde, H., Arnestad, H. M., Laberg, J. C., Skutle, A., Iversen, E., & Støylen, Inge Jarl. (2007). Outcome of pharmacological treatments of pathological gambling: A review and meta-analysis. [Meta-Analysis Review]. *Journal of Clinical Psychopharmacology, 27*(4), 357–364. doi:10.1097/jcp.013e3180dcc304d. Retrieved from http://www.ncbi.nlm.nih.gov/pubmed/17632219

Petry, N. M., Stinson, F. S., & Grant, B. F. (2005). Comorbidity of DSM-IV pathological gambling and other psychiatric disorders: Results from the National Epidemiologic Survey on Alcohol and Related Conditions. *The Journal of Clinical Psychiatry, 66*(5), 564–574. Retrieved from https://www.ncbi.nlm.nih.gov/pubmed/15889941

Pilla, M., Perachon, S., Sautel, F., Garrido, F., Mann, A., Wermuth, C. G., & Schwartz, Jean-Charles. (1999). Selective inhibition of cocaine-seeking behaviour by a partial dopamine D3 receptor agonist. *Nature, 400*(6742), 371–375. Retrieved from http://www.ncbi.nlm.nih.gov/entrez/query.fcgi?cmd=Retrieve&db=PubMed&dopt=Citation&list_uids=10432116

Potenza, M. N., Leung, H. C., Blumberg, H. P., Peterson, B. S., Fulbright, R. K., Lacadie, C. M., … Skudlarski, Pawel (2003). An fMRI Stroop task study of ventromedial prefrontal cortical function in pathological gamblers. *American Journal of Psychiatry, 160*(11), 1990–1994. Retrieved from http://www.ncbi.nlm.nih.gov/entrez/query.fcgi?cmd=Retrieve&db=PubMed&dopt=Citation&list_uids=14594746

Potenza, M. N., Steinberg, M. A., Skudlarski, P., Fulbright, R. K., Lacadie, C. M., Wilber, M. K., & Rounsaville, B. E. (2003). Gambling urges in pathological gambling: A functional magnetic resonance imaging study. *Archives of General Psychiatry, 60*(8), 828–836. doi:10.1001/archpsyc.60.8.828. Retrieved from https://www.ncbi.nlm.nih.gov/pubmed/12912766

Pushparaj, A., Kim, A. S., Musiol, M., Zangen, A., Daskalakis, Z. J., Zack, M., & Winstanley, Catharine A (2015). Differential involvement of the agranular vs granular insular cortex in the acquisition and performance of choice behavior in a rodent gambling task. *Neuropsychopharmacology, 40*(12), 2832–2842. doi:10.1038/npp.2015.133. Retrieved from http://www.ncbi.nlm.nih.gov/pubmed/25953358

Reuter, J., Raedler, T., Rose, M., Hand, I., Gläscher, J., & Büchel, C. (2005). Pathological gambling is linked to reduced activation of the mesolimbic reward system. [Comparative Study Research Support, Non-U.S. Gov't]. *Nature Neuroscience, 8*(2), 147–148. doi:10.1038/nn1378. Retrieved from http://www.ncbi.nlm.nih.gov/pubmed/15643429

Robbins, T. W. (2002). The 5-choice serial reaction time task: Behavioural pharmacology and functional neurochemistry. [Research Support, Non-U.S. Gov't Review]. *Psychopharmacology, 163*(3-4), 362–380. doi:10.1007/s00213-002-1154-7. Retrieved from http://www.ncbi.nlm.nih.gov/pubmed/12373437

Rosenberg, O., Dinur, L. K., & Dannon, P. N. (2013). Four-year follow-up study of pharmacological treatment in pathological gamblers. *Clinical Neuropharmacology, 36*(2), 42–45. doi:10.1097/WNF.0b013e31828740ea. Retrieved from http://www.ncbi.nlm.nih.gov/pubmed/23503545

Roy, A., Adinoff, B., Roehrich, L., Lamparski, D., Custer, R., Lorenz, V., & Linnoila, M. (1988). Pathological gambling. *Archives of General Psychiatry, 45*(4), 369–373. Retrieved from http://www.ncbi.nlm.nih.gov/pubmed/2451490

Schroeder, J. P., Cooper, D. A., Schank, J. R., Lyle, M. A., Gaval-Cruz, M., Ogbonmwan, Y. E., & Pozdeyev, Nikita. (2010). Disulfiram attenuates drug-primed reinstatement of cocaine seeking via inhibition of dopamine beta-hydroxylase. [Research Support, N.I.H., Extramural]. *Neuropsychopharmacology, 35*(12), 2440–2449. doi:10.1038/npp.2010.127. Retrieved from http://www.ncbi.nlm.nih.gov/pubmed/20736996

Schroeder, J. P., Alisha Epps, S. A., Grice, T. W., & Weinshenker, D. (2013). The selective dopamine beta-hydroxylase inhibitor nepicastat attenuates multiple aspects of cocaine-seeking behavior. *Neuropsychopharmacology, 38*(6), 1032–1038. doi:10.1038/npp.2012.267. Retrieved from http://www.ncbi.nlm.nih.gov/pubmed/23303068

Sibley, D. R., & Monsma, F. J. (1992). Molecular biology of dopamine receptors. *Trends in Pharmacological Sciences, 13*, 61–69.

Silveira, M. M., Malcolm, E., Shoaib, M., & Winstanley, C. A. (2015). Scopolamine and amphetamine produce similar decision-making deficits on a rat gambling task via independent pathways. *Behavioural Brain Research, 281*, 86–95. doi:10.1016/j.bbr.2014.12.029. Retrieved from http://www.ncbi.nlm.nih.gov/pubmed/25529186

Silveira, M. M., Murch, W. S., Clark, L., & Winstanley, C. A. (2016). Chronic atomoxetine treatment during adolescence does not influence decision-making on a rodent gambling task, but does modulate amphetamine's effect on impulsive action in adulthood. *Behavioural Pharmacology, 27*(4), 350–363. doi:10.1097/FBP.0000000000000203. Retrieved from https://www.ncbi.nlm.nih.gov/pubmed/26650252

Toplak, M. E., Sorge, G. B., Benoit, A., West, R. F., & Stanovich, K. E. (2010). Decision-making and cognitive abilities: A review of associations between Iowa Gambling Task performance, executive functions, and intelligence. *Clinical Psychology Review, 30*(5), 562–581. doi:10.1016/j.cpr.2010.04.002. Retrieved from https://www.ncbi.nlm.nih.gov/pubmed/20457481

Tremblay, M., & Winstanley, C. A. (2016). Anticonvulsant medications attenuate amphetamine-induced deficits in behavioral inhibition but not decision making under risk on a rat gambling task. *Behavioural Brain Research, 314*, 143–151. doi:10.1016/j.bbr.2016.08.016. Retrieved from https://www.ncbi.nlm.nih.gov/pubmed/27515288

de Visser, L., Homberg, J. R., Mitsogiannis, M., Zeeb, F. D., Rivalan, M., Fitoussi, A., & Dellu-Hagedorn, F. (2011). Rodent versions of the IOWA gambling task: Opportunities and challenges for the understanding of decision-making. *Front Neurosci, 5*, 109. doi:10.3389/fnins.2011.00109. Retrieved from http://www.ncbi.nlm.nih.gov/pubmed/22013406

Volkow, N. D., Fowler, J., Wang, G.-J., Hitzemann, R., Logan, J., Schlyer, David J., & Dewey, Stephen L. (1993). Decreased dopamine D2 receptor availability is associated with reduced frontal metabolism in cocaine abusers. *Synapse, 14*, 169–177.

Walker, B. M., Rasmussen, D. D., Raskind, M. A., & Koob, G. F. (2008). alpha1-noradrenergic receptor antagonism blocks dependence-induced increases in responding for ethanol. *Alcohol, 42*(2), 91–97. doi:S0741-8329(08)00015-3 [pii]10.1016/j.alcohol.2007.12.002. Retrieved from http://www.ncbi.nlm.nih.gov/entrez/query.fcgi?cmd=Retrieve&db=PubMed&dopt=Citation&list_uids=18358987

Wang, G. B., Zhang, X. L., Zhao, L. Y., Sun, L. L., Wu, P., Lu, L., & Shi, J. (2012). Drug-related cues exacerbate decision making and increase craving in heroin addicts at different abstinence times. *Psychopharmacology, 221*(4), 701–708. doi:10.1007/s00213-011-2617-5. Retrieved from https://www.ncbi.nlm.nih.gov/pubmed/22207241

Wee, S., Mandyam, C. D., Lekic, D. M., & Koob, G. F. (2008). Alpha 1-noradrenergic system role in increased motivation for cocaine intake in rats with prolonged access. *European Neuropsychopharmacology, 18*(4), 303–311. doi:10.1016/j.euroneuro.2007.08.003. Retrieved from http://www.ncbi.nlm.nih.gov/pubmed/17920248

Winstanley, C. A., & Clark, L. (2016). Translational models of gambling-related decision-making. *Curr Top Behav Neurosci, 28*, 93–120. doi:10.1007/7854_2015_5014. Retrieved from https://www.ncbi.nlm.nih.gov/pubmed/27418069

Zack, M., & Poulos, C. X. (2007). A D2 antagonist enhances the rewarding and priming effects of a gambling episode in pathological gamblers. *Neuropsychopharmacology, 32*(8), 1678–1686. Retrieved from http://www.ncbi.nlm.nih.gov/entrez/query.fcgi?cmd=Retrieve&db=PubMed&dopt=Citation&list_uids=17203013

Zeeb, F. D., & Winstanley, C. A. (2011). Lesions of the Basolateral Amygdala and orbitofrontal cortex differentially affect acquisition and performance of a rodent gambling task. *Journal of Neuroscience, 31*(6), 2197–2204. doi:10.1523/JNEUROSCI.5597-10.2011. Retrieved from https://www.ncbi.nlm.nih.gov/pubmed/21307256

Zeeb, F. D., & Winstanley, C. A. (2013). Functional disconnection of the orbitofrontal cortex and basolateral amygdala impairs acquisition of a rat gambling task and disrupts animals' ability to alter decision-making behavior after reinforcer devaluation. *Journal of Neuroscience, 33*(15), 6434–6443. doi:10.1523/JNEUROSCI.3971-12.2013. Retrieved from http://www.ncbi.nlm.nih.gov/pubmed/23575841

Zeeb, F. D., Robbins, T. W., & Winstanley, C. A. (2009). Serotonergic and dopaminergic modulation of gambling behavior as assessed using a novel rat gambling task. [Research Support, Non-U.S. Gov't]. *Neuropsychopharmacology, 34*(10), 2329–2343. doi:10.1038/npp.2009.62. Retrieved from http://www.ncbi.nlm.nih.gov/pubmed/19536111

Zeeb, F. D., Wong, A. C., & Winstanley, C. A. (2013). Differential effects of environmental enrichment, social-housing, and isolation-rearing on a rat gambling task: Dissociations between impulsive action and risky decision-making. *Psychopharmacology, 225*(2), 381–395. doi:10.1007/s00213-012-2822-x. Retrieved from http://www.ncbi.nlm.nih.gov/pubmed/22864967

Zeeb, F. D., Baarendse, P. J., Vanderschuren, L. J., & Winstanley, C. A. (2015). Inactivation of the prelimbic or infralimbic cortex impairs decision-making in the rat gambling task. *Psychopharmacology (Berl),*. doi:10.1007/s00213-015-4075-y. Retrieved from http://www.ncbi.nlm.nih.gov/pubmed/26387517

Zhang, X. Y., & Kosten, T. A. (2005). Prazosin, an alpha-1 adrenergic antagonist, reduces cocaine-induced reinstatement of drug-seeking. [Research Support, N.I.H., Extramural Research Support, Non-U.S. Gov't Research Support, U.S. Gov't, P.H.S.]. *Biological Psychiatry, 57*(10), 1202–1204. doi:10.1016/j.biopsych.2005.02.003. Retrieved from http://www.ncbi.nlm.nih.gov/pubmed/15866561

Zhang, X. L., Wang, G. B., Zhao, L. Y., Sun, L. L., Wang, J., Wu, P., & Lu, Lin. (2012). Clonidine improved laboratory-measured decision-making performance in abstinent heroin addicts. *PLoS ONE, 7*(1), e29084. doi:10.1371/journal.pone.0029084. Retrieved from https://www.ncbi.nlm.nih.gov/pubmed/22291886

d OPEN ACCESS

Connectivity networks in gambling disorder: a resting-state fMRI study

Tim van Timmeren [iD], Paul Zhutovsky [iD], Ruth J. van Holst [iD] and Anna E. Goudriaan [iD]

ABSTRACT

Gambling disorder (GD) is characterized by an inability to stop or control gambling behaviour and is often accompanied by gambling-related cognitive distortions. Task-based functional Magnetic Resonance Imaging (fMRI) studies have revealed abnormal responses within the prefrontal and insular cortex, and mesolimbic reward regions. Studies examining resting-state functional connectivity in GD, although limited in number, have so far applied seed-based analysis approaches which revealed altered brain functioning. Here, we applied data-driven Independent Components Analysis to resting-state multi-echo fMRI data. Networks of interest were selected by spatially correlating them to independently derived network templates. Using dual regression, we compared connectivity strength between 20 GD patients and 20 healthy controls within 4 well-known networks (the ventral attention, limbic, frontoparietal control, and default mode network) and an additional basal ganglia component. Compared to controls, GD patients showed increased integration of the right middle insula within the ventral attention network, an area suggested to play an important role in addiction-related drive. Moreover, our findings indicate that gambling-related cognitive distortions – a hallmark of GD – were positively related to stronger integration of the amygdala, medial prefrontal cortex and insula within various resting-state networks.

Introduction

Gambling disorder (GD) is a behavioural addiction characterized by an inability to stop or control gambling behaviour and is often accompanied by gambling-related cognitive distortions; that is, false beliefs about skill and chance in gambling games. Neuroimaging studies in GD have revealed abnormalities in a wide range of cognitive functions (van Timmeren, Daams, van Holst, & Goudriaan, 2018) and associated brain responses (van Holst, van den

This is an Open Access article distributed under the terms of the Creative Commons Attribution License (http://creativecommons.org/licenses/by/4.0/), which permits unrestricted use, distribution, and reproduction in any medium, provided the original work is properly cited.

Brink, Veltman, & Goudriaan, 2010). Most studies have focused on decision-making in GD, showing consistent disadvantageous risky decision-making in GD, accompanied by abnormal responses within prefrontal control regions, mesolimbic reward regions and the insula (Fauth-Bühler, Mann, & Potenza, 2017; Limbrick-Oldfield et al., 2017). However, such task-related functional Magnetic Resonance Imaging (fMRI) studies could be confounded by the fact that many decision-making tasks resemble gambling games, which are experienced differently by gamblers compared to healthy control subjects (HCs). Elicited brain responses could therefore be related to, for example, experience or motivation, rather than dysfunction. A more unbiased and practical approach to study brain activity in GD is to study 'spontaneous' fluctuations of the brain during rest. Such resting-state fMRI studies assess functional connectivity within and between circuits and systems, based on the temporal correlation of the blood oxygenation level-dependent (BOLD) signal.

Various approaches to analysing resting-state fMRI data exist, but the two most frequently used in the literature are seed-based connectivity and spatial Independent Component Analysis (ICA) methods. Seed-based connectivity analysis is a spatially model-driven approach, in which the BOLD time course of one predefined seed region is temporally correlated with the BOLD time courses of all other voxels in the brain (Joel, Caffo, Van Zijl, & Pekar, 2011). ICA-based approaches, on the other hand, decompose whole brain responses into components that are statistically maximally independent (Beckmann, DeLuca, Devlin, & Smith, 2005; Fox & Raichle, 2007) and offer a data-driven approach to detect resting-state networks. Thus, while seed-based methods strongly rely on a priori assumptions regarding the selected regions of interest, ICA is a model-free and multivariate method (Fox & Raichle, 2007). This switches the focus from evaluating the functional connectivity of single brain regions to evaluating brain connectivity in terms of all networks that are simultaneously engaged in oscillatory activity (Nickerson, Smith, Öngür, & Beckmann, 2017).

Studies examining resting-state functional connectivity in GD have so far been scarce, but have mostly relied on seed-based methods. In one of the first resting-state studies in GD, higher functional connectivity between the right middle frontal gyrus and the right striatum was observed in GD patients compared to controls using a seed-based approach (Koehler et al., 2013). Another seed-based connectivity study found that, when compared to controls, cocaine dependent patients and GD patients showed overlapping increases in local connectivity within the orbitofrontal cortex and amygdala, between the orbitofrontal cortex and the dorsomedial prefrontal cortex and striatum, and between the amygdala and insula (Contreras-Rodríguez et al., 2016). This study also revealed that cocaine dependent patients and GD patients displayed decreased connectivity between the amygdala and cerebellum. Besides increases of connectivity within the (meso)limbic and frontostriatal circuit, GD has been associated with decreased default mode network connectivity in the left superior frontal gyrus, right middle temporal gyrus, and precuneus (Jung et al., 2014). Moreover, Tschernegg et al. (2013) used a graph-theoretical approach to examine frontostriatal functional connectivity and observed increased functional connectivity between the caudate nucleus and anterior cingulate in GD patients compared to controls. To sum up, three out of four resting-state studies in GD have used seed-based methods and have generally revealed connectivity differences in GD patients, mostly in regions implicated in reward processing and cognitive control.

We here applied a group-ICA in combination with dual regression to assess the intrinsic functional connectivity in networks potentially implicated in GD. To further optimize our data-driven approach, we used functional connectivity networks derived from an independent group of 1000 healthy individuals (Yeo et al., 2011) as templates to select our resting-state networks of interest. Based on the previous seed-based findings described above, we focus on four well-known networks (Figure 1): (i) *the ventral attention network*, also referred to as the salience (Seeley et al., 2007) or cingulo-opercular network (Dosenbach et al., 2007), which is thought to modulate attention to internal and external stimuli and includes regions such as the amygdala, insula, inferior frontal gyrus and the pregenual cingulate; (ii) *the limbic network*, which is involved in processing emotions, including the amygdala, hippocampus and temporal cortices; (iii) *the frontoparietal control network* (Dosenbach et al., 2007; Vincent, Kahn, Snyder, Raichle, & Buckner, 2008), implicated in adaptive control over behaviour and associated with the dorsolateral prefrontal cortex, premotor cortex and parietal cortex; and (iv) *the default mode network*, which characterizes the resting state of the human brain and primarily comprises the anterolateral temporal cortex, parahippocampal gyrus, thalamus, pons and cerebellum, as well as part of the medial prefrontal cortex and the posterior cingulate cortex (Buckner, Andrews-Hanna, & Schacter, 2008; Greicius, Krasnow, Reiss, & Menon, 2003). While most previous resting-state studies in GD have focused on connectivity with the mesolimbic reward circuitry (e.g. Contreras-Rodríguez et al., 2016; Koehler et al., 2013), the networks that were selected using the templates from Yeo et al (2011) did not cover mesolimbic areas. Therefore, we additionally included a network encompassing the basal ganglia, which was derived from our ICA. We examined differences in connectivity strength within these identified resting-state networks between 20 GD patients and 20 HCs. Moreover, because we were interested to test whether individual variation in the strength of specific resting-state networks was related to gambling severity and gambling cognitive distortions, we also tested this within the GD group.

Materials and methods

Participants

A total of 21 individuals diagnosed with GD (17 males) were recruited from a local addiction treatment centre (Jellinek, Amsterdam), and 20 HCs (17 males) were recruited through advertisements. All data were collected between December 2015 and May 2017. The ethical review board of the Academic Medical Centre approved the study, and all participants provided written informed consent.

Patients with GD were included if they were diagnosed with, and started therapy for, GD (at least one and on average 19.6 weeks prior to participation). Patients were abstinent for an average of 6 weeks (range 0–26 weeks). All subjects underwent a structured psychiatric interview (Mini-International Neuropsychiatric Interview–Plus; Sheehan, Lecrubier, & Sheehan, 1998), which further confirmed criteria for DSM-5 Gambling Disorder in the GD group, or the lack thereof in HCs. Exclusion criteria for all subjects included: lifetime history of bipolar disorder, anxiety disorder, obsessive-compulsive disorder or schizophrenia; past six-month history of major depressive episode; current or past-year substance use disorder; current psychiatric treatment (except for GD in GD patients); the use of any psychotropic medication; positive urine screen for (meth)amphetamines, benzodiazepines, opioids, cocaine, ecstasy, PCP, methadone or cannabis; history or current treatment for neurological disorders; major physical disorders; brain trauma; exposure to neurotoxic

THE NEUROSCIENCE AND NEUROPSYCHOLOGY OF GAMBLING

factors; or any contraindications for MRI. One patient tested positive on THC use, but informed us that the subject used marijuana once, seven days prior to participation. Because our inclusion criteria allowed drug use until 72 hours prior to inclusion, this subject was included for further analyses.

All participants completed the Fagerstrom Test for Nicotine Dependence (FTND; Heatherton, Kozlowski, Frecker, & Fagerström, 1991) and the Alcohol Use Disorders Identification Test (AUDIT; Saunders, Aasland, Babor, de la Fuente, & Grant, 1993). Furthermore, in GD patients, the experience of gambling-related problems was assessed using the past-12-month Problem Gambling Severity Index (PGSI; Ferris & Wynne, 2001) and the Gamblers' Beliefs Questionnaire (GBQ; Steenbergh, Meyers, May, & Whelan, 2002). The GBQ contains 21 items (e.g. 'My choices or actions affect the game on which I am betting' or 'I am pretty accurate at predicting when a "win" will occur'), with higher scores reflecting more gambling-related distortions.

One male subject was excluded due to excessive head motion (>5 mm movement in any direction relative to the first volume) during the fMRI session, resulting in a total of 20 GDs and 20 HCs for further analysis. The groups significantly differed on gross motion ($p = 0.012$) as calculated by mean relative framewise displacement (FD) (Jenkinson, Bannister, Brady, & Smith, 2002), with GDs showing higher motion (mean = 0.187, SD = 0.162, range 0.047–0.682) than HCs (mean = 0.094, SD = 0.042, range 0.039–0.211). We additionally report analyses excluding two GD subjects with FD > 0.55 mm (following criteria similar to Satterthwaite et al., 2013), which rendered the group differences on FD non-significant ($p = 0.62$; GD-group: mean = 0.1347, SD = 0.67, range 0.047–0.301).

Procedure

Participants were in the scanner in supine position and were instructed to relax and keep their eyes open while attending to a centrally presented white fixation cross on a black projection screen for ~8 minutes. These data were collected as part of a larger study protocol including questionnaires, neuropsychological testing and multiple fMRI tasks, data of which will be presented elsewhere. The fMRI tasks, which included a combined cue reactivity/monetary incentive delay task, were performed prior to the resting-state scan.

Magnetic Resonance Imaging

MRI measurements were acquired using a 3-Tesla (T), full-body Philips Intera MRI scanner equipped with a 32-channel phased array SENSE radiofrequency (RF) receiver head coil. For resting-state data acquisition, we used a multi-echo planar sequence for its improved blood oxygenation level-dependent (BOLD) sensitivity and lower susceptibility for artifacts, especially for ventral regions (Poser, Versluis, Hoogduin, & Norris, 2006). A total of 200 BOLD scans were acquired using a T2*-weighted gradient multi-echo echoplanar imaging (EPI) sequence (Poser et al., 2006) with the following parameters: repetition time (TR) = 2375 ms; echo time (TE) = 9 / 26.4 / 43.8 ms; flip angle = 76°; field of view (FOV) = 224 x 121.8 x 224 mm; voxel size = 3 x 2.95 x 3 mm; matrix size = 76 x 73; slice thickness = 3 mm; slice gap = 0.3 mm; number of slices = 37, acquired in interleaved order. The first three scans were discarded to allow T1 saturation to reach equilibrium.

Additionally, we acquired a high resolution T1-weighted anatomical image (voxel size = 1 x 1 x 1 mm; FOV = 236.679 x 180 x 256 mm; TR = 6.862 ms; TE = 3.14 ms, 150 slices, slice thickness = 1.2 mm, sampling matrix = 212 x 212 x 150, flip angle = 8°).

Statistical analyses

Demographics and clinical data were analysed for group differences with two-sampled t-tests and Pearson's chi-square tests using SPSS 22.0 (IBM Corporation).

Preprocessing

Raw multi-echo fMRI data were first processed according to Poser et al. (2006). Realignment parameters were estimated for the images acquired at the first echo time and consequently applied to images resulting from the three other echoes using SPM12 software (Wellcome Trust Centre for Neuroimaging, London). This is compliant with recent work that suggests that motion is more appropriately controlled if realignment parameters are estimated before any interpolation is done on the data (Power, Plitt, Kundu, Bandettini, & Martin, 2017). Thirty volumes, acquired independently from the resting-state scan, were used to calculate the optimal weighting of echo times for each voxel by applying a PAID-weight algorithm (Poser et al., 2006). These weightings were then used to combine multi-echo fMRI data into single volumes.

All further processing of MRI data was performed in FSL 5.09 (FMRIB's Software Library, www.fmrib.ox.ac.uk/fsl). Preprocessing was carried out using FEAT (FMRI Expert Analysis Tool) Version 6.00. The following pre-statistics processing was applied; non-brain removal using BET (Smith, 2002); spatial smoothing using a Gaussian kernel of FWHM 6.0 mm; grand-mean intensity normalization of the entire 4D data-set by a single multiplicative factor. Registration of functional data to the high resolution structural image was carried out using the boundary based registration (BBR) algorithm (Greve & Fischl, 2009). Registration of the high resolution structural image to standard space was carried out using FLIRT (Jenkinson & Smith, 2001; Jenkinson et al., 2002) and was further refined using FNIRT nonlinear registration (Andersson, Jenkinson, & Smith, 2007a,b). Tissue segmentation was performed using FAST (Zhang, Brady, & Smith, 2001).

Because resting-state functional MRI is especially sensitive to motion artifacts (e.g. Power, Barnes, Snyder, Schlaggar, & Petersen, 2012), we used ICA-AROMA (Pruim et al., 2015b) to remove motion-related artifacts from the individual resting-state data. Previous studies have shown that cleaning based on single-subject ICA significantly increases reproducibility (Pruim, Mennes, Buitelaar, & Beckmann, 2015a). We followed the methods as described by Pruim et al. (2015b): first, ICA was used to decompose the data into a set of independent components. Next, the components that were related to head motion were identified by the AROMA algorithm and regressed out from the data. Additionally, compliant with Pruim et al. (2015b), residual (non-motion related) structured noise was regressed out by using mean white matter and cerebrospinal fluid signal as nuisance regressors. Masks were obtained using FAST's binary segmentations and eroded once. Recent work by Power, Plitt, Laumann, and Martin (2017) demonstrated that the correlation of those signals with grey matter can be high without extensive erosion, which was indeed the case (r = 0.80 for white matter; 0.55 for cerebrospinal fluid). It is important to note that by using these highly

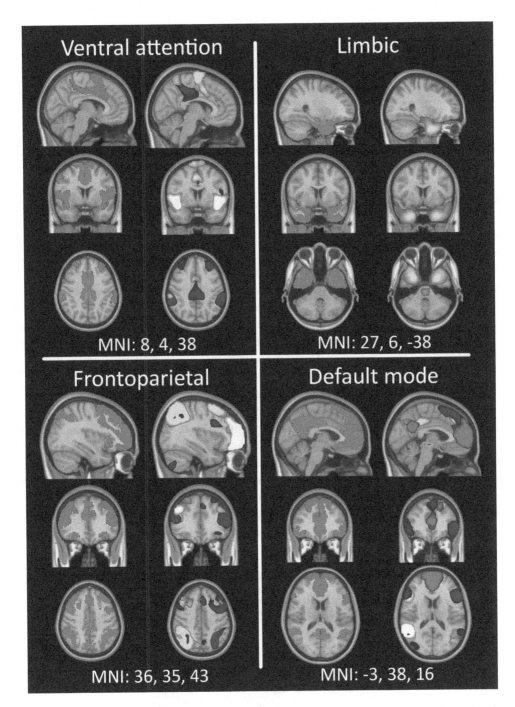

Figure 1. Reference networks (Yeo et al., 2011) are well matched to resting-state networks used in the current study. The reference network is plotted on the left in red, while individual ICs (significantly overlapping with that reference network) are plotted in contrasting colours within a single image on the right. All overlays are thresholded at $3 < z < 6$.

correlated masks as nuisance regressors, we are effectively applying global signal regression; a highly debated processing step which has benefits but can also lead to 'artefactual' anti-correlations (for a recent review, see Murphy & Fox, 2017). After high-pass filtering, the denoised data was then resampled into MNI space in 4 mm.

Independent component analysis

After preprocessing, the temporally concatenated resting-state data of all subjects were analysed using group-ICA (Beckmann & Smith, 2004) as implemented in FSL's MELODIC (3.14). The number of dimensions was estimated using the Laplace approximation to the Bayesian evidence of the model order (Beckmann & Smith, 2004; Minka, 2001) and yielded 51 components. These group components reflect a variety of structured signals that can exist simultaneously in the data: some are of interest (e.g. patterns of intrinsic functional connectivity) and others are noise (e.g. head motion and physiological noise). Identifying which components are of interest is usually done 'subjectively' by an expert. A more objective approach would be to statistically compare each component with a set of reference networks. Following Reineberg, Andrews-Hanna, Depue, Friedman, and Banich (2015), we thus compared all 51 components with a set of online available reference networks from a previous study analysing resting-state data of ~1000 participants (Yeo et al., 2011). This study parcellated the cerebral cortex's connectivity into seven robust networks. Because we did not expect connectivity differences within all of those seven networks, we a priori selected the four following networks to compare to our components: the ventral attention, limbic, frontoparietal and default mode network. Pearson's *r* was calculated for each pairwise relationship using FSL's 'fslcc' tool. Only those components that yielded a significant spatial correlation (Pearson's r > .263) with one of the four selected Yeo networks were selected for further analysis. However, the networks described by Yeo et al. (2011) cover mainly the cerebral cortex. Based on the previous GD resting-state literature (Contreras-Rodríguez et al., 2016; Jung et al., 2014; Koehler et al., 2013), we also wanted to include a component covering the basal ganglia. This component was therefore manually selected for analysis (see Figure 2), resulting in a total of five networks of interest.

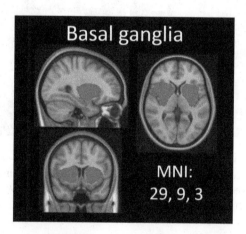

Figure 2. Basal ganglia network. This network was manually selected based on previous literature. Thresholded at 3 < z < 6.

Dual regression

To compare resting-state network activity between GD patients and HCs, and to identify how network activity varies with gambling severity (PGSI-scores) and the severity of gambling-related distortions (GBQ-scores) within the GD patients, dual regression was used (Beckmann, Mackay, Filippini, & Smith, 2009; Filippini et al., 2009). Using this approach, the set of spatial maps from the group-ICA were used to generate subject-specific versions of the spatial maps, and associated time series. These subject-specific time-courses were normalized to allow testing for shape and amplitude effects (Nickerson et al., 2017). The spatial maps were tested voxel-wise for statistically significant differences between the groups and correlations with gambling severity and gambling beliefs using dual regression's default settings and FSL randomise nonparametric permutation testing with 5000 permutations, using a threshold-free cluster enhanced (TFCE) technique to control for multiple comparisons (Nichols & Holmes, 2001). A Bonferroni correction (two-tailed) for tests over the five networks was applied to reduce the likelihood of committing a Type 1 error, resulting in a reported significance threshold of $p < 0.005$ (= 0.05 / (2 directions * 5 networks)). For the significant clusters, MNI coordinates are reported.

Results

Groups were matched on gender, age, handedness and alcohol use (Table 1). Compared to HCs, the number of education years was significantly lower in GD patients. Moreover, there were significantly more tobacco smoking GD patients than HCs, although the severity of nicotine dependence was similar across groups within smoking subjects.

Independent component analysis

A total of 11 ICA components significantly correlated with a reference network: 3 with the ventral attention network, 1 with the limbic network, 3 with the frontoparietal network and 4 with the default mode network. Figure 1 shows the four template networks of Yeo et al. (2011) next to the combined individual components (ICs). Individual plots of the ICs that were obtained using MELODIC for the four reference networks are included in the supplement (Supplementary Figures 1–4). Additionally, we included a manually selected

Table 1. Demographics.

	GDs (n = 20) Mean (SD)	HCs (n = 20) Mean (SD)	p value
Gender (male/female)	16/4	17/3	0.68[a]
Handedness (right/left)	19/1	17/3	0.29[a]
Age, years	33.8 (12.8)	38.3 (9.5)	0.22[b]
Education, years	7.8 (2.7)	9.8 (3.0)	**0.03**[b]
Smokers	10	3	**0.02**[a]
FTND in smokers	5.6 (1.7)	4.7 (.57)	0.39[b]
AUDIT	4.5 (4.0)	3.4 (2.4)	0.30[b]
GBQ	72.1 (24.8)	–	–
PGSI (12 months)	15.2 (3.8)	–	–

GDs: Gambling Disordered patients; HCs: Healthy Controls; SD: Standard Deviation; FTND: Fagerstrom test for nicotine dependence; AUDIT: Alcohol Use Disorders Identification Test; GBQ: Gamblers' Beliefs Questionnaire; PGSI: Problem Gambling Severity Index.
[a]p value of chi-square test.
[b]p value of two-sampled t-test.

component covering the basal ganglia in our analysis, which did not correlate to any of the reference networks (see Figure 2).

Dual regression

Group differences

Our dual regression analysis indicated that GD patients showed significantly increased connectivity in the ventral attention network (IC 39), specifically within the right insula (one voxel at x, y, z: 42, 2, −12, $p = 0.004$, Figure 3). No other significant group differences in any of the other networks were observed.

Association with gambling severity

Within the GD group, we did not find significant associations between gambling severity and functional connectivity strength in any of the four networks, nor the basal ganglia network.

Association with gambling beliefs

In GD patients, a significant positive association between gambling beliefs and functional connectivity strength was found in a number of networks and components (Figure 4). In the limbic network (IC33), higher GBQ scores were positively related to increased activity in the right temporal lobe, extending towards the amygdala (peak at x, y, z: 34, 2, −40, $p = 0.004$, cluster size = 17 voxels; Figure 4A). Within the frontoparietal network (IC30), GBQ score was positively related to bilateral Brodmann area 10 (BA10) (one voxel at x, y, z: 15, 63, −4, $p = 0.004$; Figure 4B). Moreover, within the default mode network (IC10),

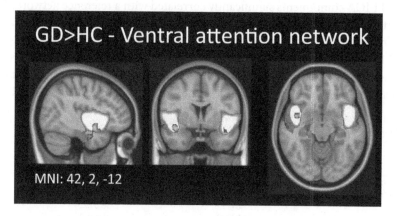

Figure 3. Increased functional connectivity in gambling disordered patients compared to healthy controls within the ventral attention network. The independent component representing part of the ventral attention network, which was used as input for dual regression, is plotted in gradient from red to yellow ($3 < z < 6$). Comparison of this spatial map between the two groups revealed increased connectivity strength in the right insula in gambling disordered patients. For visualization purposes, these results are shown in blue, thresholded at $p < 0.05$ (uncorrected). Results are superimposed on a MNI152 standard space template image; orthogonal slices through the peak voxel are shown in radiological convention (right = left).

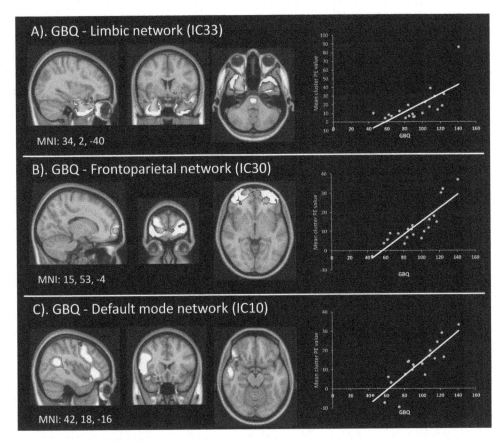

Figure 4. Number of gambling distortions covaries with resting-state networks. Spatial maps of the significant dual regression results are plotted over corresponding ICAs (see Figure 2 for details). Results in blue show regions that covary with individual GBQ scores. For visualization purposes, these results are shown in blue, thresholded at $p < 0.05$ (uncorrected). Next to these results, scatter plots showing the mean functional connectivity value (PE = parameter estimate) extracted from the significant clusters (y-axis) are plotted against the GBQ scores for each individual gambling disordered patient.

gambling beliefs were positively related to a cluster encompassing the right insula and amygdala (peak at x, y, z: 42, 18, −16, $p = 0.003$, cluster size = 4 voxels; Figure 4C).

Additional analyses without high-motion subjects

Because motion was significantly higher in the GD patients, we performed additional analyses on a subsample, excluding two high-motion (GD) subjects (mean FD > 0.55 mm). First, we investigated the relationship between motion and the ICs by computing the correlation between volume-to-volume motion (FD) and the time series outputs of stage 1 of the dual-regression. The distribution of the boxplots is centred around zero (Supplementary Figure 6), indicating that our initial analyses were relatively free of motion-related artifacts.

Additionally, we repeated the dual regression analyses without the two high-motion subjects. This rendered the results of both analyses non-significant at the initial Bonferroni-corrected threshold. However, the connectivity pattern between the two groups was similar to what was previously described, albeit at a lower threshold (Supplementary Figure 5). The reported whole-brain correlations with GBQ within the GD group disappeared after removal of those subjects. In sum, we interpret the whole-sample group difference as not being merely driven by the two high-motion subjects because (i) there was no systematic relationship between the level of motion and the selected ICs, and (ii) a similar but weaker connectivity pattern was observed after excluding two subjects, which may be due to the lower number of subjects leading to decreased power.

Discussion

The present study compared the functional architecture of five resting-state networks in GD patients with HCs. We found that, in GD patients, the bilateral insula is more strongly integrated into the ventral attention network, compared to HCs. No significant group differences were found in the other connectivity networks that we assessed. Within the GD patients, our results indicate positive relationships between the level of gambling distortions and how strongly (i) the right temporal lobe and amygdala were integrated into the limbic network; (ii) Brodmann area 10 (bilateral) was integrated into the frontoparietal control network and (iii) the right insula and amygdala were integrated into the default mode network. These findings indicate that increased insular connectivity in GD patients during (non-gambling-related) processing may be attentional, while (gambling-related) insular connectivity positively relates with gambling beliefs within the default mode network. Interestingly, any insular differences in GD do not appear to be related to frontoparietal control mechanisms.

Our finding of the right insula being more strongly integrated into the ventral attentional network in GD patients compared to HCs resonates with previous work highlighting a crucial role for the insula in GD. Previous resting-state studies in GD patients have reported increased connectivity of the insula with the right middle frontal gyrus (Koehler et al., 2013) and the amygdala (Contreras-Rodríguez et al., 2016). Task-based fMRI studies in GD patients also demonstrated increased connectivity of the left insula with the bilateral ventral striatum during a discounting task (Peters, Miedl, & Büchel, 2013) and increased activity in the insula during a cue reactivity task (i.e. watching gambling cues compared to neutral cues) which also correlated with between-subject craving scores (Limbrick-Oldfield et al., 2017). Because our resting-state block was preceded by a task containing gambling pictures, our results may partly reflect a sustained cue reactivity effect; previous work has shown that task execution preceding a resting-state scan can affect the functional structure of resting-state networks (Grigg & Grady, 2010). More generally, the insula is thought to play a critical role in several substance-related addictions and craving (Naqvi, Gaznick, Tranel, & Bechara, 2014), with insula damage disrupting nicotine addiction (Naqvi, Rudrauf, Damasio, & Bechara, 2007). Hence, the increased connectivity strength we observed in GD patients during rest is congruent with accumulating evidence for insula involvement in addiction-related states.

Gambling-related cognitive distortions are a key characteristic of GD, predicting gambling severity (Steenbergh et al., 2002) as well as duration of play and treatment outcome (Fortune & Goodie, 2012; Goodie & Fortune, 2013). Interestingly, a higher number of cognitive distortions about gambling was associated with increased involvement of different regions within a number of networks. Higher GBQ-scores were related to significantly increased involvement of the temporal lobe (extending towards the amygdala) in the limbic network; the bilateral medial prefrontal cortex (BA 10) in the frontoparietal control network; and the right insula (extending into the amygdala) in the default mode network. Although the involvement of these regions was found within different brain networks, all are directly anatomically connected: the anterior insula projects to the amygdala, which in turn receives from and projects to the bilateral medial prefrontal cortex (Flynn, 1999). These areas have been implicated in emotional awareness (Gu, Hof, Friston, & Fan, 2013) and incentive learning (Denny et al., 2014; Parkes & Balleine, 2013). There is some work directly linking increased insula activity and connectivity to gambling distortions. A typical cognitive distortion seen in gamblers is the near-miss effect, which occurs when an unsuccessful outcome is close to a win, resulting in increased motivation and the illusion of control (Clark, 2010). Amplified responses to near-misses have been observed in the bilateral anterior insula and striatum in GD patients (Clark, Lawrence, Astley-Jones, & Gray, 2009; Sescousse et al., 2016), while increased connectivity between the ventral striatum and insula during such events was related to gambling severity in regular gamblers (van Holst, Chase, & Clark, 2014). The positive relation we found between gambling distortions and connectivity strength within the insula is also in line with a lesion study showing that damage to the insula abolishes several cognitive distortions about gambling, including the near-miss effect (Clark, Studer, Bruss, Tranel, & Bechara, 2014).

Contrary to previous resting-state studies, we did not find evidence for abnormal striatal connectivity in GD compared to controls. This inconsistency may be a consequence of methodological differences. Whereas previous studies used seed-based analyses to directly test the connectivity from the striatum to other regions, we applied a data-driven ICA approach to test for differences in networks (some of which include the striatum; e.g. salience network, frontal-partietal control network and self-selected basal ganglia network). It could also be argued that using a preselected striatal seed is more sensitive to picking up abnormal striatal connectivity, while these abnormalities could remain sub-threshold when using data-driven ICA approaches. Moreover, task-based fMRI studies have consistently shown abnormal striatal functioning in GD. Perhaps striatal abnormalities are more pronounced in patients with GD when they are preforming specific tasks recruiting the striatum than during rest.

These results need to be considered in the context of some limitations. First, the reported sample size is relatively small, which renders replication of these results necessary. Second, the groups significantly differed in the level of motion. Motion-related artifacts are known to influence measures of functional connectivity, specifically of resting-state data (e.g. Power et al., 2012). Although benchmarking studies indicate that the denoising techniques deployed here, including the use of multi-echo imaging and ICA-AROMA, rank amongst the most successful (Ciric et al., 2017; Parkes, Fulcher, Yucel, & Fornito, 2018), it is impossible to completely rule out the impact of motion. Excluding two high-motion subjects in additional analyses rendered the effects non-significant. However, this could also be an issue of decreased power for the group comparison, as the increased insular connectivity within the ventral attentional was still observed at a lower (p < 0.1) threshold. Last, the number of smoking subjects in the GD group was significantly higher than in the HC group. The increased insula connectivity within the ventral attention network in the GD group could therefore also be driven by smoking status, which would correspond with the critical role of the insula in the addiction to smoking (Naqvi et al., 2007).

To our knowledge, this article is the first to investigate resting-state connectivity using an ICA approach in GD. Another strength of this study is that we used ICA-AROMA (Pruim et al., 2015b) to remove motion-related artifacts from the individual resting-state data, which has been shown to increase reproducibility (Pruim et al., 2015a). Furthermore, we used an objective and easily reproducible method to select networks based on an independent template describing the cerebral cortex created from more than 1000 subjects. To further understand how abnormal resting-state connectivity relates to cognition and behaviour in GD, future studies would benefit from including neurocognitive assessments and testing for correlations between network integrity and neurocognitive functioning.

In conclusion, in this study we used a data-driven approach to investigate resting-state connectivity in GD patients. Compared to controls, GD patients showed increased functional connectivity strength within the right middle insula, which is part of the ventral attention network, and is suggested to play an important role in addiction-related drive. Moreover, our findings indicated that increased connectivity strength in networks encompassing the amygdala, medial prefrontal cortex and insula (areas implicated in emotional awareness and incentive learning) may underlie gambling-related cognitive distortions, which are a hallmark of GD.

Author contributions

T.v.T., R.J.v.H. and A.E.G. designed the study. T.v.T. acquired the data. T.v.T. and P.Z. carried out neuroimaging data processing and analyses. T.v.T. and R.J.v.H. prepared the manuscript. All authors read, corrected and approved the final manuscript.

Conflicts of interest

Funding sources

This work was supported by NWO-ZonMw grant VIDI [grant number 91713354] to AEG.

Competing interests

The authors declared no competing interests.

Constraints on publishing

There were no constraints on publishing.

ORCID

Tim van Timmeren (iD) http://orcid.org/0000-0003-0282-8269
Paul Zhutovsky (iD) http://orcid.org/0000-0003-3737-6258
Ruth J. van Holst (iD) http://orcid.org/0000-0002-1184-9355
Anna E. Goudriaan (iD) http://orcid.org/0000-0001-8670-9384

References

Andersson, J., Jenkinson, M., & Smith, S. (2007a). Non-linear optimisation. FMRIB technical report TR07JA1. *University of Oxford FMRIB.* Retrieved from https://www.fmrib.ox.ac.uk/datasets/techrep/tr07ja1/tr07ja1.pdf

Andersson, J., Jenkinson, M., & Smith, S. (2007b). Non-linear registration, aka Spatial normalisation FMRIB technical report TR07JA2. *FMRIB Analysis Group of.* Retrieved from https://www.fmrib.ox.ac.uk/datasets/techrep/tr07ja2/tr07ja2.pdf

Beckmann, C. F., & Smith, S. M. (2004). Probabilistic Independent Component Analysis for Functional Magnetic Resonance Imaging. *IEEE Transactions on Medical Imaging, 23*(2), 137–152. doi:10.1109/TMI.2003.822821

Beckmann, C. F., DeLuca, M., Devlin, J. T., & Smith, S. M. (2005). Investigations into resting-state connectivity using independent component analysis. *Philosophical Transactions of the Royal Society B: Biological Sciences, 360*(1457), 1001–1013. doi:10.1098/rstb.2005.1634

Beckmann, C. F., Mackay, C., Filippini, N., & Smith, S. (2009). Group comparison of resting-state FMRI data using multi-subject ICA and dual regression. *Neuroimage.* Retrieved from http://web.mit.edu/fsl_v5.0.8/fsl/doc/wiki/attachments/DualRegression/CB09.pdf

Buckner, R. L., Andrews-Hanna, J. R., & Schacter, D. L. (2008). The brain's default network: Anatomy, function, and relevance to disease. *Annals of the New York Academy of Sciences, 1124,* 1–38. doi:10.1196/annals.1440.011

Ciric, R., Wolf, D. H., Power, J. D., Roalf, D. R., Baum, G. L., Ruparel, K., … Satterthwaite, T. D. (2017). Benchmarking of participant-level confound regression strategies for the control of motion artifact in studies of functional connectivity. *NeuroImage, 154*(March), 174–187. doi:10.1016/j.neuroimage.2017.03.020

Clark, L. (2010). Decision-making during gambling: An integration of cognitive and psychobiological approaches. *Philosophical Transactions of the Royal Society of London. Series B, Biological Sciences, 365*(1538), 319–330. doi:10.1098/rstb.2009.0147

Clark, L., Lawrence, A. J., Astley-Jones, F., & Gray, N. (2009). Gambling near-misses enhance motivation to gamble and recruit win-related brain circuitry. *Neuron, 61*(3), 481–490. doi:10.1016/j.neuron.2008.12.031

Clark, L., Studer, B., Bruss, J., Tranel, D., & Bechara, A. (2014). Damage to insula abolishes cognitive distortions during simulated gambling. *Proceedings of the National Academy of Sciences of the United States of America, 111*, 6098–6103. doi:10.1073/pnas.1322295111

Contreras-Rodríguez, O., Albein-Urios, N., Vilar-López, R., Perales, J. C., Martínez-Gonzalez, J. M., Fernández-Serrano, M. J., ... Verdejo-García, A. (2016). Increased corticolimbic connectivity in cocaine dependence versus pathological gambling is associated with drug severity and emotion-related impulsivity. *Addiction Biology, 21*(3), 709–718. doi:10.1111/adb.12242

Denny, B. T., Fan, J., Liu, X., Guerreri, S., Mayson, S. J., Rimsky, L., ... Koenigsberg, H. W. (2014). Insula-amygdala functional connectivity is correlated with habituation to repeated negative images. *Social Cognitive and Affective Neuroscience, 9*(11), 1660–1667. doi:10.1093/scan/nst160

Dosenbach, N. U. F., Fair, D. A., Miezin, F. M., Cohen, A. L., Wenger, K. K., Dosenbach, R. A. T., & Petersen, S. E. (2007). Distinct brain networks for adaptive and stable task control in humans. *Proceedings of the National Academy of Sciences of the United States of America, 104*(26), 11073–11078. doi:10.1073/pnas.0704320104

Fauth-Bühler, M., Mann, K., & Potenza, M. N. (2017). Pathological gambling: A review of the neurobiological evidence relevant for its classification as an addictive disorder. *Addiction Biology, 22*(4), 885–897. doi:10.1111/adb.12378

Ferris, J., & Wynne, H. (2001). *The Canadian problem gambling index: Final report*. Ottawa: Canadian Centre on Substance Abuse.

Filippini, N., MacIntosh, B. J., Hough, M. G., Goodwin, G. M., Frisoni, G. B., Smith, S. M., ... Mackay, C. E. (2009). Distinct patterns of brain activity in young carriers of the APOE- 4 allele. *Proceedings of the National Academy of Sciences, 106*(17), 7209–7214. doi:10.1073/pnas.0811879106

Flynn, F. G. (1999). Anatomy of the insula functional and clinical correlates. *Aphasiology, 13*(1), 55–78. doi:10.1080/026870399402325

Fortune, E. E., & Goodie, A. S. (2012). Cognitive distortions as a component and treatment focus of pathological gambling: A review. *Psychology of Addictive Behaviors, 26*(2), 298–310. doi:10.1037/a0026422

Fox, M. D., & Raichle, M. E. (2007). Spontaneous fluctuations in brain activity observed with functional magnetic resonance imaging. *Nature Reviews Neuroscience, 8*(9), 700–711. doi:10.1038/nrn2201

Goodie, A. S., & Fortune, E. E. (2013). Measuring cognitive distortions in pathological gambling: Review and meta-analyses. *Psychol Addict Behav, 27*(3), 730–743. doi:10.1037/a0031892

Greicius, M. D., Krasnow, B., Reiss, A. L., & Menon, V. (2003). Functional connectivity in the resting brain: A network analysis of the default mode hypothesis. *Proceedings of the National Academy of Sciences of the United States of America, 100*(1), 253–258. doi:10.1073/pnas.0135058100

Greve, D. N., & Fischl, B. (2009). Accurate and robust brain image alignment using boundary-based registration. *NeuroImage, 48*(1), 63–72. doi:10.1016/j.neuroimage.2009.06.060

Grigg, O., & Grady, C. L. (2010). Task-related effects on the temporal and spatial dynamics of resting-state functional connectivity in the default network. *PLoS ONE, 5*(10), 1–12. doi:10.1371/journal.pone.0013311

Gu, X., Hof, P. R., Friston, K. J., & Fan, J. (2013). Anterior insular cortex and emotional awareness. *The Journal of Comparative Neurology, 521*(15), 3371–3388. doi:10.1002/cne.23368

Heatherton, T. F., Kozlowski, L. T., Frecker, R. C., & Fagerström, K. O. (1991). The Fagerström Test for Nicotine Dependence: A revision of the Fagerström Tolerance Questionnaire. *British Journal of Addiction, 86*(9), 1119–1127. doi:10.1111/j.1360-0443.1991.tb01879.x

van Holst, R. J., van den Brink, W., Veltman, D. J., & Goudriaan, A. E. (2010). Why gamblers fail to win: A review of cognitive and neuroimaging findings in pathological gambling. *Neuroscience and Biobehavioral Reviews, 34*(1), 87–107. doi:10.1016/j.neubiorev.2009.07.007

van Holst, R. J., Chase, H. W., & Clark, L. (2014). Striatal connectivity changes following gambling wins and near-misses: Associations with gambling severity. *NeuroImage. Clinical, 5*, 232–239. doi:10.1016/j.nicl.2014.06.008

Jenkinson, M., & Smith, S. (2001). A global optimisation method for robust affine registration of brain images. *Medical Image Analysis, 5*(2), 143–156. doi:10.1016/S1361-8415(01)00036-6

Jenkinson, M., Bannister, P., Brady, M., & Smith, S. (2002). Improved optimization for the robust and accurate linear registration and motion correction of brain images. *NeuroImage, 17*(2), 825–841. doi:10.1016/S1053-8119(02)91132-8

Joel, S. E., Caffo, B. S., Van Zijl, P. C. M., & Pekar, J. J. (2011). On the relationship between seed-based and ICA-based measures of functional connectivity. *Magnetic Resonance in Medicine, 66*(3), 644–657. doi:10.1002/mrm.22818

Jung, M. H., Kim, J.-H., Shin, Y.-C., Jung, W. H., Jang, J. H., Choi, J.-S., … Kwon, J. S. (2014). Decreased connectivity of the default mode network in pathological gambling: A resting state functional MRI study. *Neuroscience Letters, 583C*, 120–125. doi:10.1016/j.neulet.2014.09.025

Koehler, S., Ovadia-Caro, S., Van Der Meer, E., Villringer, A., Heinz, A., Romanczuk-Seiferth, N., & Margulies, D. S. (2013). Increased functional connectivity between prefrontal cortex and reward system in pathological gambling. *PLoS ONE, 8*(12), 1–13. doi:10.1371/journal.pone.0084565

Limbrick-Oldfield, E. H., Mick, I., Cocks, R. E., McGonigle, J., Sharman, S. P., Goldstone, A. P., … Clark, L. (2017). Neural substrates of cue reactivity and craving in gambling disorder. *Translational Psychiatry, 7*(1), e992–e992. doi:10.1038/tp.2016.256

Minka, T. (2001). Automatic choice of dimensionality for PCA. *Advances in Neural Information Processing Systems.* Retrieved from http://papers.nips.cc/paper/1853-automatic-choice-of-dimensionality-for-pca.pdf

Murphy, K., & Fox, M. D. (2017). Towards a consensus regarding global signal regression for resting state functional connectivity MRI. *NeuroImage, 154*(November 2016), 169–173. https://doi.org/10.1016/j.neuroimage.2016.11.052

Naqvi, N. H., Rudrauf, D., Damasio, H., & Bechara, A. (2007). Damage to the Insula Disrupts Addiction to Cigarette Smoking. *Science (New York, N.Y.),* (January), 531–534.

Naqvi, N. H., Gaznick, N., Tranel, D., & Bechara, A. (2014). The insula: A critical neural substrate for craving and drug seeking under conflict and risk. *Annals of the New York Academy of Sciences, 1316*(1), 53–70. doi:10.1111/nyas.12415

Nichols, T. E., & Holmes, A. P. (2001). Nonparametric Permutation Tests for functional Neuroimaging Experiments: A Primer with examples. *Human Brain Mapping, 15*(1), 1–25. doi:10.1002/hbm.1058

Nickerson, L. D., Smith, S. M., Öngür, D., & Beckmann, C. F. (2017). Using dual regression to investigate network shape and amplitude in functional connectivity analyses. *Frontiers in Neuroscience, 11*(MAR), 1–18. doi:10.3389/fnins.2017.00115

Parkes, S. L., & Balleine, B. W. (2013). Incentive memory: Evidence the basolateral amygdala encodes and the insular cortex retrieves outcome values to guide choice between goal-directed actions. *The Journal of Neuroscience : The Official Journal of the Society for Neuroscience, 33*(20), 8753–8763. doi:10.1523/JNEUROSCI.5071-12.2013

Parkes, L., Fulcher, B., Yücel, M., & Fornito, A. (2018). An evaluation of the efficacy, reliability, and sensitivity of motion correction strategies for resting-state functional MRI. *NeuroImage, 171*, 415–436. doi:10.1016/j.neuroimage.2017.12.073

Peters, J., Miedl, S. F., & Büchel, C. (2013). Elevated functional connectivity in a striatal-amygdala circuit in pathological gamblers. *PloS One, 8*(9), e74353. doi:10.1371/journal.pone.0074353

Poser, B. A., Versluis, M. J., Hoogduin, J. M., & Norris, D. G. (2006). BOLD contrast sensitivity enhancement and artifact reduction with multiecho EPI: Parallel-acquired inhomogeneity-desensitized fMRI. *Magnetic Resonance in Medicine, 55*(6), 1227–1235. doi:10.1002/mrm.20900

Power, J. D., Barnes, K. A., Snyder, A. Z., Schlaggar, B. L., & Petersen, S. E. (2012). Spurious but systematic correlations in functional connectivity MRI networks arise from subject motion. *NeuroImage, 59*(3), 2142–2154. doi:10.1016/j.neuroimage.2011.10.018

Power, J. D., Plitt, M., Kundu, P., Bandettini, P. A., & Martin, A. (2017). Temporal interpolation alters motion in fMRI scans: Magnitudes and consequences for artifact detection. *Plos One, 12*(9), e0182939. doi:10.1371/journal.pone.0182939

Power, J. D., Plitt, M., Laumann, T. O., & Martin, A. (2017). Sources and implications of whole-brain fMRI signals in humans. *NeuroImage, 146*(May), 609–625. doi:10.1016/j.neuroimage.2016.09.038

Pruim, R. H. R., Mennes, M., Buitelaar, J. K., & Beckmann, C. F. (2015a). Evaluation of ICA-AROMA and alternative strategies for motion artifact removal in resting state fMRI. *NeuroImage, 112*, 278–287. doi:10.1016/j.neuroimage.2015.02.063

Pruim, R. H. R., Mennes, M., van Rooij, D., Llera, A., Buitelaar, J. K., & Beckmann, C. F. (2015b). ICA-AROMA: A robust ICA-based strategy for removing motion artifacts from fMRI data. *NeuroImage, 112*, 267–277. doi:10.1016/j.neuroimage.2015.02.064

Reineberg, A. E., Andrews-Hanna, J. R., Depue, B. E., Friedman, N. P., & Banich, M. T. (2015). Resting-state networks predict individual differences in common and specific aspects of executive function. *NeuroImage, 104*, 69–78. doi:10.1016/j.neuroimage.2014.09.045

Satterthwaite, T. D., Elliott, M. A., Gerraty, R. T., Ruparel, K., Loughead, J., Calkins, M. E., … Wolf, D. H. (2013). An improved framework for confound regression and filtering for control of motion artifact in the preprocessing of resting-state functional connectivity data. *NeuroImage, 64*(1), 240–256. doi:10.1016/j.neuroimage.2012.08.052

Saunders, J. B., Aasland, O. G., Babor, T. F., de la Fuente, J. R., & Grant, M. (1993). Development of the alcohol use disorders identification test (AUDIT): WHO collaborative project on early detection of persons with harmful alcohol consumption–II. *Addiction (Abingdon, England), 88*(6), 791–804. Retrieved from http://www.fpl.fs.fed.us/documnts/pdf2002/cowan02a.pdf

Seeley, W. W., Menon, V., Schatzberg, A. F., Keller, J., Glover, G. H., Kenna, H., … Greicius, M. D. (2007). Dissociable intrinsic connectivity networks for salience processing and executive control. *J Neurosci, 27*(9), 2349–2356. doi:10.1523/JNEUROSCI.5587-06.2007

Sescousse, G., Janssen, L. K., Hashemi, M. M., Timmer, M. H. M., Geurts, D. E. M., ter Huurne, N. P., … Cools, R. (2016). Amplified striatal responses to near-miss outcomes in pathological gamblers. *Neuropsychopharmacology, 41*(10), 2614–2623, doi:10.1038/npp.2016.43

Sheehan, D., Lecrubier, Y., & Sheehan, K. (1998). Diagnostic psychiatric interview for DSM-IV and ICD-10. *J Clin Psychiatry, 59*, 22–33. Retrieved from https://www.researchgate.net/profile/David_Sheehan2/publication/13406551_The_Mini-International_Neuropsychiatric_Interview_MINI_The_development_and_validation_of_a_structured_diagnostic_psychiatric_interview_for_DSM-IV_and_ICD-10/links/02bfe50d063159c19e0

Smith, S. (2002). Fast robust automated brain extraction. *Human Brain Mapping*. Retrieved from http://onlinelibrary.wiley.com/doi/10.1002/hbm.10062/full

Steenbergh, T. A., Meyers, A. W., May, R. K., & Whelan, J. P. (2002). Development and validation of the Gamblers' Beliefs Questionnaire. *Psychology of Addictive Behaviors : Journal of the Society of Psychologists in Addictive Behaviors, 16*(2), 143–149. Retrieved from http://www.ncbi.nlm.nih.gov/pubmed/12079253

van Timmeren, T., Daams, J. G., van Holst, R. J., & Goudriaan, A. E. (2018). Compulsivity-related neurocognitive performance deficits in gambling disorder: A systematic review and meta-analysis. *Neuroscience & Biobehavioral Reviews, 84*, 204–217. doi:10.1016/j.neubiorev.2017.11.022

Tschernegg, M., Crone, J. S., Eigenberger, T., Schwartenbeck, P., Fauth-Bühler, M., Lemènager, T., … Kronbichler, M. (2013). Abnormalities of functional brain networks in pathological gambling: A graph-theoretical approach. *Frontiers in Human Neuroscience, 7*(September), 1–10. doi:10.3389/fnhum.2013.00625

Vincent, J. L., Kahn, I., Snyder, A. Z., Raichle, M. E., & Buckner, R. L. (2008). Evidence for a frontoparietal control system revealed by intrinsic functional connectivity. *Journal of Neurophysiology, 100*(6), 3328–3342. doi:10.1152/jn.90355.2008

Yeo, B. T. T., Krienen, F. M., Sepulcre, J., Sabuncu, M. R., Lashkari, D., Hollinshead, M., … Buckner, R. L. (2011). The organization of the human cerebral cortex estimated by intrinsic functional connectivity. *Journal of Neurophysiology, 106*, 1125–1165. doi:10.1152/jn.00338.2011

Zhang, Y., Brady, M., & Smith, S. (2001). Segmentation of brain MR images through a hidden Markov random field model and the expectation-maximization algorithm. *IEEE Transactions on Medical Imaging, 20*(1), 45–57. doi:10.1109/42.906424

Amygdala grey matter volume increase in gambling disorder with depression symptoms of clinical relevance: a voxel-based morphometry study

Evangelos Zois [ID], Falk Kiefer, Sabine Vollstädt-Klein, Tagrid Lemenager, Karl Mann[‡] and Mira Fauth-Bühler

ABSTRACT
Studies on brain structure in gambling disorder (GD) have so far employed small sample sizes offering little in the investigation of co-morbid conditions such as depression. The aim of the current investigation is to examine grey matter (GM) volume alterations in GD patients with depression symptoms compared to GD without. In total, 107 gamblers with and without depression symptoms were assessed with the Beck Depression Inventory (BDI). The authors employed voxel-based morphometry (VBM) to look for GM volume differences between the groups. Group comparison showed that GD patients with higher depressive symptoms exhibited significant GM volume increase in the left amygdala ($p < 0.05$, ROI FWE corrected). Amygdala GM volume positively correlated with depression scores. The authors extend previous findings in the field acknowledging the need for subgroup formation and comparisons in GD. Brain structural alterations in GD patients with depressive symptomatology might also exist. Depression co-morbidity in GD is an interesting field for future research with implications for therapy (i.e. personalized treatment) and the development of psychological or pharmacological interventions in GD patients with and without depression co-morbidity targeting amygdala and neighbouring regions.

Introduction

Evidence suggests that mood disorders and depression in particular are the second most prevalent co-morbidity in gambling disorder (GD) after substance use disorders (SUDs) (Kessler et al., 2003, 2008). Depression might even pose as a risk factor for the development of gambling problems (Blaszczynski & McConaghy, 1989). Depression combined with GD results in higher gambling symptoms (Rømer Thomsen, Callesen, Linnet, Kringelbach, & Møller, 2009) and impulsivity (Lister, Milosevic, & Ledgerwood, 2015). Also, GD patients with depression symptoms exhibit altered brain activation during monetary reward

---

[‡]Contributed equally.

processing (Fauth-Bühler et al., 2014). Fauth-Bühler and colleagues found that GD patients with moderate to severe depression showed increased striatal and insula activation during the feedback phase of monetary reward processing compared to GD patients with no symptoms of depression (Fauth-Bühler et al., 2014). According to the pathways model of problem and pathological gambling, there is a subtype of GD patients referred to as the emotionally vulnerable. GD patients of this subtype gamble to cope with negative affect as they view gambling as escapism or an arousing mechanism (Blaszczynski & Nower, 2002). The neurobiological basis of this vulnerability could involve abnormal functioning of the amygdala and adjacent regions (Blaszczynski & Nower, 2002).

Research on brain grey matter (GM) has offered some interesting results in relation to GD. Rahman and colleagues addressed the issue of amygdala vulnerability by examining its volume in GD patients compared to controls. They found decreased volume in the patient group in amygdala and hippocampus, which negatively correlated with behavioural measures tapping impulsivity in GD (Rahman, Xu, & Potenza, 2014). Several investigations in depression patients have also focused on amygdala volume. Burke et al. (2011) found that early and late onset depressed patients had smaller amygdala volume than age-matched non-depressed participants (Burke et al., 2011). Frodl et al. (2003) examined first-episode depressed patients who showed enlarged amygdala volume compared to patients with recurrent depression (Frodl et al., 2003). In line with Frodl et al. (2003), similar findings emerged when examining amygdala volume in patients with a first depressive episode (Hamilton, Siemer, & Gotlib, 2008).

GD morphological findings to date have significantly contributed to our understanding of GD and its underlying neurobiological mechanisms. However, sample sizes employed are relatively small, not allowing subgroup comparisons (Joutsa, Saunavaara, Parkkola, Niemelä, & Kaasinen, 2011; Koehler et al., 2013). Previously, GD subgroup investigations using large samples have offered interesting findings that support the existence of different GD subgroups (Fauth-Bühler et al., 2014; Zois et al., 2017, 2014). We employed a large GD sample ($N = 107$; previously published in Zois et al., 2017) to explore the neurobiological underpinnings of GD patients with depression symptoms by subgroup definition based on scores from the Beck Depression Inventory (BDI). Amygdala has been associated with negative affect and depression (Blaszczynski & Nower, 2002; Sheline, Gado, & Price, 1998), and studies exploring brain function (Elman et al., 2012) and structure (Rahman et al., 2014) report altered activation/structure of the amygdala in GD. We were interested in extending our understanding of the relationship between GD, depression symptoms and amygdala volume. We aimed at exploring amygdala volume differences in GD patients with and without depression symptoms of clinical relevance. We expect to see differences in GM volume of the amygdala in GD patients with depression symptoms compared to those without. We also anticipate that GM amygdala volume will be associated with clinical variables of interest.

Method

Participants

In total, 107 gambling patients were included in the study. Data in this report have not been collected anew; instead, almost the same patient data sample has been previously published

(Zois et al., 2017). They were all slot-machine-playing male GD patients (with a few exceptions who were excluded from any analysis to keep our sample homogenous) recruited from the addiction day clinic at the Central Institute of Mental Health (CIMH) in Mannheim (Germany) and other inpatient treatment centres in Münzesheim (Germany), Münchwies (Germany) and CIMH. Participants met criteria for GD according to the *Diagnostic and Statistical Manual of Mental Disorders*, fourth edition (DSM-IV; Bell, 1994), were aged 18 to 70 years old and were attending treatment for GD (psychosocial interventions) at time of recruitment. Participants were excluded from the study if they had a history of severe head trauma that involved loss of consciousness, or a neurological disease that might interfere with cognition, as well as a diagnosis of any Axis I disorder according to DSM-IV using the structured clinical interview for DSM disorders (SCID-I) criteria apart from specific phobias and lifetime substance use disorder. In addition, a positive urine drug screen at the data collection point constituted an exclusion from participation in the study. SUD in patients was assessed using the SCID-I criteria. Nicotine dependence was assessed using the DSM-IV criteria for nicotine dependence. Lifetime substance use disorder (SUD) co-morbidity was not met for 60 GD patients. However, gambling patients with a lifetime alcohol dependence/misuse diagnosis were in total 31, and those with a diagnosis of poly-substance misuse/dependence were 16 (Zois et al., 2017). Specifically, 85 patients were current smokers and 1 was an ex-smoker and was excluded from the analysis as information on past smoking history was not available. Regarding depression subgroup definition we collected data using the Beck Depression Inventory (BDI) (Beck, Ward, Mendelson, Mock, & Erbaugh, 1961). We defined subgroups with depression symptoms using a median split of the overall BDI score (Fauth-Bühler et al., 2014). The median BDI score was 12. GD patients with a BDI < 12 were assigned to the BDI $_{LOW}$ group ($N = 56$) and GD patients with a BDI ≥ 12 were assigned to the BDI $_{HIGH}$ group ($N = 51$) (Fauth-Bühler et al., 2014).

Procedure

The ethics committee of the Medical Faculty Mannheim, University of Heidelberg approved the study (Ref: 2009-207 N-MA). All participants included in this investigation were taken from a large-scale study conducted in CIMH within the scope of the Baden-Württemberg study on pathological gambling. After complete description of the study to the subjects, written informed consent was obtained. The assessment included the South Oaks Gambling Screen (SOGS; Lesieur & Blume, 1987) to assess gambling severity. Subjective gambling urges/craving and gambling severity was assessed using the Yale–Brown Obsessive Compulsive Scale adapted for Pathological Gambling (PG-YBOCS; Pallanti, DeCaria, Grant, Urpe, & Hollander, 2005). The Beck Depression Inventory (Beck et al., 1961) was completed to assess depression symptomatology. Anxiety was measured using the State Trait Anxiety Inventory (STAI; Laux, Glanzmann, Schaffner, & Spielberger, 1981). Information was also collected on the age of onset of gambling disorder and gambling years in total as well as variables describing engagement in gambling activities i.e. amount of time spent on gambling activities. Data on those variables were analysed using IBM SPSS V20 (Statistical Package of the Social Sciences, Version 15.0.0, SPSS Inc., Chicago, IL, USA) with a significance threshold of $p < 0.05$.

MRI data acquisition, preprocessing and analysis

Magnetic resonance imaging (MRI) data acquisition was performed on a 3.0T MR scanner (Siemens MAGNETOM TrioTim), with a standard multi-channel receiver head coil (12-channel). 3-Dimensional *T1*-weighted structural images (Magnetization Prepared Rapid Acquisition Gradient Echo, MPRAGE) were collected over 8 minutes. The T1-weighted anatomical scans comprised 192 sagittal slices (flip angle: 9°; repetition time: 2.3 ms; echo time: 3.03 ms; field of view 256 x 256; voxel size, 1 mm x 1 mm x 1 mm). For analysis of the T1-weighted images, we used an extension of the default unified segmentation (Ashburner & Friston, 2005) as implemented in VBM8 toolbox (http://dbm.neuro.uni-jena.de/vbm/) for the Statistical Parametric Mapping software 8 (SPM8; Wellcome Department of Imaging Neuroscience Group, University College London, London, UK; http://www.fil.ion.ucl.ac.uk/spm) (default parameters). Images were bias-corrected, tissue classified, and normalized to Montreal Neurological Institute (MNI)-space using linear (12-parameter affine) and non-linear transformations, including high-dimensional diffeomorphic anatomical registration through exponentiated lie algebra (DARTEL) normalization. Normalized images were modulated with the Jacobian determinants of the deformation parameters to preserve absolute tissue volumes. Normalization using a non-linear warp refuted the need to account for total individual brain volume in group-level statistics. Images were smoothed using a Gaussian kernel of 8 mm full width at half maximum (FWHM). In order to avoid possible edge effects between GM and white matter (WM), all voxels with GM values of less than *0.1* were excluded.

Age, smoking status and SUD co-morbidity were used as covariates of no interest together with clinical variables such as gambling severity (SOGS, PG-YBOCS) and impulsivity (BIS). Based on previous amygdala findings in functional (Elman et al., 2012) and structural (Rahman et al., 2014) MRI in GD as well as depression (Frodl et al., 2003), we performed region of interest (ROI) analysis using a predefined bilateral amygdala anatomical mask (http://fmri.wfubmc.edu/software/PickAtlas) at the significance level of $p < 0.05$ FWE correcting for multiple comparisons comparing GD $_{BDI\,LOW}$ and $_{BDI\,HIGH}$ respectively. Partial correlations were performed between amygdala (bilateral anatomical mask) extracted mean regional GM volume and clinical variables (YBOCS, SOGS, STAI, BDI, BIS, gambling years, amount of debts, age of onset, hours gambled in a typical day [mean and maximum], days gambled in a month [mean], gambling-related craving). Mean amygdala GM volume was extracted using the response exploration tool REX (Duff, Cunnington, & Egan, 2007).

Results

Psychometric data

All data on demographic and clinical characteristics were assessed using independent samples *t*-test. GD $_{BDI\,HIGH}$ had significantly higher scores on most gambling-related variables including YBOCS and SOGS than the GD $_{BDI\,LOW}$ group. Also, GD $_{BDI\,HIGH}$ reported higher STAI scores than the GD $_{BDI\,LOW}$ (see Table 1).

Table 1. Demographics and clinical characteristics of GD $_{BDI\ LOW}$ and $_{HIGH}$ groups.

Variables of interest	BDI LOW (N = 56)	BDI HIGH (N = 51)	t-statistic	p-value
Age	37.1 ± 8.5	36.3 ± 9.5	.46	.65
Age of onset (gambling disorder)	26.3 ± 8.8	24.3 ± 8.4	1.07	.29
DSM-IV criteria (nicotine)	3.3 ± 2.8	4.8 ± 2.9	−2.74	.007
PG-YBOCS total (severity)	13.6 ± 7.6	19.43 ± 8.6	−3.38	.001
SOGS (severity)	9.1 ± 3.2	12.45 ± 2.9	−3.92	<.001
STAI (anxiety)	36.7 ± 9.1	51.9 ± 11.1	−15.0	<.001
Gambling years (total)	10.6 ± 8.5	12.3 ± 8.5	−.92	.36
Debts (total)	22,482 ± 41,419	28,124 ± 33,461	−.71	.48
Mean gambling hours (day)	4.5 ± 3.9	6.6 ± 6.1	−1.92	.06
Maximum gambling hours (day)	11.6 ± 12.4	10.6 ± 6.2	.20	.84
Mean days gambling (month)	13.9 ± 8.1	17 ± 8.1	−1.8	.08
Gambling craving	25.9 ± 24.2	42.7 ± 24.9	−2.94	.004
BIS (impulsivity)	68.5 ± 8.9	78.2 ± 9.8	−4.86	<.001

SOGS: South Oaks Gambling Screen; PG-YBOCS: Yale-Brown Obsessive Compulsive Scale adapted for Pathological Gambling; BIS: Barratt Impulsivity Scale; STAI: State Trait Anxiety Inventory; values represent mean and standard deviation. Test statistic used was an independent samples test.

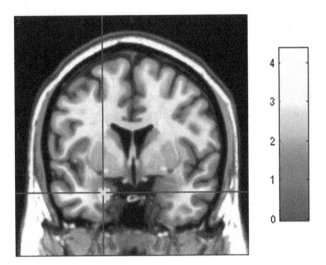

Figure 1. Significant GM volume increase in the amygdala in the DG $_{BDI\ HIGH}$ group compared with DG $_{BDI\ LOW}$. Results are ROI FWE ($p < 0.05$) corrected.

Whole brain morphometric findings

Explorative analysis revealed whole brain GM volume differences when comparing GD $_{BDI\ HIGH}$ with GD $_{BDI\ LOW}$ groups but only when applying a *0.001* uncorrected threshold to contextualize the ROI findings ($k = 20$, $t = 3.21$, $p = .001$). GD $_{BDI\ HIGH}$ compared with GD $_{BDI\ LOW}$ show increased GM volume in a cluster in the left amygdala/parahippocampus ($p = .71$, $t = 3.85$, $k = 153$) and right fusiform gyrus ($p = .97$, $t = 3.71$, $k = 35$).

Amygdala morphometric findings (ROI analysis)

ROI analysis was performed using a bilateral anatomical mask of the amygdala (Figure 1). GD patients with higher BDI scores exhibited increased GM volume compared with GD $_{BDI\ LOW}$ in the left amygdala ($x = -20$, $y = 2$, $z = -24$, $k = 125$, $t = 3.85$, $p = .005$, ROI FWE corrected).

Grey matter volume associations and clinical variables

In order to explore the relationship between clinical variables of interest and GM volume, we performed partial correlations between mean extracted GM volume from the bilateral amygdala and variables of interest controlling for age, SUD and smoking (see Table 1). A significant positive correlation was found between bilateral amygdala volume and BDI scores ($r = .417$, $p = .002$), using a Bonferroni corrected p value ($p = .004$) (Figure 2).

Discussion

Morphometric findings emerging from this analysis relate to amygdala GM volume in GD with and without depression symptomatology. GD $_{BDI\ HIGH}$ showed increased amygdala (left) GM volume compared to GD $_{BDI\ LOW}$. Extracted GM volume from a bilateral amygdala anatomical mask positively correlated with BDI scores. Psychometric data showed that GD $_{BDI\ HIGH}$ had significant higher scores than GD $_{BDI\ LOW}$ in gambling-related variables such as gambling craving/severity (SOGS, PG-YBOCS, mean number of hours one gambles in a day), as well as impulsivity (BIS) and anxiety (STAI).

Concerning the psychometric significant differences, our results as already published by our group (Fauth-Bühler et al., 2014) indicate that depressive symptoms influence gambling severity. This is in line with previous findings suggesting that GD patients with a mood disorder are more likely to have higher levels of gambling severity (el-Guebaly et al., 2006; Lister et al., 2015). Romer-Thomsen and colleagues (2009) investigated gambling severity

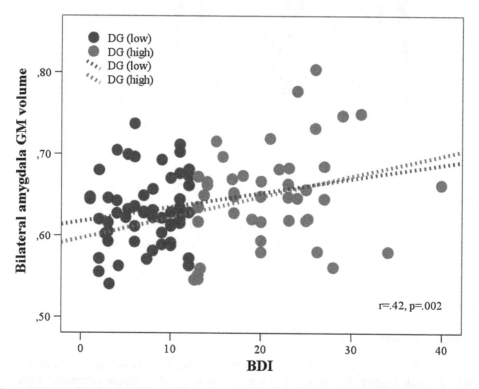

Figure 2. Scatterplot showing the significant positive correlation between bilateral amygdala GM volume and BDI scores, for the complete group of gamblers.

and depression symptoms in slot-machine GD. They found that gambling symptoms were experienced in excess in GD patients with high depression symptoms (Rømer Thomsen et al., 2009). We have also investigated slot-machine gamblers only in this report. Previous work in support of the pathways model has shown that slot-machine gamblers show emotional vulnerabilities similar to depression and anxiety (Valleur et al., 2016). This suggests that our findings might not extend to the other two subtypes of the pathways model (behaviourally addicted and the impulsive subtypes).

Regarding depression symptomatology and GM volume, no study to our knowledge has examined volumetric differences taking into account depression symptoms in GD. Recent functional neuroimaging findings published by our group demonstrate that increased depression symptoms differentiated reward processing in GD (Fauth-Bühler et al., 2014). (Fauth-Bühler et al., 2014). Specifically, we found increased dorsal striatum and insula activation at receipt of monetary reward in GD with higher depression symptoms (Fauth-Bühler et al., 2014). Current findings in amygdala volume in GD $_{BDI\ HIGH}$ also suggest that higher depression symptoms might result in higher GM volume in the amygdala.

Depressed patients show anomalies in the amygdala which manifests with either increase (Frodl et al., 2003) or decrease (Sheline et al., 1998) in volume relative to non-depressed individuals (Hamilton et al., 2008). Our results show higher amygdala volume in GD patients with higher depressive symptoms, in line with studies in depression that also report higher amygdala volume but only in those patients on antidepressants (Hamilton et al., 2008) or patients with a first depressive episode (Frodl et al., 2003). Increased GM amygdala volume in depression could be explained by neurogenesis due to antidepressant use (Hamilton et al., 2008). Yet in our GD sample, no patient was receiving such treatment. Future studies should explore this in more detail and try to disentangle whether amygdala volume alterations found relate to depression symptoms or are the result of GD itself. A speculative explanation relates to the pathways model and the emotionally vulnerable GD subtype. Patients in this cohort engage in gambling activities excessively to self-medicate and reduce emotional discomfort (Blaszczynski & McConaghy, 1989; Blaszczynski & Nower, 2002).

Amygdala has long been linked with depression. Our results potentially support this assumption by showing that volume in the amygdala is positively associated with depression symptoms. This could relate to abnormal neurobiological processes originating from amygdala projections to the prefrontal cortex (PFC). The PFC downregulates amygdala activity (Hariri et al., 2006) but when that fails, the amygdala is over-activated. Such neuronal adaptations could predispose GD patients to experience negative affect disproportionately. We assume a likely interruption in the brain inhibition track (Volkow, Wang, Tomasi, & Baler, 2013) in GD. This is perhaps demonstrated via GM volume increase in the amygdala associated with depression symptoms.

There are several limitations characterizing the current study. There were only male patients included. There was also no inclusion of depressed participants that would allow comparisons between GD patients with depression and depressed controls without gambling diagnosis. In addition, the cross-sectional design employed does not allow further analysis to explore the relationship between amygdala GM volume and relapse prediction considering such findings have recently emerged in alcohol use disorders (Zois et al., 2016). As a further limitation, we wish to emphasize that the BDI is measuring state depression symptoms and for that reason is difficult to say whether those symptoms existed prior to GD diagnosis or developed as a result of it. Thus, it remains unclear as to whether increased

amygdala volume indicates pre-morbid depression symptoms or the consequence of pro-
tracted gambling activity.

The present investigation examined GD subgroups, comparing gamblers with depressive
symptoms of clinical relevance to those without. GD patients with depression symptoms
show increased GM volume in the amygdala. Also, amygdala volume correlated with BDI
scores. Our findings suggest that depression co-morbidity in GD is an interesting research
area with implications for therapy and treatment. However, additional work is needed to
draw any conclusions on whether amygdala and adjacent regions in GD patients form the
neurobiological basis of depression co-morbidity in GD. Further work in the field will also
validate existing theoretical prepositions in behavioural addictions that acknowledge the
existence of subgroups in GD. Taken together, our results might have useful implications
for the development of new therapeutic interventions in GD focusing on personalized
treatment targeting the amygdala and neighbouring regions.

Conflicts of interest

Funding sources

The study was supported financially by the Ministry for Work and Social Affairs (Ministerium
für Arbeit und Sozialordnung, Familien und Senioren), Baden-Württemberg, Germany
[grant number 53–5072–7.1].

Competing interests

None of the authors report financial relationships with commercial interests or any other
potential conflicts of interest.

Constraints on publishing

None of the authors reported any constraints on publishing.

ORCID

Evangelos Zois ⓘ http://orcid.org/0000-0003-4279-0672

References

Ashburner, J., & Friston, K. J. (2005). Unified segmentation. *NeuroImage, 26*(3), 839–851. doi:10.1016/j.neuroimage.2005.02.018

Beck, A. T., Ward, C. H., Mendelson, M., Mock, J., & Erbaugh, J. (1961). An inventory for measuring depression. *Archives of General Psychiatry, 4*(6), 561–571.

Bell, C. C. (1994). DSM-IV: Diagnostic and statistical manual of mental disorders. JAMA: The. *Journal of the American Medical Association, 272*(10), doi:10.1001/jama.1994.03520100096046.

Blaszczynski, A., & McConaghy, N. (1989). Anxiety and/or depression in the pathogenesis of addictive gambling. *International Journal of the Addictions, 24*(4), 337–350.

Blaszczynski, A., & Nower, L. (2002). A pathways model of problem and pathological gambling. *Addiction, 97*(5), 487–499.

Burke, J., McQuoid, D. R., Payne, M. E., Steffens, D. C., Krishnan, R. R., & Taylor, W. D. (2011). Amygdala volume in late-life depression: Relationship with age of onset. *American Journal of Geriatric Psychiatry, 19*(9), 771–776. doi:10.1097/JGP.0b013e318211069a

Duff, E. P., Cunnington, R., & Egan, G. F. (2007). REX: Response exploration for neuroimaging datasets. *Neuroinformatics, 5*(4), 223–234. doi:10.1007/s12021-007-9001-y

Elman, I., Becerra, L., Tschibelu, E., Yamamoto, R., George, E., & Borsook, D. (2012). Yohimbine-induced amygdala activation in pathological gamblers: A pilot study. *PLoS One, 7*(2), e31118. doi:10.1371/journal.pone.0031118

Fauth-Bühler, M., Zois, E., Vollstädt-Klein, S., Lemenager, T., Beutel, M., & Mann, K. (2014). Insula and striatum activity in effort-related monetary reward processing in gambling disorder: The role of depressive symptomatology. *NeuroImage: Clinical, 6*, 243–251. doi:10.1016/j.nicl.2014.09.008

Frodl, T., Meisenzahl, E. M., Zetzsche, T., Born, C., Jäger, M., Groll, C., & Bottlender, Ronald (2003). Larger amygdala volumes in first depressive episode as compared to recurrent major depression and healthy control subjects. *Biological Psychiatry, 53*(4), 338–344.

el-Guebaly, N., Patten, S. B., Currie, S., Williams, J. V., Beck, C. A., Maxwell, C. J., & Wang, J. L. (2006). Epidemiological associations between gambling behavior, substance use & mood and anxiety disorders. *Journal of Gambling Studies, 22*(3), 275–287. doi:10.1007/s10899-006-9016-6

Hamilton, J. P., Siemer, M., & Gotlib, I. H. (2008). Amygdala volume in major depressive disorder: A meta-analysis of magnetic resonance imaging studies. *Molecular Psychiatry, 13*(11), 993–1000. doi:10.1038/mp.2008.57

Hariri, A. R., Brown, S. M., Williamson, D. E., Flory, J. D., de Wit, H., & Manuck, S. B. (2006). Preference for immediate over delayed rewards is associated with magnitude of ventral striatal activity. *Journal of Neuroscience, 26*(51), 13213–13217. doi:10.1523/JNEUROSCI.3446-06.2006

Joutsa, J., Saunavaara, J., Parkkola, R., Niemelä, S., & Kaasinen, V. (2011). Extensive abnormality of brain white matter integrity in pathological gambling. *Psychiatry Research: Neuroimaging, 194*(3), 340–346. doi:10.1016/j.pscychresns.2011.08.001

Kessler, R. C., Berglund, P., Demler, O., Jin, R., Koretz, D., Merikangas, K. R., & National Comorbidity Survey, R. (2003). The epidemiology of major depressive disorder: Results from the National Comorbidity Survey Replication (NCS-R). *JAMA, 289*(23), 3095–3105. doi:10.1001/jama.289.23.3095

Kessler, R. C., Hwang, I., LaBrie, R., Petukhova, M., Sampson, N. A., Winters, K. C., & Shaffer, H. J. (2008). DSM-IV pathological gambling in the National Comorbidity Survey Replication. *Psychol Med, 38*(9), 1351–1360. doi:10.1017/S0033291708002900

Koehler, S., Ovadia-Caro, S., van der Meer, E., Villringer, A., Heinz, A., Romanczuk-Seiferth, N., & Margulies, D. S. (2013). Increased functional connectivity between prefrontal cortex and reward system in pathological gambling. *PLoS One, 8*(12), e84565. doi:10.1371/journal.pone.0084565

Laux, L., Glanzmann, P., Schaffner, P., & Spielberger, C. (1981). *Das State-Trait-Angstinventar. Theoretische Grundlagen und Handanweisung*. Weinheim: Beltz Test GmbH.

Lesieur, H. R., & Blume, S. B. (1987). The South Oaks Gambling Screen (SOGS): A new instrument for the identification of pathological gamblers. *Am J Psychiatry, 144*(9), 1184–1188.

Lister, J. J., Milosevic, A., & Ledgerwood, D. M. (2015). Psychological characteristics of problem gamblers with and without mood disorder. *The Canadian Journal of Psychiatry, 60*(8), 369–376. doi:10.1177/070674371506000806

Pallanti, S., DeCaria, C. M., Grant, J. E., Urpe, M., & Hollander, E. (2005). Reliability and validity of the pathological gambling adaptation of the yale-brown obsessive-compulsive scale (PG-YBOCS). *Journal of Gambling Studies, 21*(4), 431–443. doi:10.1007/s10899-005-5557-3

Rahman, A. S., Xu, J., & Potenza, M. N. (2014). Hippocampal and amygdalar volumetric differences in pathological gambling: A preliminary study of the associations with the behavioral inhibition system. *Neuropsychopharmacology, 39*(3), 738–745. doi:10.1038/npp.2013.260

Rømer Thomsen, K., Callesen, M. B., Linnet, J., Kringelbach, M. L., & Møller, A. (2009). Severity of gambling is associated with severity of depressive symptoms in pathological gamblers. *Behavioural Pharmacology, 20*(5-6), 527–536. doi:10.1097/FBP.0b013e3283305e7a

Sheline, Y. I., Gado, M. H., & Price, J. L. (1998). Amygdala core nuclei volumes are decreased in recurrent major depression. *NeuroReport, 9*(9), 2023–2028.

Valleur, M., Codina, I., Vénisse, J. L., Romo, L., Magalon, D., Fatséas, M., & Chéreau-Boudet, Isabelle (2016). Towards a validation of the three pathways model of pathological gambling. *Journal of Gambling Studies, 32*(2), 757–771. doi:10.1007/s10899-015-9545-y

Volkow, N. D., Wang, G. J., Tomasi, D., & Baler, R. D. (2013). Unbalanced neuronal circuits in addiction. *Current Opinion in Neurobiology, 23*(4), 639–648. doi:10.1016/j.conb.2013.01.002

Zois, E., Kortlang, N., Vollstädt-Klein, S., Lemenager, T., Beutel, M., Mann, K., & Fauth-Bühler, M. (2014). Decision-making deficits in patients diagnosed with disordered gambling using the Cambridge Gambling task: The effects of substance use disorder comorbidity. *Brain and Behavior, 4*(4), 484–494. doi:10.1002/brb3.231

Zois, E., Vollstädt-Klein, S., Hoffmann, S., Reinhard, I., Bach, P., Charlet, K., ... Kiefer, F. (2016). GATA4 variant interaction with brain limbic structure and relapse risk: A voxel-based morphometry study. *European Neuropsychopharmacology, 26*(9), 1431–1437. doi:10.1016/j.euroneuro.2016.06.011

Zois, E., Kiefer, F., Lemenager, T., Vollstädt-Klein, S., Mann, K., & Fauth-Bühler, M. (2017). Frontal cortex gray matter volume alterations in pathological gambling occur independently from substance use disorder. *Addiction Biology, 22*(3), 864–872. doi:10.1111/adb.12368

Relating neural processing of reward and loss prospect to risky decision-making in individuals with and without gambling disorder

Iris M. Balodis[†], Jakob Linnet[†], Fiza Arshad, Patrick D. Worhunsky, Michael C. Stevens [ID], Godfrey D. Pearlson and Marc N. Potenza

ABSTRACT

Neuroimaging studies demonstrate alterations in fronto-striatal neurocircuitry in gambling disorder (GD) during anticipatory processing, which may influence decision-making impairments. However, to date little is known about fronto-striatal anticipatory processing and emotion-based decision-making. While undergoing neuroimaging, 28 GD and 28 healthy control (HC) participants performed the Monetary Incentive Delay Task (MIDT). Pearson correlation coefficients assessed out-of-scanner Iowa Gambling Task (IGT) performance with the neural activity during prospect (A1) processing on the MIDT across combined GD and HC groups. The HC and GD groups showed no significant difference in out-of-scanner IGT performance, although there was a trend for higher IGT scores in the HC group on the last two IGT trial blocks. Whole-brain correlations across combined HC and GD groups showed that MIDT BOLD signal in the ventral striatum/caudate/ventromedial prefrontal cortex and anterior cingulate regions during the prospect of winning positively correlated with total IGT scores. The GD group also contained a higher proportion of tobacco smokers, and correlations between neural activations in prospect on the MIDT may relate in part to gambling and/or smoking pathology. In this study, fronto-striatal activity during the prospect of reward and loss on the MIDT was related to decision-making on the IGT, with blunted activation linked to disadvantageous decision-making. The findings from this work are novel in linking brain activity during a prospect-of-reward phase with performance on a decision-making task in individuals with and without GD.

[†]These authors contributed equally

Introduction

Gambling disorder (GD) is a behavioural addiction characterized by persistent and recurrent betting that leads to clinically significant impairment or distress (DSM-5; American Psychiatric Association, 2013, p. 585). GD is linked to disadvantageous decision-making on measures such as the Iowa Gambling Task (IGT) (Grant, Contoreggi, & London, 2000; Petry, 2001; Cavedini, Riboldi, Keller, D'Annucci, & Bellodi, 2002; Goudriaan, Oosterlaan, de Beurs, & van den Brink, 2005, Goudriaan et al. 2006, Linnet, Rojskjaer, Nygaard, & Maher, 2006; Roca et al., 2008), which has been linked to ventral striatal function (Linnet, Peterson, Doudet, Gjedde, & Møller, 2010; Linnet et al. 2011a, b; Linnet et al., 2012).

Ventral striatal activity differences in GD (as compared to healthy control [HC] groups) may be linked to differences in reward anticipation. The IGT consists of four card decks (A, B, C and D) associated with reward and punishment contingencies, with the objective of IGT performance being to maximize gains. Decks with immediately smaller rewards are associated with long-term gains, while decks with immediately larger rewards are associated with long-term losses. During IGT performance, people may learn over time to select preferentially from advantageous (leading to long-term gains) versus disadvantageous (leading to long-term losses) decks as they acquire knowledge of the reward contingencies associated with each of the four decks. During IGT performance, decision-making may be guided by neurobiological feedback that may include both conscious and subconscious processes, with individual differences noted. People show individual differences in the magnitudes of increased anticipatory skin conductance responses (SCRs) in relation to encountering risky decisions, prior to having conscious or declarative knowledge that choices may be risky (Bechara, Damasio, Damasio, & Anderson, 1994; Bechara, Damasio, Tranel, & Damasio, 1997; Bechara, Dolan, & Hindes, 2002; Bechara, Tranel, & Damasio, 2000). Individuals with lesions in the ventromedial prefrontal cortex (vmPFC) often demonstrate low anticipatory SCRs prior to the behavioural response of card selection and also perform disadvantageously on the IGT, perhaps due to insensitivities in processing risk-related signals. Studies of individuals with substance-use disorders (SUDs) (Bechara, 2003; Bechara & Damasio, 2002; Bechara et al., 2001) or GD (Goudriaan et al. 2006) show reduced anticipatory SCRs compared to HC subjects, suggesting a possible deficient anticipatory neurobiological signal related to risk-reward decision-making in addictions. Therefore, anticipatory neurobiological processes that may help guide decision-making warrant further examination as related to IGT performance.

Brain imaging studies suggest altered brain functions of reward anticipation in GD, which may relate to poor decision-making and disadvantageous IGT performance. IGT performance in individuals with SUDs with or without GD has been linked to cortico-striatal circuitry, with blunted activation of the vmPFC observed in addicted individuals (Tanabe et al., 2007). Given that IGT performance involves risk-reward decision-making, the neural correlates of reward and loss processing also warrant consideration. A meta-analysis by Luijten, Schellekens, Kuhn, Machielse, and Sescousse (2017) showed that anticipatory processing in SUDs and GD is characterized by decreased striatal activation when compared with HC subjects. Balodis et al. (2012) found reduced anticipatory BOLD activation toward gains and losses in the medial prefrontal cortex (mPFC, including vmPFC), anterior cingulate and left ventral striatum of individuals with GD compared with HC subjects during performance of the Monetary Incentive Delay Task (MIDT). Choi et al. (2012)

found reduced anticipatory BOLD activation during MIDT performance in the caudate in individuals with GD compared with HC subjects and those with obsessive-compulsive disorder (OCD). Romanczuk-Seiferth et al. (2015) found reduced anticipatory BOLD activation in the right ventral striatum toward loss anticipation in individuals with GD compared with HC subjects and those with alcohol-use disorder during MIDT performance. Sescousse et al. (2013) found that individuals with GD had a blunted anticipatory BOLD activation response in the ventral striatum toward erotic images, but not toward monetary cues, compared with HC subjects. Additional studies of the processing of near-miss losses and when making decisions to chase or accept losses also implicate the vmPFC and ventral striatum (Worhunsky, Malison, Rogers, & Potenza, 2014; Worhunsky, Potenza, & Rogers, 2017). While these studies provide evidence for reduced anticipatory BOLD activation in GD toward gains and losses, reduced BOLD activation is also involved in other aspects of decision-making in GD including those related to temporal discounting (e.g. Miedl et al., 2015) and response perseveration (e.g. de Ruiter et al., 2009). Furthermore, some studies report relatively increased activation of the ventral striatum and (vmPFC) during reward anticipation in GD. For instance, van Holst, Veltman, Buchel, van den Brink, and Goudriaan (2012) found that individuals with GD had significantly increased anticipatory BOLD activation in the bilateral ventral striatum and left orbitofrontal cortex toward gain-related expected value compared to HC subjects during performance of a monetary guessing task.

As noted above, the MIDT is a widely used task to assess the neural correlates of reward and loss processing. Although not observed across all studies, relatively blunted activation of the ventral striatum has been observed in multiple addictive disorders during anticipatory phases of reward processing (Balodis & Potenza, 2015). While the original MIDT assessed two phases of reward processing, our modified version permits the modelling of three phases: prospect, anticipation and consumption/outcome, which we have termed A1, A2 and OC, respectively (Andrews et al., 2011). The A1 and A2 phases were designated as such as they may be considered as two forms of anticipation, with the former anticipating task performance (needing to push the button while the target is on screen) and the latter anticipating reporting of performance outcome (having successfully won or avoided loss, or not). The designation of prospect for the A1 phase is derived from its position following information given to participants about the type of trial (i.e. a win or loss trial, along with high, low or null values). The ability to parse two anticipation phases is important as each is linked not only to specific psychological features of reward loss processing, but also to specific neural correlates in individuals family history positive for alcoholism (Andrews et al., 2011), with GD (Balodis et al., 2012) and with binge-eating disorder (Balodis et al., 2013).

While there is evidence for altered brain functions of reward anticipation in GD, little is currently known about the possible association between neural correlates of reward and loss processing as assessed using functional magnetic resonance imaging (fMRI) and decision-making deficits on behavioural tasks such as the IGT. In the present study, we aimed to study relationships between anticipatory processing of rewards and losses on the MIDT and out-of-scanner measures of risk-reward decision-making on the IGT. Given differences in the neural correlates of A1 and A2 phases of the MIDT, we examined both phases with respect to IGT performance. Given prior findings, we hypothesized that anticipatory BOLD responses in the ventral striatum during anticipatory phases of the MIDT, and particularly A2 given prior findings in GD (Balodis et al., 2012), would be positively associated with IGT performance. We hypothesized that this tendency would be observed in both GD and

Table 1. Demographic information for gambling disorder (GD) and healthy control (HC) groups.

	GD	HC
N	28	28
Male/Female	19/9	19/9
Age (SD)	40.61 (10.6)	41.36 (10.21)
White/Black/Asian/American Indian	18/10	20/6/1/1
Non-Hispanic/Hispanic	26/2	27/1
Years of education	13.79 (1.8)	14.82 (2.53)
Current smoker	14	7
SOGS*	13.3(3.9)	0.7 (1.25)

SD = Standard deviation.
*$P < 0.05$.

HC groups given findings of blunted ventral striatal activation that transcends diagnostic groupings (Balodis & Potenza, 2015; Balodis et al., 2013), including HC subjects at greater risk for addictions (Andrews et al., 2011). Given the association between vmPFC activation and IGT performance and mPFC contributions to MIDT processing including in but not limited to anticipatory phases, we hypothesized that vmPFC activation during anticipatory phases of reward processing would also be positively correlated with IGT performance.

Methods

Participants included 28 individuals who met criteria for GD and 28 healthy control (HC) participants (demographic information displayed in Table 1). Participants consisted of a community sample recruited through advertisements and flyers in the New Haven area. GD status was assessed with the Structured Clinical Interview for Pathological Gambling, which has clinical validity and reliability in GD populations (Grant, Steinberg, Kim, Rounsaville, & Potenza, 2004); other co-occurring disorders were assessed via a Structured Clinical Interview for DSM-IV Disorders (First, Spitzer, Gibbon, & Williams, 2002). In the GD group, 14 individuals identified as tobacco smokers, as compared with 7 individuals in the HC group ($X^2_{(1,56)} = 0.053$). The following other co-occurring disorders were noted: in the GD group, seven individuals met criteria for past alcohol dependence, seven for past alcohol abuse, two for past opioid dependence, one for past cannabis abuse, two for past cannabis dependence, four for past cocaine dependence, one for past substance-induced mood disorder, two for past major depression, one for current obsessive/compulsive disorder, one for current specific phobia, one for current social phobia, one for current alcohol abuse, one for current cocaine dependence, one for current alcohol dependence, one for current generalized anxiety disorder, one for past phencyclidine abuse and one for past stimulant abuse. In the HC group, one individual reported past panic disorder.

Urine toxicology at the time of scanning confirmed that participants were free of illicit substances. All participants provided written informed consent. Participants completed the MIDT and the IGT on separate days. The study was approved by the University's Human Investigations Committee.

Monetary Incentive Delay Task (MIDT) experimental procedure

All participants completed the MIDT. The task and experimental methods have previously been described (Andrews et al., 2011; Balodis et al., 2012). In brief, participants completed two runs of the MIDT in two 10-minute sessions, with each run consisting of 55 trials, and each trial lasting 12 seconds each. The current study focused on the anticipatory phases (A1W for win prospect, A1L for loss prospect, A2W for win anticipation and A2L for loss anticipation). The A1 phase modelled the period when participants viewed a cue signalling the potential win or loss of money (either $1 or $5) and then fixated on a crosshair, anticipating working to win or avoid loss via button press.

fMRI volume acquisitions were time-locked to the offset of each cue, and trial types were pseudorandomly ordered within each session. Task difficulty was based on practice reaction times collected prior to the scanning session and set so that participants would experience a positive outcome on 66% of trials. All participants were informed that their compensation for the task was performance-based. The main effects of the MIDT in 13 individuals in the GD group have previously been published (Balodis et al., 2012). The focus of the current manuscript is on the correlation of prospect-related processing activity on the MIDT with IGT performance.

Image acquisition and analysis

Images were obtained on a Siemens 3 Tesla scanner (Trio; Siemens AG, Erlangen, Germany) at the University's Magnetic Resonance Research Center at the University School of Medicine. Localizer images were acquired aligning the eighth slice parallel to the plane transecting the anterior and posterior commissures. Functional images were acquired with a T2*-weighed blood oxygen level dependent (BOLD) sequence with a TR of 1500 ms, TE of 27, flip angle of 60°, 64 x 64 in-plane matrix, field of view of 220 x 220 and 25 4 mm slices with a 1 mm skip. High-resolution 3D MPRAGE structural images were also acquired with a TR of 2530 ms, TE of 3.34 ms, flip angle of 7°, 256 x 256 in-plane matrix, and 176 1 mm slices. Voxel size in the T1 scan was 3 mm. Each MIDT fMRI run comprised 486 volumes, including an initial rest period of 9 seconds for signal stability, which was subsequently removed from analyses. Functional images were processed using SPM5 (Welcome Functional Imaging Laboratory, London, UK), normalized to the Montreal Neurological Institute template, and smoothed with a 6-mm kernel full-width at half maximum. First-level modelling was conducted using robust regression to reduce the influence of strong outliers. Motion parameters and high-pass filter parameters were included as additional regressors of no interest. The Neuroelf analysis package (www. neuroelf.net) was used for second-level random-effects analysis. Correction for multiple comparisons was conducted using Monte-Carlo simulation (i.e. AlphaSim), using a combined voxelwise and cluster threshold to result in a family-wise-error (FWE) rate of 5%. Statistical analyses used a robust general linear model approach and each phase of each trial type was separately modelled. Analyses combined 'Win $1' and 'Win $5' trials, 'Lose $1' and 'Lose $5' trials, and 'Win $0' and 'Lose 0' trials in reward (W), penalty (L) and neutral (N) conditions in order to increase power. Specific correlations consisted of the contrasts A1W > A1N, A1L > A1N, A2W > A2N, and A2L > A2N correlated with IGT scores. Whole-brain correlations were conducted across and within each group. Correlations were conducted across groups initially and within-group analyses were conducted post hoc if positive findings were observed.

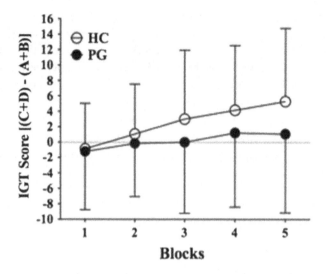

Figure 1. Behavioural performance on the Iowa Gambling Task (IGT) in gambling disorder (GD) and healthy control (HC) participants. A repeated-measures ANOVA demonstrates a significant effect of trial blocks [$F_{4,216} = 162.5, p < .05$], but no Block X Group interaction ($p > .05$). There was no significant between-group difference [$F_{1,54} = 2.18, p > .05$], although the HC group showed a trend of increasing scores over trial blocks. The GD group did not demonstrate a significant increase in IGT score across the five trial blocks.

Iowa Gambling Task and experimental procedure

The IGT is a computerized card game, which simulates real-life decision-making in the way that it factors reward and punishment. The IGT consists of four card decks (A, B, C and D). In decks A and B ('disadvantageous decks') choosing a card is followed by an immediately high gain of money, but at unpredictable trials the selection is followed by a high penalty, leading to a net loss over time. In decks C and D ('advantageous decks') the immediate gain is smaller, but the future loss is also smaller, leading to a net gain over time. The IGT score is calculated as the number of cards selected from advantageous decks minus those from disadvantageous decks ((C + D) − (A + B)), usually measured across 5 blocks of 20 trials (1–20, 21–40 and so forth) for a total of 100 cards. A repeated-measures ANOVA tested group and block differences on the IGT. Participants were not reimbursed for IGT task performance.

Results

Behavioural performance on the IGT in GD and HC participants

A repeated-measures ANOVA demonstrated a significant effect of Trial Block [$F_{4,216} = 162.5$, $p < .05$], but no Block X Group interaction ($p > .05$). There was no significant between-group difference [$F_{1,54} = 2.18, p > .05$], although the HC group showed a trend of increasing scores over most trial blocks ($p < .10$). The GD group did not demonstrate a significant increase in IGT score across the 5 trial blocks ($p > .10$) (Figure 1).

THE NEUROSCIENCE AND NEUROPSYCHOLOGY OF GAMBLING

Total IGT score correlations with MIDT prospect phase (A1 phase)

GD and HC combined

A1W Phase

Positive correlations between IGT scores and the A1W > A1N0 contrast were observed in three main clusters in the cingulate cortex (Table 2; Figure 2). The first one was in the left anterior cingulate, extending bilaterally into the right anterior cingulate, anteriorly into the orbitofrontal cortex, and posteriorly into the medial and inferior frontal gyri, the caudate, ventral striatum and the left lentiform nucleus. The second cluster was observed bilaterally in the posterior cingulate, extending bilaterally into the culmen, posteriorly into the left cuneus, and anteriorly into the right thalamus, insula, precuneus, and the middle temporal, lingual, and cingulate gyri. The third cluster was observed in the dorsal posterior cingulate cortex, extending bilaterally into the paracentral lobule, the right precentral gyrus, and the left insula, paracentral lobule, precuneus, caudate, superior parietal lobule, the cingulate gyrus, and the superior and middle temporal gyri.

Relationship with smoking status

To examine possible effects in A1W related to smoking status, 14 individuals who reported smoking were removed from the GD group and 7 individuals were removed from the HC group. The combined group of non-smokers (N = 35) did not show any significant correlations between IGT performance and neural activations during the A1W phase (Supplemental Materials, Supplemental Table 1). Examining the GD group of non-smokers alone (n = 14) did not result in any correlations surviving correction during the A1W phase (Supplemental Materials, Supplemental Table 1).

A1L phase

A positive correlation was observed in the left ventral striatum, extending bilaterally into the caudate, and ventrally into the right putamen, lentiform nucleus, medial frontal gyrus, and the parahippocampal gyrus (Table 2; Figure 2).

Relationship with smoking status

To examine possible effects in A1L related to smoking status, 14 individuals who reported smoking were removed from the GD group and 7 individuals were removed from the HC group. The combined group of non-smokers (N = 35) showed significant correlations between IGT performance and neural activations during the A1L phase in 3 clusters (Supplemental Materials, Supplemental Table 1). Specifically, inverse correlations were observed between IGT performance and neural activations involving the middle frontal gyrus, the cingulate gyrus extending to the posterior cingulate and the superior temporal gyrus, respectively. Examining the GD group of non-smokers alone (n = 14) did not result in any correlations surviving correction during the A1L phase (Supplemental Materials, Supplemental Table 1).

Table 2. Correlation between total Iowa Gambling Task (IGT) scores with A1Win (A1W) and A1Loss (A1L) activity on the Monetary Incentive Delay Task (MIDT) in combined HC and GD participants (N = 56).

HC + GD combined	Structure	BA	L/R	x	y	z	k	Peak r-value
Total IGT scores								
A1W > N	Anterior Cingulate/Lentiform Nucleus/Orbitofrontal cortex/Medial Frontal Gyrus/Claustrum/Inferior Frontal Gyrus/Caudate/Ventral Striatum	32	L	−12	36	6	521	0.488
	Posterior Cingulate/Thalamus/Precuneus/Culmen/Middle Temporal Gyrus/Insula/Cingulate Gyrus/Cuneus/Middle Occipital Gyrus/Lingual Gyrus	30	L	−6	−54	3	560	0.427
	Dorsal Posterior Cingulate Cortex/Cingulate Gyrus/Insula/Paracentral Lobule/Precuneus/Precentral Gyrus/Caudate/Middle Temporal Gyrus/Superior Parietal Lobule/Superior Temporal Gyrus/Paracentral Lobule	31	L	−18	−44	30	461	0.427
A1L > N	Ventral Striatum/ Caudate/Putamen/Lentiform Nucleus/Medial Frontal Gyrus/Parahippocampal Gyrus	–	L	−9	6	−6	300	0.473

BA = Brodmann's area

k = voxel size

r = Pearson correlation coefficient

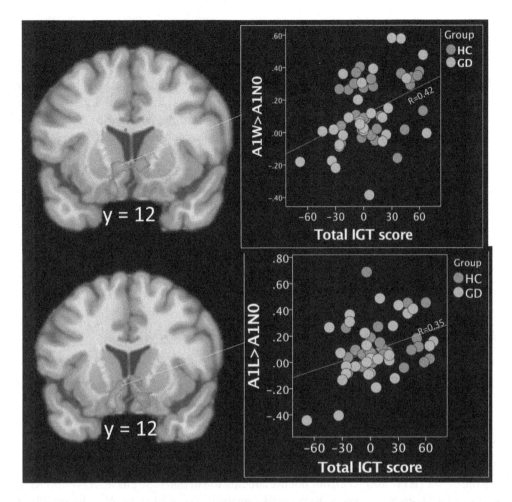

Figure 2. Positive correlation between ventral striatal activity during the prospect of winning and total IGT score in HC and GD participants (N = 56). Whole brain correlations demonstrate that increased ventral striatal activity during the winning prospect (A1W; relative to neutral A1L > N0) and the losing prospect (A1L > A1N0) are associated with higher IGT scores across both HC and GD groups. Scatterplots depict percent blood-oxygen-level-dependent (BOLD) signal change in the ventral striatum cluster correlated with the total IGT score. All contrast maps are thresholded at an uncorrected level of $p < 0.05$ two-tailed and using a Monte Carlo simulation, family-wise-error-corrected at $p < 0.05$. The right side of the brain is on the right.

GD versus HC comparison

HC group

A1W
 No correlations were observed at $p = 0.05$ with a k-threshold of 223.
A1L
 No correlations were observed at $p = 0.05$ with a k-threshold of 223.

GD Group

A1W phase

Positive correlations were observed between the total IGT scores and activation during the MIDT in four main clusters (Table 3; Figure 3). The first cluster was seen bilaterally in the anterior cingulate, with the activation extending bilaterally into the orbitofrontal cortex, medial frontal cortex, caudate, insula, and anteriorly into the left inferior frontal gyrus, lentiform nucleus, precuneus, inferior parietal lobule, precentral gyrus and the paracentral lobule. The second cluster was observed bilaterally in the cuneus, extending into the middle occipital gyrus, cuneus, anteriorly into the left inferior occipital, superior occipital, middle temporal and inferior temporal gyri, medially into the left posterior cingulate, laterally into the left precuneus, and into the right lingual gyrus. The third cluster depicted activations in the right paracentral lobule, extending laterally into the inferior parietal lobule, middle temporal gyrus, precuenus, cuneus, and anteriorly into the middle temporal, superior temporal, and precental gyri. The fourth main cluster was observed in the right precentral gyrus, extending into claustrum, anteriorly into the middle frontal, superior frontal, and precentral gyri, and bilaterally into the medial frontal gyrus.

Entire PG and HC sample

A2W and A2L

No significant correlations were observed between IGT performance and the neural correlates of reward processing in the entire sample in the A2W and A2L contrasts.

Discussion

In the current study, we found that striatal activity during the prospect of reward and loss on the MIDT (A1W and A1L), but not the anticipation of outcome phase (A2W and A2L), correlated with decision-making performance on the IGT. Correlations were also significant within the GD group but not the HC group. Differences in neural correlates were observed when smoking status was considered. These findings suggest that impaired striatal activation in the formulation of prospects is associated with impaired decision-making across GD and HC groups and within GD participants, with smoking status representing an important consideration. These findings suggest possible biological mechanisms for disadvantageous decision-making in people generally and in GD specifically.

It is important to note that findings were observed in the prospect anticipatory phases (A1W and A1L) as opposed to the anticipatory phase related to outcome notification (A2W and A2L). The A2 phase has been linked to blunted ventral striatal signalling in GD (Balodis et al., 2012) and HC subjects at elevated risk for addictions (i.e. those with a positive family history for alcoholism (Andrews et al., 2011). It is possible that the prospect phase of reward and loss processing may be particularly relevant to IGT performance in both GD and HC subjects. We should note that the correlation between IGT performance and MIDT prospect processing in GD and HC does not preclude group differences between GD and HC participants. It is possible that GD subjects may cluster around the lower end of the correlation and HC subjects may cluster around the higher end of the correlation, as suggested by our data (Figure 2). Regardless, the findings suggest that decision-making may link to

Table 3. Correlation between total IGT scores with A1W and A2L activity on the MIDT in GD participants ($N = 28$).

PG	Structure	BA	L/R	x	y	z	k	Peak r-value
Total IGT scores								
A1W > N	Anterior Cingulate/Limbic Lobe/Cingulate Gyrus/Inferior Frontal Gyrus/Medial Frontal Gyrus/Orbitofrontal Cortex/Lentiform Nucleus/Precuneus/Insula/Caudate/Inferior Parietal Lobule/Precentral Gyrus/Paracentral Lobule	24	L	0	30	6	1064	0.651
	Cuneus/Middle Occipital Gyrus/Inferior Occipital Gyrus/Precuneus/Posterior Cingulate/Inferior Temporal Gyrus/Middle Temporal Gyrus/Lingual Gyrus/Superior Occipital Gyrus	18	L	−9	−99	21	645	0.65
	Paracentral Lobule/Inferior Parietal Lobule/Middle Temporal Gyrus/Precuneus/Precentral Gyrus/Superior Temporal Gyrus/Cuneus/Angular Gyrus	5	R	12	−40	60	515	0.637
	Precentral Gyrus/Claustrum/Middle Frontal Gyrus/Superior Frontal Gyrus/Medial Frontal Gyrus	6	R	59	−5	42	531	0.6
A2L > N	Uncus/Middle Frontal Gyrus/Orbitofrontal Cortex/Superior Frontal Gyrus/Medial Frontal Gyrus/Parahippocampal Gyrus/Inferior Frontal Gyrus	28	L	−33	0	−33	774	−0.745
	Cingulate Gyrus/Precentral Gyrus/Postcentral Gyrus/Paracentral Lobule/Precuneus/Supramarginal Gyrus/Inferior Parietal Lobule	31	R	18	−27	45	360	−0.687

BA = Brodmann's area

k = voxel size

r = Pearson correlation coefficient

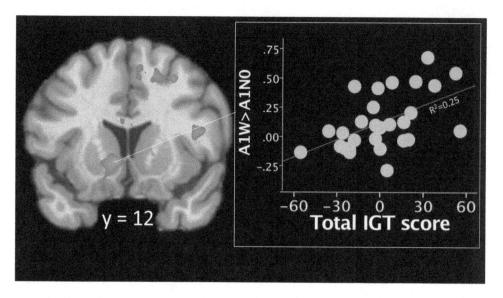

Figure 3. Positive correlation between ventral striatal activity during the prospect of winning and total IGT score in GD participants (*n* = 28). This whole brain correlations demonstrates that increased ventral striatal activity during the winning prospect (A1W; relative to neutral A1L > N0) is associated with higher IGT scores across the GD group. Scatterplot depicts percent blood-oxygen-level-dependent (BOLD) signal change in the ventral striatum cluster correlated with the total IGT score ($R^2 = 0.25$, $p < 0.05$). All contrast maps are thresholded at an uncorrected level of $p < 0.05$ two-tailed and using a Monte Carlo simulation, family-wise-error-corrected at $p < 0.05$. The right side of the brain is on the right.

biological processes underlying the processing of the prospects of monetary rewards and losses. While individual differences in the neural correlates of prospect formulation may be particularly relevant to GD, they may also be relevant to HC subjects, particularly those at elevated risk for engaging in addictive behaviours, although this notion is somewhat speculative given the current data. However, the notion that smoking status may influence neural processes relating to prospect formation and risky decision-making warrants further consideration and study.

In the present study, we found that activation of the ventral striatum during the prospect phase of considering working for both gaining monetary reward and avoiding monetary losses was linked to performance on the IGT, suggesting that this area may contribute to processing of both positive and negative prospects relating to advantageous decision-making. The results resonate with the original findings by Knutson, Fong, Bennett, Adams, and Hommer (2003) of recruitment of the ventral striatum in anticipation (involving both prospect and anticipation, in the original MIDT) of monetary rewards, which could suggest that a reduced anticipatory BOLD response of both positive and negative outcomes is a biological marker for decision-making processes that have been linked to addictive disorders. This notion is consistent with findings from the meta-analysis conducted by Luijten et al. (2017).

The association between anticipatory striatal BOLD response and advantageous decision-making is consistent with the SCR literature (Bechara et al., 1997). Both within the GD group, and across the GD and HC groups, individuals with lower prospect-related BOLD response performed poorer on the IGT.

Nevertheless, it is notable that smoking status appears to contribute to the current findings, as the correlation between prospect-reward-related striatal activation and IGT scores was no longer significant once smokers were removed from analyses. Individuals with GD who smoke may represent an important subgroup with respect to problem-gambling severity (Petry & Oncken, 2002), co-occurring psychopathology (Potenza, Steinberg, et al., 2004) and clinical interventions (Grant et al., 2014). Multiple MIDT studies demonstrate alterations in anticipatory responding, particularly in striatal areas in smoking populations (Garrison, Yip, et al., 2017; Nestor, McCabe et al., 2018). Indeed, a recent study demonstrated that acute nicotine increased striatal anticipatory responses on the MIDT (Moran, Stoeckel, et al., in press), with incentive responsiveness relating to greater nicotinic influences on salient stimuli. These findings emphasize the importance of considering smoking status and recency of smoking when conducting neuroimaging studies in populations of individuals who smoke, including studies of conditions that frequently co-occur with tobacco-use disorders like GD. Such considerations may be particularly relevant to understanding constructs related to addictive disorders including incentive responsiveness.

Several limitations should be considered in the interpretation of the present results.

First, we compared MIDT performance in the scanner with IGT performance outside the scanner. Therefore, the association between MIDT measures and IGT performance is an indirect measure, as MIDT and IGT performances were recorded at different times.

Second, we do not have SCR data available in relation to IGT performance in the present study. Therefore, we do not know if the prospect-related BOLD response on the MIDT is associated with SCR responses on the IGT.

Third, there is a trend toward between-group differences on the last blocks of the IGT. It is possible that we were not able to detect between-group differences due to the sample size in our study. The present study involved 56 individuals equally distributed in GD and HC groups. While this sample size is of sufficient power in relation to neuroimaging studies, and while some IGT studies find significant differences between GD and HC groups with smaller samples sizes, we also note that some IGT studies with smaller sample size do not detect significant differences, (Linnet et al., 2010). In line with this possibility, Bechara and Damasio (2002) compared 46 individuals with SUDs and 49 HC subjects, while (Goudriaan et al., 2006) compared 46 individuals with GD with 47 HC subjects.

Fourth, we do not know how the present data may relate to declarative knowledge on the IGT. The original IGT studies reported an association between more advantageous IGT performance and declarative knowledge, where individuals who were able to describe which decks were better performed better, suggesting that they were learning the task.

Fifth, individuals with GD had more co-morbidity than did healthy control subjects. Co-occurring disorders are common in GD, with over 95% of individuals estimated to have one or more co-occurring disorders (Kessler et al. 2008). While we cannot exclude the possibility that the present results are related to other types of co-morbidity than GD, particularly tobacco-use disorders, we note that co-morbidity is a common aspect of GD. While this limits the attribution of findings to GD per se, the sample studied is arguably more clinically relevant than a group of GD subjects without co-occurring disorders, increasing the clinical relevance of the findings.

Finally, we note that other explanations for differences in the neural underpinnings of formulating or experiencing prospects could account for relationships with disadvantageous IGT performance. For instance, disadvantageous decision-making on the IGT could relate to a general insensitivity for rewards or losses, and individuals with GD who may have experienced tolerance to risk-reward decisions involving lower monetary stakes may be particularly likely to demonstrate such differences. This currently speculative possibility warrants additional direct examination.

In conclusion, these findings highlight how reduced neural activations relating to reward- and loss-related prospects may relate to disadvantageous decision-making (i.e. lower IGT scores). Future studies should investigate whether this altered signalling may relate to the development or progression of GD or to recovery from it. Future studies should also focus on tobacco smoking as related to gambling, decision-making and addictions, particularly when trying to understand and help people with GD. The findings are novel in linking brain activity during a prospect phase of reward and loss processing with performance on a well-validated decision-making task.

Conflicts of interest

None of the authors have any relevant conflicts of interests.

Competing interests

Dr Potenza has consulted for Ironwood, Lundbeck, Shire, INSYS, Rivermend Health, Opiant/Lakelight Therapeutics, and Jazz Pharmaceuticals; has received research support (to Yale) from Pfizer, Mohegan Sun Casino and the National Center for Responsible Gaming; has participated in surveys, mailings or telephone consultations related to drug addiction, impulse-control disorders or other health topics; has consulted for gambling and legal entities on issues related to impulse-control/addictive disorders; provides clinical care in a problem gambling services programme; has performed grant reviews for the National Institutes of Health and other agencies; has edited journals and journal sections; has given academic lectures in grand rounds, CME events and other clinical or scientific venues; and has generated books or book chapters for publishers of mental health texts.

Constraints on publishing

The authors declared no constraints on publishing. No funding agencies had input into the content of this article.

Funding sources

This work was supported in part by R01 DA019039 from the National Institutes of Health; the Connecticut Mental Health Center; and a Center of Excellence in Gambling Research Award from the National Center for Responsible Gaming. IMB was partially supported by the Peter Boris Centre for Addictions Research. This work was also supported by the Connecticut Department of Mental Health and Addiction Services and the Connecticut Council on problem Gambling.

ORCID

Michael C. Stevens ⓘ http://orcid.org/0000-0002-3799-5465

References

American Psychiatric Association [DSM 5]. (2013). *Diagnostic and statistical manual of mental disorders: DSM 5*. Washington, DC.

Andrews, M. M., Meda, S. A., Thomas, A. D., Potenza, M. N., Krystal, J. H., Worhunsky, P., ... Pearlson, G. D. (2011). Individuals family history positive for alcoholism show functional magnetic resonance imaging differences in reward sensitivity that are related to impulsivity factors. *Biological Psychiatry, 69*(7), 675–683.

Balodis, I. M., & Potenza, M. N. (2015). Anticipatory reward processing in addicted populations: A focus on the monetary incentive delay task. *Biological Psychiatry, 77*(5), 434–444.

Balodis, I. M., Kober, H., Worhunsky, P. D., Stevens, M. C., Pearlson, G. D., & Potenza, M. N. (2012). Diminished frontostriatal activity during processing of monetary rewards and losses in pathological gambling. *Biological Psychiatry, 71*(8), 749–757.

Balodis, I. M., Kober, H., Worhunsky, P. D., White, M. A., Stevens, M. C., Pearlson, G. D., ... Potenza, M. N. (2013). Monetary reward processing in obese individuals with and without binge eating disorder. *Biological Psychiatry, 73*(9), 877–886.

Bechara, A. (2003). Risky business: Emotion, decision-making, and addiction. *Journal of Gambling Studies, 19*(1), 23–51.

Bechara, A., & Damasio, H. (2002). Decision-making and addiction (part I): Impaired activation of somatic states in substance dependent individuals when pondering decisions with negative future consequences. *Neuropsychologia, 40*(10), 1675–1689.

Bechara, A., Damasio, A. R., Damasio, H., & Anderson, S. W. (1994). Insensitivity to future consequences following damage to human prefrontal cortex. *Cognition, 50*(1–3), 7–15.

Bechara, A., Damasio, H., Tranel, D., & Damasio, A. R. (1997). Deciding advantageously before knowing the advantageous strategy. *Science, 275*(5304), 1293–1295.

Bechara, A., Tranel, D., & Damasio, H. (2000). Characterization of the decision-making deficit of patients with ventromedial prefrontal cortex lesions. *Brain, 123*(11), 2189–2202.

Bechara, A., Dolan, S., Denburg, N., Hindes, A., Anderson, S. W., & Nathan, P. E. (2001). Decision-making deficits, linked to a dysfunctional ventromedial prefrontal cortex, revealed in alcohol and stimulant abusers. *Neuropsychologia, 39*(4), 376–389.

Bechara, A., Dolan, S., & Hindes, A. (2002). Decision-making and addiction (part II): Myopia for the future or hypersensitivity to reward? *Neuropsychologia, 40*(10), 1690–1705.

Cavedini, P., Riboldi, G., Keller, R., D'Annucci, A., & Bellodi, L. (2002). Frontal lobe dysfunction in pathological gambling patients. *Biological Psychiatry, 51*(4), 334–341.

Choi, J. S., Shin, Y. C., Jung, W. H., Jang, J. H., Kang, D. H., Choi, C. H., ... Kwon, J. S. (2012). Altered brain activity during reward anticipation in pathological gambling and obsessive-compulsive disorder. *PLoS One, 7*(9), e45938.

De Ruiter, M. B., Veltman, D. J., Goudriaan, A. E., Oosterlaan, J., Sjoerds, Z., & Van Den Brink, W. (2009). Response perseveration and ventral prefrontal sensitivity to reward and punishment in male problem gamblers and smokers. *Neuropsychopharmacology, 34*(4), 1027.

First, M., Spitzer, R., Gibbon, M., & Williams, J. (2002). *Structured clinical interview for DSM-IV-TR Axis I disorders, research version, non-patient edition. (SCID-I/NP)*. New York, NY, Biometrics Research, New York State Psychiatric Institute.

Garrison, K. A., Yip, S. W., Balodis, I. M., Carroll, K. M., Potenza, M. N., & Krishnan-Sarin, S. (2017). Reward-related frontostriatal activity and smoking behavior among adolescents in treatment for smoking cessation. *Drug & Alcohol Dependence, 177*, 268–276.

Goudriaan, A. E., Oosterlaan, J., de Beurs, E., & van den Brink, W. (2005). Decision making in pathological gambling: A comparison between pathological gamblers, alcohol dependents, persons with Tourette syndrome, and normal controls. *Cognitive Brain Research, 23*(1), 137–151.

Goudriaan, A. E., Oosterlaan, J., de Beurs, E., & van den Brink, W. (2006). Psychophysiological determinants and concomitants of deficient decision making in pathological gamblers. *Drug and Alcohol Dependence, 84*(3), 231–239.

Grant, S., Contoreggi, C., & London, E. D. (2000). Drug abusers show impaired performance in a laboratory test of decision making. *Neuropsychologia, 38*(8), 1180–1187.

Grant, J. E., Steinberg, M. A., Kim, S. W., Rounsaville, B. J., & Potenza, M. N. (2004). Preliminary validity and reliability testing of a structured clinical interview for pathological gambling. *Psychiatry Research, 128*(1), 79–88.

Grant, J. E., Odlaug, B. L., & Schreiber, L. (2014). Pharmacological treatments in pathological gambling. *British journal of clinical pharmacology, 77*(2), 375–381.

Kessler, R. C., Hwang, I., LaBrie, R., Petukhova, M., Sampson, N. A., Winters, K. C., & Shaffer, H. J. (2008). DSM-IV pathological gambling in the National Comorbidity Survey Replication. *Psychological Medicine, 38*(9), 1351–1360.

Knutson, B., Fong, G. W., Bennett, S. M., Adams, C. M., & Hommer, D. (2003). A region of mesial prefrontal cortex tracks monetarily rewarding outcomes: Characterization with rapid event-related fMRI. *NeuroImage, 18*(2), 263–272.

Linnet, J., Rojskjaer, S., Nygaard, J., & Maher, B. A. (2006). Episodic chasing in pathological gamblers using the Iowa gambling task. *Scandinavian Journal of Psychology, 47*(1), 43–49.

Linnet, J., Peterson, E. A., Doudet, D., Gjedde, A., & Møller, A. (2010). Dopamine release in ventral striatum of pathological gamblers losing money. *Acta Psychiatrica Scandinavica, 122*, 326–333.

Linnet, J., Moller, A., Peterson, E., Gjedde, A., & Doudet, D. (2011a). Dopamine release in ventral striatum during Iowa Gambling Task performance is associated with increased excitement levels in pathological gambling. *Addiction, 106*(2), 383–390.

Linnet, J., Moller, A., Peterson, E., Gjedde, A., & Doudet, D. (2011b). Inverse association between dopaminergic neurotransmission and Iowa Gambling Task performance in pathological gamblers and healthy controls. *Scandinavian Journal of Psychology, 52*(1), 28–34.

Linnet, J., Mouridsen, K., Peterson, E., Møller, A., Doudet, D., & Gjedde, A. (2012). Striatal dopamine release codes uncertainty in pathological gambling. *Psychiatry Research: Neuroimaging, 204*, 55–60.

Luijten, M., Schellekens, A. F., Kuhn, S., Machielse, M. W., & Sescousse, G. (2017). Disruption of reward processing in addiction : An image-based meta-analysis of functional magnetic resonance imaging studies. *JAMA Psychiatry, 74*(4), 387–398.

Miedl, S. F., Wiswede, D., Marco-Pallarés, J., Ye, Z., Fehr, T., Herrmann, M., & Münte, T. F. (2015). The neural basis of impulsive discounting in pathological gamblers. *Brain imaging and behavior, 9*(4), 887–898.

Nestor, L. J., McCabe, E., Jones, J., Clancy, L., & Garavan, H. (2018). Smokers and ex-smokers have shared differences in the neural substrates for potential monetary gains and losses. *Addiction biology, 23*(1), 369–378.

Petry, N. M. (2001). Substance abuse, pathological gambling, and impulsiveness. *Drug & Alcohol Dependence, 63*(1), 29–38.

Petry, N. M., & Oncken, C. (2002). Cigarette smoking is associated with increased severity of gambling problems in treatment-seeking gamblers. *Addiction, 97*(6), 745–753.

Potenza, M. N., Steinberg, M. A., McLaughlin, S. D., Wu, R., Rounsaville, B. J., Krishnan-Sarin, S., ... O'Malley, S. S. (2004). Characteristics of tobacco-smoking problem gamblers calling a gambling helpline. *American Journal on Addictions, 13*(5), 471–493.

Romanczuk-Seiferth, N., Koehler, S., Dreesen, C., Wüstenberg, T., & Heinz, A. (2015). Pathological gambling and alcohol dependence: neural disturbances in reward and loss avoidance processing. *Addiction biology, 20*(3), 557–569.

Roca, M., Torralva, T., Lopez, P., Cetkovich, M., Clark, L., & Manes, F. (2008). Executive functions in pathologic gamblers selected in an ecologic setting. *Cognitive and Behavioral Neurology, 21*(1), 1–4.

Sescousse, G., Barbalat, G., Domenech, P., & Dreher, J. C. (2013). Imbalance in the sensitivity to different types of rewards in pathological gambling. *Brain, 136*(8), 2527–2538.

Tanabe, J., Thompson, L., Claus, E., Dalwani, M., Hutchison, K., & Banich, M. T. (2007). Prefrontal cortex activity is reduced in gambling and nongambling substance users during decision-making. *Human brain mapping, 28*(12), 1276–1286.

van Holst, R. J., Veltman, D. J., Buchel, C., van den Brink, W., & Goudriaan, A. E. (2012). Distorted expectancy coding in problem gambling: Is the addictive in the anticipation? *Biological Psychiatry, 71*(8), 741–748.

Worhunsky, P. D., Malison, R. T., Rogers, R. D., & Potenza, M. N. (2014). Altered neural correlates of reward and loss processing during simulated slot-machine fMRI in pathological gambling and cocaine dependence. *Drug and Alcohol Dependence, 145*, 77–86.

Worhunsky, P. D., Potenza, M. N., & Rogers, R. D. (2017). Alterations in functional brain networks associated with loss-chasing in gambling disorder and cocaine-use disorder. *Drug and Alcohol Dependence, 178*, 363–371.

A review of opioid-based treatments for gambling disorder: an examination of treatment outcomes, cravings, and individual differences

Darren R. Christensen

ABSTRACT
Although pharmacological treatments for gambling disorder have shown some promise, questions remain regarding the relationships between primary outcome measures, cravings and sensitivities. In this review of the clinical literature of opioid treatments for gambling disorder an analysis is presented on primary outcome measures, dosing schedules, the reasons for drop-out, and adverse effects. This review of the extant literature shows a relationship between craving and primary outcome measures that appears to be mediated by individual differences, and mirrors the complexity found in the alcohol dependence literature. This relationship implies that individual differences mediate the effectiveness of opioid treatments and indicates that tailored 'precision medicine' treatments are possible for gambling disorder. For example, modifying dosing schedules based on personal and familial histories of co-morbidities (e.g. alcohol dependence or prior substance use), and using pharmacologies implicated in reducing impulsive behaviour might increase treatment effectiveness. Future basic science and applied research examining the interactions between pharmacologies and neurotransmitters may elucidate a possible pharmacological treatment taxonomy for gambling disorder.

Introduction

Gambling disorder is often associated with substance-dependence disorders as both share similar clinical symptoms such as tolerance and withdrawal, cravings, difficulties with cutting back use, and significant impairments in major life areas (American Psychiatric Association, 1994, 2013). Epidemiological research has found that a wide variety of addictions (e.g. alcohol, tobacco, heroin), are risk factors for developing problem gambling behaviours (Johansson, Grant, Kim, Odlaug, & Gotestam, 2009). For example, 15–20% of treatment-seeking problem gamblers report current alcohol problems (Dowling et al., 2015a). Further, treatments for alcohol dependence also show efficacy for problematic gambling, such as 12-step approaches and cognitive-behavioural therapies (Petry & Roll,

2001). Therefore, as gambling and alcohol problems share many similarities, a hypothesis has been proposed that a common neurological basis underlies both disorders (Grant, Odlaug, & Schreiber, 2012). This possibility has been extended to problem gambling treatment, where pharmacological treatments for alcohol and substance abuse may also be effective treatments for gambling disorder.

Recent systematic reviews and meta-analyses of the pharmacological treatment literature for gambling disorder (Aboujaoude & Salame, 2016; Grant et al., 2012; Hodgins, Stea, & Grant, 2011; Pallesen, Molde, Arnestad, et al., 2007; Problem Gambling Research & Treatment Centre, 2011; van den Brink, 2012; Victorri-Vigneau et al., 2017) suggest that opioid antagonist drugs (i.e. drugs that block the opioid receptor from responding to endogenous or exogenous opioids), are more effective than other types of medications (e.g. anti-depressants, anti-psychotics, mood stabilizers, glutamatergic drugs). However, a recent meta-analysis of the pharmacological treatment literature suggests the earlier studies were analytically flawed; later studies using more rigorous intention to treat analyses showed no statistical effect compared to placebo (Bartley & Bloch, 2013). Further, Bartley and Bloch (2013) reported significant heterogeneity across studies, especially in studies with smaller sample sizes.

Although these results suggest that the pharmacology literature is ambiguous, they confirm the general heterogeneous nature of problem gambling (Lindberg, Fernie, & Spada, 2011). Theoretically, the pathways model of problem and pathological gambling (Blaszczynski & Nower, 2002) suggests multiple and divergent pathways for developing these conditions. Likewise, studies of gambling epidemiology (Lorains, Cowlishaw, & Thomas, 2011) and treatment-seeking populations (Dowling et al., 2015a, 2015b) empirically indicate a diffuse experience of problem gambling. Further, problematic gamblers appear to regularly move between gambling severity classes (Williams et al., 2014), possibly indicating that gamblers experience a range of gambling phenomenologies as they transition through gambling severities (Christensen, Jackson, Dowling, Volberg, & Thomas, 2015). Consequently, merely examining problem gambling from a treatment vs. placebo analysis, is likely to miss the range of complexities inherent in the problem gambling population.

Neurological research

One research approach that has shown complex and sometimes contradictory results is the investigations of brain region activation to gambling stimuli. For example, Goudriaan, de Ruiter, van den Brink, Oosterlaan, and Veltman (2010) found problem gamblers elicited greater activation in occipital, temporal and limbic areas compared to controls when viewing gambling and neutral imagery. However, Potenza et al. (2003) found problem gamblers elicited decreases in activation in cortical and thalamic regions compared to controls, whilst de Ruiter et al. (2009) found problem gamblers elicited decreases in the dorsal prefrontal cortex for gains and losses, and Miedl, Peters, and Buchel (2012) found problem gamblers elicited decreases in both the prefrontal cortex and the ventral tegmental area for delayed rewards. Further, a study examining neural connectivity found problem gamblers to have enhanced integration in reward regions and less integration in executive functioning regions compared to controls (Tschernegg et al., 2013).

Moreover, several neurotransmitters are associated with gambling disorder (Grant, 2016). An obvious research target is dopamine. Dopamine is implicated in various behaviours related to substance use (i.e. learning, motivation, and feelings of pleasure; Robbins & Everitt, 1996), although the evidence for gambling disorder is mixed. For example, use of raclopride (which binds to dopamine receptors D2/D3) found no significant differences in striatal dopamine receptor binding between gambling-disordered subjects and controls (Clark et al., 2012). However, 'urgency' was negatively associated with raclopride binding in the gambling disorder group (Clark et al., 2012). This evidence suggests that, unlike the substance use literature, which has strong associations between dopamine receptor D2 down-regulation and chronic substance use (Grant et al., 2016), gambling disorder may follow a different pattern of dopamine receptor binding.

There is also research that has investigated the link between drug reward and other neurotransmitters. Similar to the research on dopamine, research investigating glutamate transmission suggests that glutamate is associated with the experiences of pleasure, reinforcement and relapse (Grant et al., 2016). Further, glutamate and dopamine are concurrently released in the mesolimbic pathway which includes brain structures associated with decision-making and reward (Advokat, Comaty, & Julien, 2014). Interestingly, early evidence suggests that problem gamblers have elevated rates of glutamate acids in cerebrospinal fluid compared to controls (Nordin, Gupta, & Sjodin, 2007). Further, a case study that reported the use of amantadine, an N-methyl-D-aspartate antagonist with a weak dopaminergic release, found a 43–64% reduction in gambling severity symptoms (Pettorruso et al., 2012).

Like glutamate, norepinephrine is implicated in the creation of associations, particularly during decision-making in challenging conditions (Aston-Jones & Cohen, 2005; Bouret & Sara, 2005). For example, Pallanti et al. (2010) assessed the neuroendocrine growth hormone (NGH) during a drug challenge using an adrenergic receptor agonist and found a reduced NGH response in pathological gamblers compared to controls 120 to 150 minutes post-challenge. Further, during placebo trials, the NGH response was significantly smaller in pathological gamblers than in controls. This suggests an abnormal responsivity in pathological gamblers, possibly indicating a higher than normal noradrenergic release (Pallanti et al., 2010).

Serotonin is also a research target for gambling disorder. Several studies have linked mood disorders with gambling, including three recent systematic reviews and meta-analyses (Dowling et al., 2015a, 2015b; Lorains et al., 2011), although the human neuroimaging evidence is weak. Results suggest that when examining the relationship between gambling severity and serotonin receptor affinity in the ventral striatum, putamen and anterior cingulate, no differences were found between pathological gamblers and controls (Potenza et al., 2013). Further, when pathological gamblers were scanned with high-resolution positron emission tomography to identify a serotonin transporter tracer, no differences were found between gamblers and controls (Majuri et al., 2017). Similarly, a selective serotonin reuptake inhibitor made no discernible impact on response inhibition compared to the other groups (i.e. atomoxetine, placebo), but performance was impaired on a probabilistic learning task; participants were more likely to shift responding away from the correct stimulus after receiving misleading feedback (Chamberlain et al., 2006). This suggests that although serotonin is implicated in gambling, possibly in conjunction with dopamine in the striatum, further research is necessary to specify the serotonin induced effects related to gambling disorder.

Non-human research examining hedonic pleasure indicates that opioid receptors in the nucleus accumbens and the ventral pallidum appear important in the amplification of 'liking' food rewards (Pecina, Smith, & Berridge, 2006). As discussed earlier, opioid antagonists have been shown to attenuate the urge to gamble and gambling behaviour in human subjects (for a recent review, see Victorri-Vigneau et al., 2017). Further, a functional magnetic resonance imaging (fMRI) study investigating an opioid antagonist challenge during a gambling task found healthy controls to report decreases in pleasure ratings for larger rewards as well as decreases in neural activation to increasing rewards in the rostral anterior cingulate cortex (Petrovic et al., 2008). Moreover, the opioid antagonist challenge resulted in higher negative valuations for losses at all dose concentrations with increased activity in the anterior insula and caudal anterior cingulate cortex. It is thought the co-occurrence of mu and delta opioid and dopamine receptors in the mesolimbic system facilitates the experience of pleasure and urges (Victorri-Vigneau et al., 2017), while the adaptation to dopamine release is implicated in the development of tolerance (Nutt, 2014). Further, the kappa opioid subtype receptors are implicated in negative reinforcement states in opposition to the mu and delta opioid subtypes (Shippenberg, 2009). In addition, the effects of opioid-based medications may be influenced by dopamine levels, possibly related to impulsivity (Shippenberg, 2009; Victorri-Vigneau et al., 2017). For example, administration of naltrexone appears to reduce alcohol induced dopamine levels in brain regions associated with feelings of pleasure, possibly by blocking mid-brain dopamine activity through reductions in endogenous opioids (Benjamin, Grant, & Pohorecky, 1993; Nutt, 2014).

Consequently, an empirically based pharmacological taxonomy might assist in a more tailored approach to matching possible pharmacologies to problem gambling subgroups. However, making a thorough analysis of all the possible factors likely to contribute to problem gambling or differentiate problem gamblers is a large and multistage process. Therefore, this review examines an abbreviated but important list of factors that might better explain the mixed evidence from the pharmacology treatment literature. Focusing on recent opioid antagonist studies, this review examines all treatment studies investigating opioid-based treatments for gambling disorder rather than only randomized controlled trials. Targeting the relationships between dosing regimens, craving and clinical outcomes, this review attempts to characterize the responsiveness of problem gamblers to pharmacologic treatments and looks to provide context for these findings from the alcohol literature. This review differs from others as it focuses on study designs and the relationships between treatment outcomes and indications of individual responsiveness, including the number and reasons for drop-out and adverse effects. The objectives of this review are to investigate (1) the range of study dosages and their effectiveness; (2) relationships between gambling craving and measures of gambling behaviour and symptomatology; (3) reasons for drop-out; and (4) reported adverse effects from opioid-based treatments.

Methodology

Search strategy

Manuscripts were sourced from a variety of health science and gambling-related databases (i.e. PsychINFO, PubMed, PsycARTICLES, Ovid HealthSTAR, MEDLINE, ScienceDirect and Google Scholar). Manuscripts were selected using the search terms 'gambling' and 'treatment' and with at least one of 'naltrexone', 'nalmefene', 'opioid' or 'antagonist' in the title of the manuscript. Searches were restricted from 1 January 2000 to 25 August 2017 and to English-language manuscripts. This resulted in 28 entries. Manuscripts were inspected and duplicates ($n = 7$) and reviews ($n = 7$) were removed. This resulted in 14 manuscripts. Only peer-reviewed articles published in academic journals that evaluated opioid-based treatments for problem gambling were included. Two manuscripts were excluded. One was a government report (Toneatto, Brands, Selby, & Sinclair, 2004), and the other did not evaluate treatment efficacy (Castren, Salonen, Alho, Lathi, & Simojoki, 2015). This resulted in 12 studies. No ethical approval was requested for this review.

Data extraction

The following data were extracted from the included studies: opioid-based medication (naltrexone, nalmefene), type of study control (none, type, specific control group), co-occurring treatment (specific treatment(s), treatment type), randomization of participants (yes, no), concurrent disorders (specific, or whether there were exceptions to inclusion or exclusion criteria), dosage amounts (milligram; start, average, maximum), dosing schedule (daily, as needed), length of trial (number of weeks, as needed), eligible and reported participants (number), baseline gambling severity (average score and standard deviation), gambling craving (average score and standard deviation; baseline, treatment end), primary outcome measure (average diagnostic criteria reported score and standard deviation or percentage and level; baseline, treatment end), reasons for drop-out (number), and adverse effects (percentage).

Results

Table 1 lists the opioid-based medication, whether a control group was used, co-occurring treatments, whether participants were randomized to conditions, and whether a concurrent disorder was specified or whether exceptions were made for other disorders to the inclusion or exclusion criteria for the 12 studies. The most common opioid-based treatment for gambling disorder was naltrexone ($n = 10$), with two other studies using nalmefene. Half of the studies were double-blind placebo studies ($n = 6$), with the remaining either having no control group ($n = 4$) or other drug therapies as the control group ($n = 2$; bupropion or selective serotonin reuptake inhibitors). Half of the studies reported co-occurring treatments ($n = 6$), where the most common was cognitive behavioural therapy ($n = 2$), although two studies reported other drug therapies. Most of the studies were randomized ($n = 7$), and only three studies reported a specific concurrent disorder (alcohol abuse or dependence, Parkinson's disease and hypomania), although five studies reported exceptions to inclusion or exclusion criteria (i.e. simple phobia, nicotine dependence, positive urine specimen for cannabis, depression or alcohol abuse).

Table 2 lists the dosages for the opioid therapy, the dosing schedule, the length of the trial, the number of participants in the trial, and the baseline gambling severity for the 12 studies. Approximately half of the studies used a range of dosages ($n = 7$), where the range for the naltrexone studies was between 25 mg and 250 mg, and the range for the nalmefene studies was between 5 mg and 100 mg. The majority of studies reported a daily dosing schedule ($n = 10$), with two studies reporting an as needed dosing schedule. The length of the trials

Table 1. Study design.

Study	Opioid-based medication	Control	Co-occurring treatment	Randomization	Concurrent disorder (specific, exception to inclusion or exclusion criteria)
Kim & Grant, 2001;	Naltrexone	None		–	–, –
Kim et al., 2001;	Naltrexone	Double-blind placebo		Yes	-, simple phobia and/or nictotine dependence
Dannon et al. 2005	Naltrexone	Bupropion, blind rater		Yes	–, –
Grant et al., 2006;	Nalmefene	Double-blind placebo		Yes	–, nicotine dependence, positive urine specimen for cannabis
Grant et al., 2008;	Naltrexone	Double-blind placebo	Ondansetron	Yes	–, positive urine specimen for cannabis
Toneatto et al., 2009;	Naltrexone	Double-blind placebo	CBT	Yes	Alcohol abuse or dependence, nicotine use or dependence
Grant et al., 2010;	Nalmefene	Double-blind placebo		Yes	–, –
Lathi, Halme, Pankakoski, Sinclair, and Alho, 2010	Naltrexone	None	MBI	–	–, –
Bosco et al., 2012;	Naltrexone	None	L-Dopa, sertraline/ venlafaxine/ paroxetine	No [a]	Parkinson's disease, depression/alcohol abuse
Piz et al., 2013;	Naltrexone	None	CBT[b]	No [a]	Hypomania, –
Kovanen et al., 2016;	Naltrexone	Double-blind placebo	Psychosocial support	Yes	–
Patrascu, Fainarea Alboaie, Androne, & Bratu-Bizic, 2017	Naltrexone	SSRI		–	–

- No data.
CBT: Cognitive behavioural therapy.
MBI: Motivational brief intervention.
SSRI: Selective serotonin reuptake inhibitor.
[a]Case studies.
[b]Although it is possible these sessions might have ended before Naltrexone was given.

ranged from 6 to 20 weeks, where 4 studies reported a 1-week placebo lead-in before the beginning of the drug treatment. The number of participants reported ranged from a single case study (i.e. Piz et al., 2013) to a couple of studies with more than 100 participants (i.e. Grant, Odlaug, Potenza, Hollander, & Kim, 2010; Grant et al., 2006). Across studies, baseline gambling severity was calculated with different measures. The most common assessment tool or classification system was the *Diagnostic and Statistical Manual for Mental Disorders* (DSM). Average baseline severity for the DSM (American Psychiatric Association, 1994, 2013) ranged from the endorsement of 6.1 to 8.5 criteria (i.e. DSM-5 severity of 'moderate' to 'severe').

Table 3 lists the baseline and treatment end craving scores, and the baseline and treatment end primary outcome measure scores across studies. Typically, the Gambling Symptom Assessment Score (G-SAS total score, or where reported the urge subscale) (Kim et al., 2001) and the Problem Gambling version of the Yale Brown Obsessive Compulsive (PG-YBOCS) (Pallanti et al., 2005) urge/thought subscale were used to measure gambling cravings. At baseline the average G-SAS total score ranged from 26.9 (i.e. Grant, Kim, & Hartman, 2008) to 50.78 (Kim, Grant, Adson, & Shin, 2001), while at treatment end the average G-SAS total score ranged from 12.42 (Grant et al., 2006) to a 95% confidence interval of 19.11 to 20.32 (Grant et al., 2010; 20 mg).

Table 2. Study details.

Study	Dosage mg	Dosing schedule	Length of trial	Tx number (opioid based)	Baseline gambling severity
	(start, average, max)			(eligible[a], reported)	(average, sd)[a]
Kim & Grant, 2001;	25, 157 , 250	Daily	6 weeks Tx	17, 17	DSM-IV (8.5, 1.2)[c]
Kim et al., 2001;	25, 187.50, 250	Daily	1-week placebo lead-in, 11 weeks Tx	20, 20	SOGS (15.15, 3.53)
Dannon et al., 2005;	25, –, 150	Daily	12 weeks Tx	19, 19	DSM-IV (–, –), SOGS (–, –)
Grant et al., 2006;	25, 50, 100	Daily	16 weeks Tx	104, 104	PG-YBOCS (25 mg, 22.8, 4.1; 50 mg 23.6, 5.4; 100 mg 23.1, 5.2)[d]
Grant et al., 2008;	25, 75[b], 150	Daily	1-week placebo lead-in, 17 weeks Tx	58, 58	PG-YBOCS (16.9, 6.6)[e]
Toneatto et al., 2009;	25, 100, 250	Daily	1-week placebo lead-in, 11 weeks Tx	27, 27	DSM-IV (6.1, 2.6)
Grant et al., 2010;	5, –, 40	Daily	1-week placebo lead-in, 16 weeks Tx	159, 159	PG-YBOCS (20 mg: 21.17; 40 mg 20.75)
Lathi et al., 2010;	50	PRN	16 weeks Tx	39, 39	SOGS: 14.0; DSM-IV 8.0
Bosco et al., 2012;	50	Daily	PRN	Case studies (n = 3)	DSM-IV (–, –)
Piz et al., 2013;	100	Daily	PRN	Case study	–
Kovanen et al., 2016;	50	PRN	20 weeks Tx	50, 50	DSM-IV (7.2, 1.5)
Patrascu et al., 2017	50	Daily	12 weeks Tx	6, 6	DSM-5 (–, –)

- No data.
[a] Eligible includes those who completed baseline assessments.
[b] The midpoint between the two middle conditions: 50 mg and 100 mg.
[c] SOGS also assessed gambling severity at baseline.
[d] SOGS and G-SAS also assessed gambling severity at baseline.
[e] G-SAS and CGI-S also assessed gambling severity at baseline.
Tx: Treatment.
PRN: As needed.
DSM-IV: *Diagnostic and Statistical Manual of Mental Disorders*-IV.
DSM-5: *Diagnostic and Statistical Manual of Mental Disorders*-5.
SOGS: South Oaks Gambling Screen.
PG-YBOCS: Problem Gambling version of the Yale-Brown Obsessive Compulsive Scale.
CGI-S: Clinical Global Impression Scale.
G-SAS: Gambling Symptom Assessment Scale.

The most common primary outcome measure was the PG-YBOCS, where PG-YBOCS average scores ranged at baseline from 16.3 (Dannon, Lowengrub, Musin, Gonopolski, & Kotler, 2005) to 23.8 (Kovanen et al., 2016). At treatment end, the PG-YBOCS average scores ranged from 6.99 (Grant et al., 2006; 25 mg) or a 95% confidence interval of 6.06–7.21 (Grant et al., 2010; 40 mg) to a 95% confidence interval of 11.34–12.30 (Grant et al., 2010, 20 mg).

Table 4 lists the reasons for treatment drop-out across studies. These include high enzyme levels, placebo response, lost to follow-up, pregnancy, treatment side effects, personal/scheduling issues and study withdrawal, treatment viewed as ineffective or patient loss of trust, hallucinations, Parkinson's disease or manic disorder, participants failing to start, or drop-out reasons not stated. The most numerous reasons for drop-out appear to be study-specific. For studies that reported multiple drop-out reasons, the most numerous for each study were: treatment side effects $n = 50$ (Grant et al., 2006), not stated $n = 37$ (Grant et al., 2010), placebo response $n = 22$ (Kim et al., 2001), personal reasons/scheduling/withdrawal issues $n = 20$ (Grant et al., 2008) and lost to follow-up $n = 5$ (Kovanen et al., 2016).

Table 5 lists the percentage of adverse effects by study. These include nausea/dizziness/vomiting, drowsiness, insomnia, anxiety, dry mouth, headache, diarrhea, constipation, decreased appetite, decreased libido, vivid dreams, fatigue, perspiration, hallucinations,

Table 3. Craving and primary outcome measures.

Study	Gambling craving		Primary outcome measure	
	baseline (average, sd)[a]	Tx end (average, sd)[a]	baseline (average, sd)[a]	Tx end (average, sd)[a]
Kim & Grant, 2001; Kim et al., 2001;	G-SAS urge strength (6.12, 1.27); G-SAS (50.78, 10.62)	G-SAS urge strength (1.41, 1.46); –[d]	CGI-PT (3.09, 0.99) –[b]	CGI-PT (1.51, 0.91) 75% (much improved or better) Y-BOCS (12.2, 5.3)
Dannon et al., 2005; Grant et al., 2006;	–; G-SAS (25 mg: 31.3, 6.7; 50 mg: 32.4, 7.6; 100 mg: 31.4, 6.9)	–; G-SAS (25 mg: 12.42; 50 mg: 13.16; 100 mg: 16.08)	Y-BOCS (16.3, 4.7) PG-YBOCS (25 mg: 22.8, 4.1; 50 mg 23.6, 5.4; 100 mg 23.1, 5.2)	–; PG-YBOCS (25mg: 6.99: 50mg 9.18; 100mg 9.30)
Grant et al., 2008; Toneatto et al., 2009;	G-SAS (26.9, 8.28)[c] –	G-SAS (15.7, 9.47)[c] –	PG-YBOCS (16.9, 6.6) Sessions per month 16.4 (13.6), expenditure per day $120.2 ($208.7) CAD	PG-YBOCS score (9.7, 8.12) Sessions per month (11.4, 11.4), Ex-penditures per day ($47, $78) CAD
Grant et al., 2010;	G-SAS (20 mg: 28.89; 40 mg: 28.24)[c]	G-SAS 95% CI (20 mg: 19.11–20.32; 40 mg: 14.98–16.44)[c]	PG-YBOCS (20 mg: 21.17, 40 mg: 20.75)	PG-YBOCS 95% CI (20mg: 11.34-12.30, 40mg: 6.06-7.21)
Lathi et al., 2010;	–	–	PG-YBOCS 87% 'moderate to severe'	PG-YBOCS 16% reported 'severe' symptoms
Bosco et al., 2012;	–	–	Gambling (-, -)	Abstinent, partial abstinence
Piz et al., 2013;	–	–	Gambling (500–2000) € 2–3 weekly	3€ year
Kovanen et al., 2016;	PG-YBOCS Thoughts/urges (12.3, 3.0)	PG-YBOCS Thoughts/urges (3.5, 4.0)	PG-YBOCS (23.8, 6.0)	PG-YBOCS (10.3, 7.6)
Patrascu et al., 2017	–	–	PGSI	PGSI (decreased average score by 4.5 points)

- No data.

[a] Where reported.

[b] Visually represented.

[c] PG-YBOCS urge/thought subscale was also reported.

[d] Change score reported.

Tx: Treatment.

DSM-IV: *Diagnostic and Statistical Manual of Mental Disorders-IV*.

DSM-5: *Diagnostic and Statistical Manual of Mental Disorders-5*.

SOGS: South Oaks Gambling Screen.

Y-BOCS: Yale-Brown Obsessive Compulsive Scale.

PG-YBOCS: Problem Gambling version of the Yale-Brown Obsessive Compulsive Scale.

CGI-PT: Clinical Global Impression Scale – Patient version.

PGSI: Problem Gambling Severity Index.

G-SAS: Gambling Symptom Assessment Scale.

Table 4. Reasons for drop-out.

Study	Reasons for TX drop-out (number)										
	high enzyme levels	placebo response	lost to follow up	pregnant	TX side effects	personal reasons/ scheduling issues/ withdrawal	Tx not effective/ Loss of trust	Hallucinations	Parkinson's/ Manic	Not started	Not stated
Kim & Grant, 2001;					3						
Kim et al., 2001;	5	22	6	1	2	2					
Dannon et al., 2005;					6						
Grant et al., 2006;			33		50		2			10	12
Grant et al., 2008; [c]					5	20	3				
Toneatto et al., 2009; [d]								1			
Grant et al., 2010;		6	7		17	12				1	37
Lathi et al., 2010;											20
Bosco et al., 2012;											
Piz et al., 2013; [a]											
Kovanen et al., 2016;			5		2	3	3		2		3
Patrascu et al., 2017; [b]											

[a]None reported.
[b]Three participants were reported as discontinued but medication group was not specified.
[c]Probably both drug conditions.
[d]Only one drop-out number reported, no group stated.

Table 5. Adverse effects.

Study	Adverse effects %																
	Nausea/ dizziness/ vomitting	Drowsi-ness	Insomnia	Anxiety	Dry Mouth	Head-ache	Diarrhea	Consti-pation	Decreased Appetite	Decreased Libido	Vivid Dreams	Fatigue	Perspira-tion	Halluci-nations	Urinary Frequency	Restless-ness	Other
Kim & Grant, 2001;	47	38	38				41										
Kim et al, 2001;	45	35	15	20	40	30	20	20	25	35	40						
Dannon et al, 2005; [a]																	
Grant et al, 2006;	64.7	4.5	31.4		7.6			8.3	4.5				5.1		5.7		
Grant et al, 2008;	70.6[b]		12.1		13.8	39.7	13.8	5.2									
Toneatto et al, 2009;	14.8				7.4	7.4						14.8		3.7			
Grant et al, 2010; [c]																	
Lathi et al., 2010; [c]																	
Bosco et al, 2012; [a]																	
Piz et al, 2013; [d]																	
Kovanen et al., 2016;	26[e]		8			22	26[e]									12	4
Patrascu et al., 2017; [d]																	

[a] Side effects were listed as a group.
[b] Combined group: reported as nausea 60.3%, dizziness 10.3%.
[c] Not listed.
[d] None reported.
[e] Nausea and diarrhoea were reported together so diarrhoea is reported twice.

124   THE NEUROSCIENCE AND NEUROPSYCHOLOGY OF GAMBLING

urinary frequency, restlessness and other. The most common adverse effects across all studies were the group nausea/dizziness/vomiting, where the range was 14.8% (Toneatto, Brands, & Selby, 2009) to 70.6% (Grant et al., 2008). In addition, other highly reported adverse effects were diarrhea 41% (Kim & Grant, 2001), vivid dreams 40% and dry mouth 40% (Kim et al., 2001), headache 39.7% (Grant et al., 2008) and insomnia 31.4% (Grant et al., 2006).

Discussion

In this review, naltrexone was the most common opioid antagonist treatment for problem gambling. Most of the studies included other treatments, typically cognitive behavioural therapy, although two studies included additional pharmacological treatments. Co-morbidities were typically treated as either specific co-occurring disorders or as exceptions to inclusion and exclusion criteria. Approximately half of the studies used a range of dosing concentrations, with the majority using a daily dosing schedule rather than an as required dosing schedule. The length of the trials varied from 6 to 20 weeks, as did the number of participants, from 1 to more than 100, and whether a placebo lead-in was used before treatment. This indicates a wide variety of study designs. Across studies, average DSM-5 gambling severity was 'moderate' to 'severe'. Across studies, gambling urge and the primary outcome scores reduced by approximately 50% from baseline to treatment end. Reasons for drop-out were varied, and possibly study-specific, with treatment side effects being the most numerous reason for drop-out. The most common side effects were the group nausea/dizziness/vomiting (objective 3).

These results indicate a few consistent findings. First, opioid antagonist treatments for problematic gambling appear effective, at least when comparing baseline to treatment end. This effect appears to be relatively consistent across a range of trial durations and is congruent with the literature that examines alcohol craving reductions, especially for those with high baseline craving levels (Jaffe et al., 1996). However, as identified in some studies (Grant et al., 2010) and in a recent meta-analysis (Bartley & Bloch, 2013), these results can dissipate when compared against a placebo group. Further, there was a noticeable placebo response recorded in the reasons for drop-out, suggesting that the experience of participating in a drug treatment study has an effect on gambling behaviour.

Second, the average changes in craving scores from baseline to treatment end appear to follow the changes in the primary outcomes (objective 2). This indicates that craving and gambling symptoms track each other, suggesting craving is an important factor in the recovery from problem gambling. This confirms standard research practice of measuring both outcomes (e.g. Grant et al., 2008, 2010), and indicates that craving scores are possible proxy scores for problem gambling. This has an important clinical implication, as gambling abstinence is typically a difficult behaviour to objectively measure. Further, participants may be more comfortable reporting craving scores than gambling behaviour. Therefore, measuring craving scores may provide a more accurate indication of gambling abstinence.

Third, and perhaps surprisingly, there appears to be some evidence that dosing concentrations and schedules appear unrelated to treatment outcomes (objective 1). For example, for the two studies that reported dosage subgroups, although baseline gambling outcome measures were relatively similar across dosing subgroups, there were differences in the treatment end scores. Specifically, Grant et al. (2006) reported the lowest dose to have the most improved primary outcome score, while Grant et al. (2010) reported the highest dose to have the most improved primary outcome score. Although, the earlier study subgroup dosing treatment end scores were somewhat similar (i.e. 2 mg: 6.99, 50 mg: 9.18, 100 mg: 9.30), the later study subgroup dosing treatment end scores reported the lower dose to be approximately twice the size of the higher dose (i.e. 20 mg: 11.34–12.30, 40 mg: 6.06–7.21). Further, Grant et al. (2010) reported this change was statistically significant for the 40 mg dosage group as compared to the placebo group.

Moreover, decreases in primary outcome measures were reported for a range of dosage concentrations and for a range of trial lengths. For example, both the shortest (Kim & Grant, 2001) and the longest trial (Kovanen et al., 2016), excluding case studies, reported reductions in cravings and primary outcomes. This result indicates that the reduction in craving is relatively quick, and appears to follow, at the optimal dose, the relatively rapid pharmacokinetics of naltrexone; maximum concentration is within 1 hour of administration, 5% drug systematic circulation, and 127 ml/min renal clearance, and also the moderate duration of the drug; a 4-hour half-life (Apotex Inc., 2015; Meyer, Straughn, Lo, Schary, & Whitney, 1984). Consequently, if craving is related to gambling symptoms and naltrexone appears to reduce gambling craving and behaviour, where naltrexone quickly reaches its maximum concentration, these results suggest a relatively quick mechanism of action and a temporally close relationship between naltrexone administration and reductions in gambling symptomatology.

These temporally close relations are congruent with the literature which links greater impulsive, and typically rapid, behaviour with problem gambling (Dussault, Brendgen, Vitarom, Wanner, & Tremblay, 2011). For example, in a pilot fMRI study, when problem gamblers chose an immediate outcome in a delay discounting task, greater activation was recorded in striatal brain regions (i.e. the putamen and insula), regions functionally associated with reinforcement learning and interoceptive awareness, processes that are implicated in gambling behaviour and addiction (Ell, Marchant, & Irvy, 2006; Gaznick, Tranel, McNutt, & Bechara, 2014; Ledgerwood et al., 2014; Xue, Lu, Levin, & Bechara, 2010). Therefore, gambling cue elicitation and brain function also appears to have a temporally close relationship.

Fourth, participants across studies reported a variety of adverse effects (objective 4). Although the most numerous was the group nausea/dizziness/vomiting, participants reported virtually every known side effect of opioid antagonists. This suggests that participants have very individual responses and sensitivities to opioid antagonists, where the numerous adverse effects possibly mirror the complexity reported in the dose concentration and treatment outcome results. Therefore, using a variety of dosing options might be helpful to address this issue as adverse effects are often related to adherence and drop-out (Kranzler, Stephenson, Montejano, Wang, & Gastfriend, 2008). For example, a case study of naltrexone as a treatment for problem gambling found oral naltrexone was ineffective for the client so the client stopped taking the drug, but when the client switched to injectable naltrexone the drug resulted in gambling abstinence for the remainder of treatment and at follow-up (Yoon & Kim, 2013).

Conclusion

The general effectiveness of opioid antagonists reported in the individual studies and some systematic reviews (van den Brink, 2012) has been challenged in recent meta-analyses (Bartley & Bloch, 2013), and to a lesser degree in this review. Although these results are contradictory, these results suggest that participants appear to have individual responses to opioid antagonists. This review supports most of the theoretical and empirical gambling literature that suggests problem gamblers are a heterogeneous group. This review implies that problem gamblers have individual responses to drug treatments and multiple biological factors appear to influence these responses.

Links between alcohol and gambling literatures

A related literature that has examined these issues in greater depth is the biological, genetic, epigenetic and pharmacologic research into the risk factors for alcohol abuse and dependence. Typically, the alcohol literature indicates multiple influences on alcohol use and dependence. For example, genetic associations for alcohol sensitivities (Crabbe, 2003; Dick et al., 2002), genetic influences on the speed of alcohol metabolism (Luczak, Glatt, & Wall, 2006), consumption patterns (Bobashev, Liao, Hampton, & Helzer, 2014) and emotional dysregulation (Petit et al., 2015) are all related to alcohol dependence. Consequently, alcohol dependence is thought to result from the interaction between multiple factors, manifested as various alcohol dependence trajectories (Windle & Davies, 1999).

There is also evidence to suggest a high degree of association between alcohol dependence and problem gambling. For example, in a genome-wide study the researchers found a polygenic risk relationship between alcohol dependence and pathological gambling (Lang et al., 2016). Further, biometric fitting analyses found a 0.29 to 0.44 genetic correlation between alcohol use disorder and gambling disorder, where one-half to two-thirds of the association was due to genetic vulnerability (Slutske, Ellingson, Richmond-Rakerd, Zhu, & Martin, 2013). Moreover, familial analyses have found elevated prevalence rates of gambling disorders among relatives. For example, family members were over three times more likely to report a lifetime estimate of gambling disorder compared to controls (Black, Monahan, Temkit, & Shaw, 2006), while the data from the Vietnam Era Twin Registry indicated the estimated heritability of gambling disorder to be 50–60% (Lobo & Kennedy, 2009).

However, the genetic influence on gambling disorder appears complex. Although no specific genome-wide association has been found for gambling disorder (Lang et al., 2016; Lind et al., 2012), some evidence suggests associations with protein coding gene variants (i.e. MT1X, ATN1 and VLDLR; Lind et al., 2012), genes responsible for encoding mitochondrial enzymes involved in the deamination of amines (i.e. MAO-A; Ibanez, de Castro, Fernandez-Piqueras, Blanco, & Saiz-Ruiz, 2000), the dopamine receptor gene DRD3 (Lobo et al., 2015), the DRD4 gene (Comings et al., 1999), a protein coding gene involved in degradation of catecholamines and methylation (i.e. COMT; Grant, Leppink, Redden, Odlaug, & Chamberlain, 2015) and a serotonin transporter polymorphism (5-HTTLPR; de Castro, Ibanez, Saiz-Ruiz, & Fernandez-Piqeras, 2002). This complexity may operate in similar ways to the genetic influence of various genes associated with alcohol dependence, where, acting at proximal and intermediate levels of influence, genes associated with alcohol dependence appear to block and combine to reduce and magnify drug effects, indicating multi-level and interactive processes (Dick et al., 2007).

As previously stated, there is some evidence that genetic variants can affect the speed of alcohol metabolism, affecting the experience of adverse effects, consequently working as a protective barrier (Luczak et al., 2006). Similarly, genes implicated in the regulation of monoamines responsible for modulating neurotransmitters associated with emotion, cognition and reward are associated with addiction vulnerability (Ducci & Goldman, 2012).

THE NEUROSCIENCE AND NEUROPSYCHOLOGY OF GAMBLING

For example, COMT is associated with reducing dopamine in the prefrontal cortex, possibly reducing executive functioning (Giakoumaki, Roussos, & Bitsios, 2008; Malhotra et al., 2002), and the likelihood of inhibiting impulsive gambling behaviour (Goudriaan, Oosterlaan, de Beurs, & Van den Brink, 2004). Likewise, serotonin transporters are implicated in the regulation of mood, appetite and impulse control (Ducci & Goldman, 2012). The serotonin transporter polymorphism 5-HTTLPR is associated with influencing the activity of the amygdala, increasing responsiveness to fearful stimuli (Mueller et al., 2011), and increasing alcohol consumption during stressful conditions (Barr et al., 2003). Consequently, the activation of the gene 5-HTTLPR may increase the motivation of gambling to escape (Francis, Dowling, Jackson, Christensen, & Wardle, 2015), analogous to the motivation of consuming alcohol to relax (Advokat et al., 2014).

Evidence from electrophysiologic research suggests alcohol dependence is related to brain wave form patterns. For example, alcohol dependence is related to lower P3 wave forms, associated with emotion dysregulation (Edenberg et al., 2004). Similarly, problem gamblers also appear to have different electrophysiological responses compared to controls. For example, problem gamblers have stronger electrophysiological responses than controls as they approach a win (Hewig et al., 2010).

Some psychophysiological studies have reported high bio-behavioural reactions to substance cues (MacKillop & Monti, 2007), although these responses are highly variable among individuals (Avants, Margolin, Kosten, & Cooney, 1995), with some research suggesting that reactions to drug cues are idiosyncratic and reflect reinforcement histories rather than drug pharmacodynamics (Carter & Tiffany, 1999). Likewise, problem gamblers have been recorded with greater neural activation towards gambling-related cues in brain structures related to attention, emotional processing and cognitive control (Crockford, Goodyear, Edwards, & Quickfall, 2005; Goudriaan et al., 2010). However, there is some evidence of both hyper- and hypoactivation in several brain regions to gambling-related cues by problem gamblers. For example, gambling-disordered individuals were recorded with lower neural activation in the ventral striatum and ventral prefrontal cortex in response to monetary gains compared to monetary losses (Reuter et al., 2005), while in a probabilistic choice task, gambling-disordered individuals were recorded with greater dorsal striatum activity during the anticipation phase of large rewards compared to small rewards (van Holst, Veltman, Buchel, van den Brink, & Goudriaan, 2012b). Further, there is some evidence that gambling-disordered individuals have attentional biases to specific, possibly individually salient cues. For example, van Holst, van Holstein, van den Brink, Veltman, and Goudriann (2012a) reported that problem gamblers compared to healthy controls showed more activation in the left dorsal-lateral prefrontal cortex, the right ventral striatum and right anterior cingulate when responding to gambling versus neutral images. However, van Holst et al. (2012a) reported healthy controls compared to problem gamblers had more activation in the bilateral dorsal-lateral prefrontal cortex, right dorsal-lateral prefrontal cortex and right anterior cingulate during gambling inhibition trials compared to neutral inhibition trials. These results suggest that problem gamblers have varied neural activation to gambling stimuli, possibly developed during earlier gambling experiences (Volkow, Fowler, & Wang, 2003).

Importantly, there also appears to be a high environment and genetic interaction, where experience can have an important influence on the predisposition, sensitivity and likelihood of alcohol dependence (Rose, Dick, Viken, Pulkkien, & Kaprio, 2001). Consequently, the risks of alcohol dependence are considered multifactorial, with biological, psychological and social processes influencing the likelihood of alcohol dependence. Similarly, there are significant interactions between the gambling environment, gambling activities, gambling motives and gambling prevalence. Evidence suggests that there are positive associations between gambling accessibility and gambling involvement, where greater gambling accessibility results in a greater risk of problem gambling, although other factors mediate these relationships (Vasiliadis, Jackson, Christensen, & Francis, 2013). Therefore, at least at face value, there seems to be a significant degree of correspondence between both disorders. The nascent evidence for opioid antagonists as effective treatments for both disorders, the elevated rates of co-morbid substance use and gambling disorder, the significant degree of genetic, consumption and environmental interactions for both disorders, and the same hypoactivation in similar brain regions for both disorders suggest that these phenomena parallel each other. This indicates the possibility that both disorders are a function of similar biological processes. Consequently, the evidence of multiple genetic factors influencing the incidence of alcohol dependence might also exist for gambling disorder.

Opioid use disorder and gambling

Although systematic reviews and meta-analyses report problem gamblers have elevated rates of substance use disorders (Dowling et al., 2015a; Lorains et al., 2011), no existing neuroimaging studies appear to examine the relationship between opioid use and gambling disorders. However, a sparse literature exists comparing brain function between substance use and gambling disorders. Notably, some reviews suggest substance use and gambling disorders have reduced activation in striatal regions during reward anticipation (Balodis & Potenza, 2015; Blum, Braverman, Holder, et al., 2000), although differences in striatal activation occur during reward outcomes (Luijten, Schellekens, Kuhn, Machielse, & Sescousse, 2017). Interestingly, opioid use history and consumption patterns are important predictors of opioid use disorder (Cochran et al., 2014). Similarly, gambling intensity (e.g. gambling frequency and spend) is thought to be a strong predictor of later problem gambling (el-Guebaly et al., 2015). Consequently, the correlates, predictors and neurological similarities and differences between opioid use and gambling disorders are areas requiring further study.

Heterogeneous gambling sensitivities

The diffuse nature of the likelihood and risks for alcohol dependence offers a perspective from which to view the pharmacologic treatment literature for problem gambling. Considering the multifactorial nature of alcohol use, and the strong influence of environment and experience, similar distinctions are possible in the problem gambling population. This is perhaps best illustrated in the dominant theoretical model for gambling disorder. Blaszczynski and Nower (2002) proposed an etiological model of gambling disorder in which biological, psychological, behavioural and social factors independently and collectively influence the etiology of gambling disorder. This model suggests that the common reinforcing gambling experience of variable and regular wins elicits sustained gambling behaviour. The model also includes emotional responses, personality differences and a social framework as components in the three pathways to problematic gambling. However, a recent analysis from a five-year longitudinal survey of gamblers suggest that problem gambling etiology is primarily determined by the intensity of gambling play (el-Guebaly et al., 2015). This suggests a dose-dependent effect where greater gambling intensity increases the likelihood of gambling problems. Further, this relationship may also result in the possibility of dose-dependent treatments; higher intensities of gambling problems require higher treatment dosages.

There is some evidence to support the dose-dependent hypothesis from the current review. Specifically, the study with the lowest percentage of adverse effects used a titration procedure to adjust dosage concentrations (Toneatto et al., 2009); importantly, the population in this study had both alcohol and gambling disorders. However, the study that reported the most numerous percentage of adverse effects also followed a titration process, although these were problem gamblers with few co-morbidities (Kim et al., 2001). It is possible that gambling-disordered populations with histories of alcohol dependence are more homogeneous and can better tolerate pharmacological treatments for problem gambling than gambling-disordered populations without or with few co-morbidities.

Similarly, as the efficacy of opioid-based medications appears related to craving scores, effective dosing concentrations are likely to mirror craving levels. Further, for those participants whose gambling is triggered by external cues, like receiving a pay-cheque or seeing an advertisement for a casino, other approaches that work to minimize impulsive behaviours might be useful. Pharmacological treatments for impulsivity have often focused on stimulants, especially for the treatment of attention deficit hyperactivity disorder in children (Grant & Chamberlain, 2015). However, this pharmacological approach has received little attention in the gambling literature, perhaps because of the potential for this drug to result in increases in impulsive behaviour (Grant & Chamberlain, 2015), and the possibility of substance use and dependence (Gahr & Plener, 2016). Nevertheless, individuals with a gambling disorder appear to report multiple dimensions of impulsivity (MacKillop et al., 2014), suggesting a strong link between problem gambling and impulsive behaviour. Moreover, as gambling disorders appear heterogeneous, multiple treatment options are likely to be necessary to meet the diffuse nature of the disorder in the treatment-seeking population, and the apparent idiosyncratic responses to gambling stimuli.

Diverse gambling treatments

Consequently, jurisdictions will need to develop a varied response to gambling issues, including offering individualized pharmacological treatments that meet a range of gambling experiences, psychological traits, personality issues, co-morbidities and drug sensitivities. Future research examining gambling typologies that mirror the effects of the available drugs might be productive. For example, selective inhibition of norepinephrine might be suitable for those with impulsivity but not craving issues, opioid-antagonists for those with cravings or concurrent alcohol dependence, and serotonin reuptake inhibitors for those with mood issues. Nevertheless, it is clear there is a need to improve the tailoring of treatment options for treatment seekers. These include counselling and self-help approaches, peer support, and government policies to reduce the potential harms from gambling. Ultimately, pharmacological treatments, like other treatment approaches, need to 'personalize' treatment to better align with the personal histories, preferences and sensitivities of treatment seekers to maximize treatment efficacy. For example, the typical psychosocial problem gambling counselling approach is cognitive behavioural therapy. This approach attempts to tailor the treatment experience to the client's unique experiences, triggers, thought processes and communication styles to make the treatment more 'personal' and relevant to the client. Similarly, like cognitive behavioural therapy, pharmacological treatments might profit from matching the typical effects of specific drugs to a client's gambling experiences, psychological traits and pharmacological sensitivities.

This can be manifested across a variety of implementations including variable dose concentrations based on gambling intensity, sensitivities to adverse effects, targeting populations that appear responsive to pharmacology (i.e. opioid-based treatments for co-morbid alcohol use and gambling disorders), and novel pharmacologies for specific gambling triggers (i.e. selective norepinephrine inhibitors for gamblers who are reactive to intermittent stimuli), among others. For example, one of the earliest investigations of naltrexone as a treatment for problem gambling was a case report investigating naltrexone as a treatment for an individual with alcohol dependence and pathological gambling (Crockford & el-Guebaly, 1998). Forty-eight hours after naltrexone dosing began, the individual reported a cessation in alcohol and gambling cravings with a co-occurring decrease in obsessive compulsive scores for alcohol and gambling. These decreases continued for the next four weeks. This suggests that specific pharmacological treatments for individuals with select issues appears to be a profitable approach, given the heterogeneous nature of the gambling population (Lorains et al., 2011). These biological, sensitivity and psychological differences suggest that individually tailored pharmacologic treatments are likely to be productive when designing drug treatments for problem gambling. These might be as simple as a titration procedure, or as complex as a combination of genetic, psychological, pharmacologic and social treatments. Nevertheless, the evidence from a range of sources suggest that any treatment for problem gambling requires a person-centred 'precision-medicine' approach.

Limitations and strengths

This study has limitations. As this is a partial review of the extant literature, the connections between the results of the selected studies and suggestions for clinical practice are provisory, and further research is required to substantiate these claims. Also, only a small selection of the possible predictors of problem gambling were investigated in this review. Other variables associated with problem gambling that need investigation include age, gambling activity, gender, socio-economic status, trauma, gambling experiences and accessibility, among others (Williams et al., 2014). Further, possible sub-analyses were not conducted (i.e. co-morbidities, experimental vs. case studies, control groups). Future studies will need to examine these and other variables for their contribution to the effectiveness of drug treatments (e.g. gambling histories, specific populations, novel pharmacologies), and the possibility of gambling typologies that have implications for separate or combined pharmacological treatments (i.e. selective norepinephrine inhibitors for reactive gamblers). However, this will require laboratory analyses and applied research approaches to elucidate the possibility of pharmacological typologies. For example, examining neurotransmitter (e.g. dopamine) emission during a triggering event while under a norepinephrine inhibitor challenge will test the veracity that stimulant-based medications are possible treatment approaches for problem gambling. The current search was restricted to trials from 2000. There were earlier studies examining the effectiveness of pharmacology on problem gambling, but these were excluded as the impetus for drug treatments began in the early 2000s. Also, the G-SAS total score includes other measures of gambling symptomatology, so is somewhat confounded as a pure measure of craving. Finally, as this was a review based on specific selection criteria, it is limited in the scope of the analyses and the ability for this approach to investigate the effects of various contributing factors.

The strengths of this study are related to the design of the current review. This review focused on the relationships between dose concentration, craving scores and the primary outcomes. Importantly, the changes in craving scores matched the changes in the primary outcomes. This seems an obvious association but appears to be a secondary issue for trials, and especially in the reviews of the literature. Consequently, craving level might be a proxy measure for current gambling status, as disclosing current craving might be easier for the client than disclosing current gambling behaviour and losses. Also, collating the number of treatment drop-outs and percentage of adverse effects tests the hypothesis of the idiosyncratic nature of drug treatment efficacy and problem gambler sensitivities. Hopefully, the key conclusion from this review – that the diverse responsiveness to dosage concentrations suggests an idiosyncratic response to pharmacologic treatments – will promote more nuanced and comprehensive pharmacological treatments in future gambling disorder studies.

Conflicts of interest

Funding sources

No funding was received for this study.

Competing interests

The author reports no competing interests.

Constraints on publishing

The author reports no constraints on publishing.

References

Aboujaoude, E., & Salame, W. O. (2016). Naltrexone: A pan-addiction treatment? *CNS Drugs, 30*, 719–733.

Advokat, C. D., Comaty, J. E., & Julien, R. M. (2014). *Julien's primer of drug action: A comprehensive guide to the actions, uses, and side effects of psychoactive drugs* (13th ed.). New York, NY: Worth Publishers.

American Psychiatric Association. (1994). *Diagnostics and Statistical Manual for Mental Disorders IV*. Washington, DC: Author.

American Psychiatric Association. (2013). *Diagnostic and statistical manual of mental disorders V*. Washington, DC: Author.

Apotex Inc. (2015). *Product monograph: Apo-naltrexone. Naltrexone hydrochloride tablets usp. 50 mg. Opioid antagonist*. Toronto, ON.: Apotex Inc.

Aston-Jones, G., & Cohen, J. D. (2005). Adaptive gain and the role of the locus coeruleus-norepinephrine system in optimal performance. *The Journal of Comparative Neurology, 493*, 99–110.

Avants, S. K., Margolin, A., Kosten, T. R., & Cooney, N. L. (1995). Differences between responders and nonresponders to cocaine cues in the laboratory. *Addictive Behaviors, 20*, 215–224.

Balodis, I. M., & Potenza, M. N. (2015). Anticipatory reward processing in addicted populations: A focus on the monetary incentive delay task. *Biological Psychiatry, 77*, 434–444.

Barr, C. S., Newman, T. K., Becker, M. L., Parker, C. C., Champoux, M., Lesch, K. P., … Higley, J. D. (2003). The utility of the non-human primate: Model for studying gene by environment interactions in behavioral research. *Genes, Brain, and Behavior, 2*, 336–340.

Bartley, C. A., & Bloch, M. H. (2013). Meta-analysis: Pharmacological treatment of pathological gambling. *Expert Review of Neurotherapeutics, 13*, 887–894.

Benjamin, D., Grant, E. R., & Pohorecky, L. A. (1993). Naltrexone reverses ethanol-induced dopamine release in the nucleus accumbens in awake, freely moving rats. *Brain Research, 621*, 137–140.

Black, D. W., Monahan, P. O., Temkit, M., & Shaw, M. (2006). A family study of pathological gambling. *Psychiatry Research, 141*(3), 295–303.

Blaszczynski, A., & Nower, L. (2002). A pathways model of problem and pathological gambling. *Addiction, 97*, 487–499.

Blum, K., Braverman, E. R., Holder, J. M., Lubar, J. F., Monastra, V. J., Miller, D., … Comings, D. E. (2000). Reward deficiency syndrome: A biogenetic model for the diagnosis and treatment of impulsive, addictive, and compulsive behaviors. *Journal of Psychoactive Drugs, 32*(suppl):1–112.

Bobashev, G., Liao, D., Hampton, J., & Helzer, J. E. (2014). Individual patterns of alcohol use. *Addictive Behaviors, 39*, 934–940.

Bosco, D., Plastino, M., Colica, C., Bosco, F., Arianna, S., Vecchio, A., … Consoli, D. (2012). Opioid antagonist naltrexone for the treatment of pathological gambling in Parkinson disease. *Clinical Neuropharmacology, 35*, 118–120.

Bouret, S., & Sara, S. J. (2005). Network reset: A simplified overarching theory of locus coeruleus noradrenaline function. *Trends in Neurosciences, 28*, 574–582.

Carter, B. L., & Tiffany, S. T. (1999). Meta-analysis of cue-reactivity in addiction research. *Addiction, 94*, 327–340.

Castren, S., Salonen, A. H., Alho, H., Lathi, T., & Simojoki, K. (2015). Past-year gambling behaviour among patients receiving opioid substitution treatment. *Substance Abuse Treatment, Prevention, and Policy, 10*, 4.

Chamberlain, S. R., Muller, U., Blackwell, A. D., Clark, L., Robbins, T. R., & Sahakian, B. J. (2006). Neurochemical modulation of response inhibition and probabilistic learning in humans. *Science, 311*, 861–863.

Christensen, D. R., Jackson, A. C., Dowling, N. A., Volberg, R. A., & Thomas, S. A. (2015). An examination of a proposed DSM-IV pathological gambling hierarchy in a treatment seeking population: Similarities with substance dependence and evidence for three classification systems. *Journal of Gambling Studies, 31*, 787–806.

Clark, L., Stokes, P. R., Wu, K., Michalczuk, R., Benecke, A., Watson, B. J., … Lingford-Hughes, A. R. (2012). Striatal dopamine D_2/D_3 rceptor binding in pathological gambling is correlated with mood-related impulsivity. *NeuroImage, 63*, 40–46.

Cochran, B. N., Flentje, A., Heck, N. C., Van Den Bos, J., Perlman, D., Torres, J., … Carter, J. (2014). Factors predicting development of opioid use disorders among individuals who receive an initial opioid prescription: Mathematical modeling using a database of commercially-insured individuals. *Drug Alcohol Dependence, 138*, 202–208.

Comings, D. E., Gonzalez, N., Wu, S., Gade, R., Muhleman, D., Saucier, G., … MacMurray, J. P. (1999). Studies of the 48 bp repeat polymorphism of the DRD4 gene in impulsive, compulsive, addictive behaviors: Tourette syndrome, ADHD, pathological gambling, and substance abuse. *American Journal of Medical Genetics, 88*, 358–368.

Crabbe, J. C. (2003). Finding genes for complex behaviors: Progress in mouse models of the addictions. In R. Plomin, J. DeFries, I. Craig, & P. McGuffin (Eds.), *Behavioral genetics in the postgenomic era* (pp. 291–308). Washington, DC: American Psychological Association.

Crockford, D. N., & el-Guebaly, N. (1998). Naltrexone in the treatment of pathological gambling and alcohol dependence. *The Canadian Journal of Psychiatry, 43*, 86.

Crockford, D. N., Goodyear, B., Edwards, J., Quickfall, J., & el-Guebaly, N. (2005). Cue-induced brain activity in pathological gamblers. *Biological Psychiatry, 58*, 787–795.

Dannon, P. N., Lowengrub, K., Musin, E., Gonopolski, Y., & Kotler, M. (2005). Sustained-release bupropion vs. naltrexone in the treatment of pathological gambling. *Journal of Clinical Psychopharmacology, 25*, 593–596.

de Castro, I. P., Ibanez, A., Saiz-Ruiz, J., & Fernandez-Piqeras, J. (2002). Concurrent positive association between pathological gambling and functional DNA polymorphisms at the MAO-A and the 5-HT transporter genes. *Molecular Psychiatry, 7*, 927–928.

de Ruiter, M. B., Veltman, D. J., Goudriaan, A. E., Oosterlaan, J., Sjoerds, Z., & van den Brink, W. (2009). Response preservation and ventral prefrontal sensitivity to reward and punishment in male problem gamblers and smokers. *Neuropsychopharmacology, 34*, 1027–1038.

Dick, D. M., Nurnberger, J., Jr, Edenberg, H. J., Goate, A., Crowe, R., Rice, J., … Foroud, T. (2002). Suggestive linkage on chromosome 1 for a quantitative alcohol-related phenotype. *Alcoholism: Clinical and Experimental Research, 26*, 1453–1460.

Dick, D. M., Wang, J. C., Plunkett, J., Aliev, F., Hinrichs, A., Bertelsen, S., … Goate, A. (2007). Family-based association analyses of alcohol dependence phenotypes across DRD2 and neighbouring gene ANKK1. *Alcoholism: Clinical and Experimental Research, 31*, 1645–1653.

Dowling, N. A., Jackson, A. C., Cowlishaw, S., Francis, K., Merkouris, S., & Christensen, D. R. (2015a). Prevalence of psychiatric comorbidity in treatment-seeking problem gambling: A systematic review and meta-analysis. *Australian and New Zealand Journal of Psychiatry, 49*, 6.

Dowling, N. A., Jackson, A. C., Cowlishaw, S., Francis, K., Merkouris, S., & Christensen, D. R. (2015b). The prevalence of comorbid personality disorders in treatment-seeking problem gamblers: A systematic review and meta-analysis. *Journal of Personality Disorders, 29*, 735–754.

Ducci, F., & Goldman, D. (2012). The genetic bases of addictive disorders. *Psychiatric Clinics of North America, 35*, 495–519.

Dussault, F., Brendgen, M., Vitarom, F., Wanner, B., & Tremblay, R. E. (2011). Longitudinal links between impulsivity, gambling problems and depressive symptoms: A transactional model from adolescence to early adulthood. *Journal of Child Psychology and Psychiatry, 52*, 130–138.

Edenberg, H. J., Dick, D. M., Xuei, X., Tian, H., Almasy, L., Bauer, L. O., … Begleiter, H. (2004). Variations in GABRA2, encoding the alpha 2 subunit of the GABA(A) receptor, are associated with alcohol dependence and with brain oscillations. *The American Journal of Human Genetics, 74*, 705–714.

el-Guebaly, N., Casey, D. M., Currie, S. R., Hodgins, D. C., Schopflocher, D. P., Smith, G. J., & Williams, R. J. (2015). *The Leisure, Lifestyle, & Lifecycle Project (LLLP): A Longitudinal Study of Gambling in Alberta.* Final Report for the Alberta Gambling Research Institute. February 2015.

Ell, S. W., Marchant, N. L., & Irvy, R. B. (2006). Focal putamen lesions impair learning in rule-based, but not information-integration categorization tasks. *Neuropsychologia, 44*, 1737–1751.

Francis, K. L., Dowling, N. A., Jackson, A. C., Christensen, D. R., & Wardle, H. (2015). Gambling motives: Application of the reasons for gambling questionnaire in an Australian population survey. *Journal of Gambling Studies, 31*, 807–823.

Gahr, M., & Plener, P. L. (2016). Methylphenidate abuse: An overview. In V. R. Reedy (Ed.), *Neuropathology of drug addictions and substance misuse: Volume 3: General processes and mechanisms, prescription medications, Caffeine and Areca, poly drug misuse, emerging addictions and non-drug addiction* (pp. 651–659). London: Elsevier.

Gaznick, N., Tranel, D., McNutt, A., & Bechara, A. (2014). Basal ganglia plus Insula damage yields stronger disruption of smoking addiction Than Basal Ganglia damage alone. *Nicotine*, 445–453.

Giakoumaki, S. G., Roussos, P., & Bitsios, P. (2008). Improvement of prepulse inhibition and executive function by the COMT inhibitor tolcapone depends on COMT Val158Met polymorphism. *Neuropsychopharmacology, 33*, 3058–3068.

Goudriaan, A. E., de Ruiter, M. B., van den Brink, W., Oosterlaan, J., & Veltman, D. J. (2010). Brain activation patterns associated with cue reactivity and craving in abstinent problem gamblers, heavy smokers and healthy controls: An fMRI study. *Addiction Biology, 15*, 491–503.

Goudriaan, A. E., Oosterlaan, J., de Beurs, E., & Van den Brink, W. (2004). Pathological gambling: A comprehensive review of biobehavioral findings. *Neuroscience & Biobehavioral Reviews, 28*, 123–141.

Grant, J. E. (2016). Neurobiology of disordered gambling. *Current Addiction Reports, 3*, 445–449.

Grant, J. E., & Chamberlain, S. R. (2015). Psychopharmacological options for treating impulsivity. *Psychiatric Times, 32*, 58–65.

Grant, J. E., Leppink, E. W., Redden, S. A., Odlaug, B. L., & Chamberlain, S. R. (2015). COMT genotype, gambling activity, and cognition. *Journal of Psychiatric Research, 68*, 371–376.

Grant, J. E., Odlaug, B. L., & Chamberlain, S. R. (2016). Neural and psychological underpinnings of gambling disorder: A review. *Progress in Neuro-Psychopharmacology & Biological Psychiatry, 65*, 188–193.

Grant, J. E., Odlaug, B. L., Potenza, M. N., Hollander, E., & Kim, S. W. (2010). Nalmefene in the treatment of pathological gambling: Multicentre, double-blind, placebo-controlled study. *British Journal of Psychiatry, 197*, 330–331.

Grant, J. E., Potenza, M. N., Hollander, E., Cunnigham-Williams, R., Nurminen, T., Smits, G., & Kallio, A. (2006). Multicenter Investigation of the Opioid Antagonist Nalmefene in the Treatment of Pathological Gambling. *American Journal of Psychiatry, 163*, 303–312.

Grant, J. E., Kim, S.W., & Hartman, B. K. (2008). A double-blind, placebo-controlled study of the opiate antagonist naltrexone in the treatment of pathological gambling urges. *The Journal of Clinical Psychiatry, 69*, 783–789.

Grant, J. E., Odlaug, B. L., & Schreiber, R. N. (2012). Pharmacological treatments in pathological gambling. *British Journal of Clinical Pharmacology, 77*, 375–381.

Hewig, J., Kretschmer, N., Trippe, R. H., Hecht, H., Coles, M. G. H., Holroyd, C. B., & Miltner, W. (2010). Hypersensitivity to reward in problem gamblers. *Biological Psychiatry, 67*, 781–783.

Hodgins, D. C., Stea, J. N., & Grant, J. E. (2011). Gambling disorders. *Lancet, 378*, 1874–1884.

Ibanez, A., de Castro, I. P., Fernandez-Piqueras, J., Blanco, C., & Saiz-Ruiz, J. (2000). Pathological gambling and DNA polymorphic markers at MAO-A and MAO-B genes. *Molecular Psychiatry, 5*, 105–109.

Jaffe, A. J., Rounsaville, G., Chang, G., Schottenfeld, R. S., Meyer, R. E., & O'Malley, S. S. (1996). Naltrexone, relapse prevention, and supportive therapy with alcoholics: An analysis of patient treatment matching. *Journal of Consulting and Clinical Psychology, 64*, 1044–1053.

Johansson, A., Grant, J. E., Kim, S. W., Odlaug, B. L., & Gotestam, K. G. (2009). Risk factors for problematic gambling: A critical literature review. *Journal of Gambling Studies, 25*, 67–92.

Kim, S. W., & Grant, J. E. (2001). An open naltrexone treatment study in pathological gambling disorder. *International Clinical Psychopharmacology, 16*, 285–289.

Kim, S. W., Grant, J. E., Adson, D. E., & Shin, Y. C. (2001). Double-blind naltrexone and placebo comparison study in the treatment of pathological gambling. *Biological Psychiatry, 49*, 914–921.

Kovanen, L. Basnet, S., Castren, S., Pankakoski, M., Saarikoski, T., Alho, H., & Lahti, T. (2016). A randomised, double-blind, placebo-controlled trial of as-needed naltrexone in the treatment of pathological gambling. *European Addiction Research, 22*, 70–79.

Kranzler, H. R., Stephenson, J. J., Montejano, L., Wang, S., & Gastfriend, D. R. (2008). Persistence with oral naltrexone for alcohol treatment: Implications for health-care utilization. *Addiction, 103*, 1801–1808.

Lang, M., Lemenager, T., Streit, F., Fauth-Buhler, M., Frank, J., Juraeva, D., … Mann, K. F. (2016). Genome-wide association study of pathological gambling. *European Psychiatry, 36*, 38–46.

Lathi, T., Halme, J. T., Pankakoski, M., Sinclair, D., & Alho, H. (2010). Treatment of pathological gambling with naltrexone pharmacotherapy and brief intervention: A pilot study. *Psychopharmacology Bulletin, 43*, 35–44.

Ledgerwood, D. M., Knezevic, B., White, R., Khatib, D., Petry, N. M., & Diwadkar, V. A. (2014). Monetary delay discounting in a behavioral addiction sample: An fMRI pilot study. *Drug and Alcohol Dependence, 140*, e117–e118.

Lind, P. A., Zhu, G., Montgomery, G. W., Madden, P. A. F., Heath, A. C., Martin, N. G., & Slutske, W. S. (2012). Genome-wide association study of quantitative disordered gambling trait. *Addiction Biology, 18*, 511–522.

Lindberg, A., Fernie, B. A., & Spada, M. M. (2011). Metacognitions in problem gambling. *Journal of Gambling Studies, 27*, 75–81.

Lobo, D. S., & Kennedy, J. L. (2009). Genetic aspects of pathological gambling: A complex disorder with shared genetic vulnerabilities. *Addiction, 104*(9), 1454–1465.

Lobo, D. S., Aleksandrova, L., Knight, J., Casey, D. N., el-Guebaly, N., & Kennedy, J. L. (2015). Addiction-related genes in gambling disorders: New insights from parallel human and pre-clinical models. *Molecular Psychiatry, 20*, 1002–1010.

Lorains, F. K., Cowlishaw, S., & Thomas, S. A. (2011). Prevalence of comorbid disorders in problem gambling ad pathological gambling: Systematic review and meta-analysis of population studies. *Addiction, 106*, 490–498.

Luczak, S. E., Glatt, S. J., & Wall, T. L. (2006). Meta-analyses of ALDH2 and ADH1B with alcohol dependence in Asians. *Psychological Bulletin, 132*, 607–621.

Luijten, M., Schellekens, A. F., Kuhn, S., Machielse, M. W. J., & Sescousse, G. (2017). Disruption o reward processing in addiction. *An image-based meta-analysis of functional magnetic resonance imaging studies, 74*, 387–398.

MacKillop, J., Miller, J. D., Fortne, E., Maples, J., Lance, C. E., Campbell, W. K., & Goodie, A. S. (2014). Multidimensional examination of impulsivity in relation to disordered gambling. *Experimental and Clinical Psychopharmacology, 22*, 176–185.

MacKillop, J., & Monti, P. M. (2007). Advances in the scientific study of craving for alcohol and tobacco: From scientific study to clinical practice. In P. M. Kavanagh (Ed.), *Translation of Addictions Sciences in Practice* (pp. 189–209). Amsterdam: Elsevier Press.

Majuri, J., Joutsa, J., Johansson, J., Voon, V., Parkkola, R., Alho, H., … Kaasinen, V. (2017). Serotonin transporter density in binge eating disorder and pathological gambling: A PET study with [¹¹C] MADAM. *European Neuropsychopharmacology, 27*, 1281–1288.

Malhotra, A. K., Kestler, L. J., Mazzanti, C., Bates, J. A., Goldberg, T., & Goldberg, D. (2002). A functional polymorphism in the COMT gene and performance on a test of prefrontal cognition. *American Journal of Psychiatry, 159*, 652–654.

Meyer, M. C., Straughn, A. B., Lo, N. M. W., Schary, W. L., & Whitney, C. C. (1984). Bioequivalence, dose-proportionality, and pharmacokinetics of naltrexone after oral administration. *The Journal of Clinical Psychiatry, 45*, 15–19.

Miedl, S. F., Peters, J., & Buchel, C. (2012). Altered neural rewards representations in pathological gamblers revealed by delay and probability discounting. *Archives of General Psychiatry, 69*, 177–186.

Mueller, A., Armbruster, D., Moser, D. A., Canli, T., Lesch, K.-P., Brocke, B., & Kirschbaum, C. (2011). Interaction of serotonin transporter gene-linked polymorphic region and stressful life events predicts cortisol stress response. *Neuropsychopharmacology, 36*, 1332–1339.

Nordin, C., Gupta, R. C., & Sjodin, I. (2007). Cerebrospinal fluid amino acids in pathological gamblers and healthy controls. *Neuropsychobiology, 56*, 152–158.

Nutt, D. J. (2014). The role of the opioid system in alcohol dependence. *Journal of Psychopharmacology, 28*, 8–22.

Pallanti, S., Bernardi, S., Allen, A., Chaplin, W., Watner, D., DeCaria, C. M., & Hollander, E. (2010). Noradrenergic function in pathological gambling: Blunted growth hormone response to clonidine. *Journal of Psychopharmacology, 24*, 847–853.

Pallanti, S., DeCaria, C. M., Grant, J. E., Urpe, M., & Hollander, E. (2005). Reliability and validity of the pathological gambling adaptation of the Yale-Brown Obsessive-Compulsive Scale (PG-YBOCS). *Journal of Gambling Studies, 21*, 431–443.

Pallesen, S., Molde, H., Arnestad, H. M., Laberg, J. C., Skutle, A., Iversen, E., … Holsten, F. (2007). Outcome of pharmacological treatments of pathological gambling: A review and meta-analysis. *Journal of Clinical Psychopharmacology, 27*, 357–364.

Patrascu, M. C., Fainarea Alboaie, A. F., Androne, F. T., & Bratu-Bizic, R. E. (2017). Comparative efficacy analysis of naltrexone and selective serotonin reuptake inhibitors in pathological gambling treatment. *European Neuropsychopharmacology, 27*, S82–S83.

Pecina, S., Smith, K. S., & Berridge, K. C. (2006). Hedonic hot spots in the brain. *The Neuroscientist, 12*, 500–511.

Petit, G., Luminet, O., Maurage, F., Tecco, J., Lechantre, S., Ferauge, M., ... de Timary, P. (2015). Emotion regulation in alcohol dependence. *Alcoholism: Clinical and Experimental Research, 39*, 2471–2479.

Petrovic, P., Pleger, B., Seymour, B., Kloppel, S., De Martino, B., Critchley, H., & Dolan, R. J. (2008). Blocking central opiate function modulates hedonic impact and anterior cingulate response to rewards and losses. *Journal of Neuroscience, 28*, 10509–10516.

Petry, N. M., & Roll, J. M. (2001). A behavioural approach to understanding and treating pathological gambling. *Seminars in Clinical Neuropsychiatry, 6*, 177–183.

Pettorruso, M., Martinotti, G., Di Nicola, M., Onofrj, M., Di Giannantonio, M., Conte, G., & Janiri, L. (2012). Amantadine in the treatment of pathological gambling: A case report. *Frontiers in Psychiatry, 3*, article 102.

Piz, L., Maremmani, A. G. I., Rovai, L., Bacciardi, S., Rugani, F., & Maremmani, I. (2013). Successful long-term (3-year) treatment of gambling with naltrexone. A case report. *Heroin Addiction and Related Clinical Problems, 15*, 47–54.

Potenza, M. N., Steinberg, M. A., Skudlarski, P., Fulbright, R. K., Lacadie, C. M., Wilber, M. K., ... Wexler, B. E. (2003). Gambling urges in pathological gambling: A functional magnetic resonance imaging study. *Archives of General Psychiatry, 60*, 826–836.

Potenza, M. N., Walderhaug, E., Henry, S., Gallezot, J.-D., Planeta-Wilson, B., Ropchan, J., & Neumeister, A. (2013). Serotonin 1B receptor imaging in pathological gambling. *The World Journal of Biological Psychiatry, 14*, 139–145.

Problem Gambling Research and Treatment Centre (2011). *Guidelines for Screening, Assessment and Treatment in Problem Gambling*. Clayton, Victoria: Melbourne and Monash Universities.

Reuter, J., Taedler, T., Rose, M., Hand, I., Glascher, J., & Buchel, C. (2005). Pathological gambling is linked to reduce activation of the mesolimbic reward system. *Nature Neuroscience, 8*, 147–148.

Robbins, T. W., & Everitt, B. J. (1996). Neurobehavioural mechanisms of reward and motivation. *Current Opinion in Neurobiology, 6*, 228–236.

Rose, R. J., Dick, D. M., Viken, R. J., Pulkkien, L., & Kaprio, J. (2001). Drinking or abstaining at age 14? A genetic epidemiological study. *Alcoholism: Clinical and Experimental Research, 25*, 1594–1604.

Shippenberg, T. S. (2009). The dynorphin/kappa opioid receptor system: A new target for the treatment of addiction and affective disorders? *Neuropsychopharmacology, 34*, 247.

Slutske, W. S., Ellingson, J. M., Richmond-Rakerd, L. S., Zhu, G., & Martin, N. G. (2013). Shared genetic vulnerability for disordered gambling and alcohol use disorder in men and women: Evidence from a national community-based Australian twin study. *Twin Research and Human Genetics, 16*, 525–534.

Toneatto, T., Brands, B., Selby, P., & Sinclair, D. (2004). *A randomized, double-blind, placebo-controlled trial of naltrexone in the treatment of concurrent alcohol dependence and pathological gambling*. Final Report submitted to the Ontario Problem Gambling Research Centre.

Toneatto, T., Brands, B., & Selby, P. (2009). A randomized, double-blind, placebo-controlled trial of naltrexone in the treatment of concurrent alcohol use disorder and pathological gambling. *American Journal on Addictions, 18*, 219–225.

Tschernegg, M., Crone, J. S., Eigenberger, T., Schwartenbeck, P., Fauth-Buhler, M., Lemenager, T., ... Kronbichler, M. (2013). Abnormalities of functional brain networks in pathological gambling: A graph-theoretical approach. *Frontiers in Human Neuroscience, 7*, 625.

van den Brink, W. (2012). Evidence-based pharmacological treatment of substance use disorders and pathological gambling. *Current Drug Abuse Reviews, 5*, 3–31.

van Holst, R. J., van Holstein, M., van den Brink, W., Veltman, D. J., & Goudriann, A. E. (2012a). Response inhibition during cure reactivity in problem gamblers: an fMRI study. *PLoS ONE, 7*, e30909.

van Holst, R. J., Veltman, D. J., Buchel, C., van den Brink, W., & Goudriaan, A. E. (2012b). Distorted expectancy coding in problem gambling: Is the addictive in the anticipation? *Biological Psychiatry, 71*, 741–748.

Vasiliadis, S. D., Jackson, A. C., Christensen, D., & Francis, K. (2013). Physical accessibility of gambling opportunity and its relationship to gaming involvement and problem gambling: A systematic review. *Journal of Gambling Issues, 18*, 1–46.

Victorri-Vigneau, C., Spiers, A., Calliet, P., Bruneau, M., IGNACE-consortium, Challet-Bouju, G., & Grall-Bronnec, M. (2017). Opioid antagonists for pharmacological treatment of gambling disorder: Are the relevant? *Current Neuropharmacology, 15*, 1–15.

Volkow, N. D., Fowler, J. S., & Wang, G. J. (2003). The addicted human brain: Insights from imaging studies. *Journal of Clinical Investigation, 111*, 1444–1451.

Williams, R. J., Hann, R., Schopflocher, D., West, B., McLaughlin, P., White, N., … Flexhaug, T. (2014). *Quinte Longitudinal Study of Gambling and Problem Gambling.* Report prepared for the Ontario Problem Gambling Research Centre.

Windle, M., & Davies, P. (1999). Developmental theory and research. In K. E. Leonard & T. H. Blane (Eds.), *Psychological Theories of Drinking and Alcoholism* (pp. 164–202). New York, NY: Guilford Press.

Xue, G., Lu, Z., Levin, I. P., & Bechara, A. (2010). The impact of prior risk experiences on subsequent risky decision-making: The role of the insula. *NeuroImage, 50*, 709–716.

Yoon, G., & Kim, S. W. (2013). Monthly injectable naltrexone for pathological gambling. *American Journal of Psychiatry, 170*, 682–683.

Index

Note: *Italic* page numbers refer to figures.

acetylcholine: muscarinic agents 60; nicotinic agents 61
alcohol dependence 114, 126–130
amphetamine 52, 56, 72
amygdala 24, 26, 49, 71–72, 78–82, 87–88, 90–91, 93–94, 127; morphometric findings 91
Andrews-Hanna, J. R. 76
atomoxetine 57–58, 116

Baarendse, P. J. 57
Balodis, I. M. 98
Banich, M. T. 76
Bartley, C. A. 115
baseline gambling severity 118–119
Beck Depression Inventory II 28
behavioural addictions 24, 70, 94, 98; rehabilitation centre 26
Bellodi, L. 50
biobehavioural research 2
Blaszczynski, A. 128
Bloch, M. H. 115
brain morphometric findings 91
Buchel, C. 99, 115
Burke, J. 88
buspirone 56–57

Carter, A. 3
Cavedini, P. 50
Choi, J. S. 98
citalopram 57–59
clinical variables 88, 90, 92
connectivity networks 70, 72, 80
co-occurring disorders 100, 109, 124
cravings 2–3, 35, 80, 114, 117, 124–125, 129, 131

D'Annucci, A. 50
data extraction 118
decision-making 7–8, 10–11, 14–16, 46, 48–50, 58, 61, 71, 97–99, 106, 108, 110, 116
depression symptomatology 89, 92
depression symptoms 87–89, 93–94

depressive disorders 28, 58
Depue, B. E. 76
De Ruiter, M. B. 115
disulfiram 51, 57
dopamine receptor interventions 52
drug abuse co-morbidities 34
dual regression 71, 77–78

electronic gaming machines (EGMs) 3
emotion regulation failure 35

Fagerström Test 28
Friedman, N. P. 76
Frodl, T. 88
functional connectivity 71, 81

gambling disorder patients 6
Gambling-Related Cognitions Scale 24, 28
gambling-related cognitive distortions 23, 26, 70, 80, 82
gambling severity 25, 35, 72, 77–78, 81, 89–90, 92, 115–116
gambling treatments 129
Goudriaan, A. E. 99, 115
Grant, J. E. 124–125
grey matter (GM) 24, 29–30, 74, 87–88, 92
grey matter volume (GMV) 24, 26, 30–32, 33, 34
group differences 14, 17, 24, 29, 31, 73–74, 78, 106
group matching 29, 31

Harrigan, K. 3
Hayasaka, S. 36
heterogeneous gambling sensitivities 128
high-motion subjects 79–81
5-hydroxytryptophan (5-HTP) 58

image acquisition 101
impulsivity 23, 25–28, 33, 57, 61, 87, 90, 92, 117, 129

INDEX

independent component analysis 76–77
individual differences 24–25, 34, 52, 98, 108, 114
inhibitory control 6–17, 35
interpersonal problems 7–8, 15–17
inverse efficiency score (IES) 10, 12–13
Iowa Gambling Task (IGT) 46, 48–51, 55, 58, 98–100, 102, 106, 108–109

Keller, R. 50
Kuhn, S. 98

Laumann, T. O. 74
Livingstone, C. 3
Luijten, M. 98
Lynam, D. R. 28

Machielse, M. W. 98
Martin, A. 74
Miedl, S. F. 115
Monetary Incentive Delay Task (MIDT) 98–101, 106, 109
monetary rewards 87, 93, 108
mood disorders 87, 92
motivational theories 7–9
MRI acquisition protocol 29
MRI data acquisition 90
MRI preprocessing 29
MultiCAGE CAD-4 28

naltrexone 51, 59–61, 117–118, 124–125, 130
Navas, J. F. 35
negative interpersonal scenes 6, 8–11, 13–16
networks 34, 71–72, 76–78, 80–82
neural processing 97
neurological research 115
neurotoxic effects 2, 24, 34
neurotransmitter receptor agents 56
norepinephrine 51, 57, 116, 129
Nower, L. 128

obsessive-compulsive disorder (OCD) 99
online gambling 3
Oosterlaan, J. 115
opioid antagonists 51, 59, 61, 117, 125–126, 128
opioid-based treatments 114, 117, 130
opioids 51, 59, 72, 118
opioid use disorder 128

Pallanti, S. 116
pathological gambling 28, 36, 45, 88–89, 100, 115, 126, 130
patients with gambling disorder (PGD) 24–27, 30–36
Peters, J. 115

pharmacological treatments 45, 51, 59, 115, 124, 129–130
Plitt, M. 74
Potenza, M. N. 115
Power, J. D. 74
predictive validity 48, 51
problem gamblers 2, 115–117, 125–127, 129
Problem Gambling Severity Index (PGSI) 73, 77
Pruim, R. H. R. 74
psychometric data 90, 92
psychometric instruments 28

rat gambling task (rGT) 45–46, 47, 48–52, 55–61
reduced anticipatory BOLD activation 98–99
regional grey matter volume 23–24, 32
Reineberg, A. E. 76
reliability 50–52, 100
Riboldi, G. 50
rodent gambling task 52
Romanczuk-Seiferth, N. 99
Rømer Thomsen, K. 92

sample characteristics 12, 26
Schellekens, A. F. 98
serotonin 56–59, 61, 116
Sescousse, G. 98–99
Silveira, M. M. 58
smoking status 81, 90, 103, 106, 108–109
South Oaks Gambling Screen 27–28, 89
statistical analyses 11–12, 29–30, 74, 101
structural differences 24, 34
suboptimal group 51, 59–60
substance-use disorders (SUDs) 33, 87, 89, 92, 98, 109

total intracranial volume (TIV) 30–31, 36
Tschernegg, M. 71

UPPS-P Impulsive Behavior Scale 28

Van den Brink, W. 99, 115
Van Holst, R. J. 3, 99
Veltman, D. J. 99, 115
ventral attention network 72, 77–78, 80–82
ventromedial prefrontal cortex 49–50, 98
voxel-based morphometry (VBM) 24, 29, 31–32, 36

Wechsler Adult Intelligence Scale 28
Whiteside, S. P. 28

Yeo, B. T. T. 72, 76
Yücel, M. 3